T0333435

ANATOMY OF A MASSACRE

ANATOMY OF A MASSACRE

HOW THE SS GOT AWAY WITH WAR CRIMES IN ITALY

CHRISTIAN JENNINGS

The History Press

This book is dedicated to the inspirational, inimitable Sylvia Scheul, who believed in it from the start and has done everything to support it. One afternoon in Sant'Anna di Stazzema, she looked down from the mountains and olive groves towards the cobalt blue of the Tyrrhenian Sea. She knew, with characteristic wisdom, what this book had to be about. More humanity than history, she said. I hope I've done the story justice.

Jacket illustrations
Front: The Pardini family (Museo Storico di Sant'Anna di Stazzema); *back:* The Sant'Anna di Stazzema memorial stone (Author's collection).

First published 2021

The History Press
97 St George's Place, Cheltenham,
Gloucestershire, GL50 3QB
www.thehistorypress.co.uk

British Library Cataloguing in Publication Data.
A catalogue record for this book is available from the British Library.

ISBN 978 0 7509 9519 1

Typesetting and origination by The History Press
Printed and bound in Great Britain by TJ Books Limited, Padstow, Cornwall.

Acknowledgements

As always, a lot of thanks must go to my exceptional literary agent in London, Andrew Lownie. Many thanks too to Mark Beynon and Simon Wright at The History Press, who immediately saw the importance of this story, and then published it with clear-minded verve, style and commitment. Along the way, my brothers and sisters have ridden shotgun, especially Luke, Anthony, James and Flora. In Turin, thanks to my friends Giulia Avataneo, Katiuscia Sacco, Otilia Cheslerean and Amor Ben. Thanks as well to the efficient and very helpful staff of the museums, archives and libraries in Italy, especially those at the museum at Sant'Anna di Stazzema.

Contents

MAPS

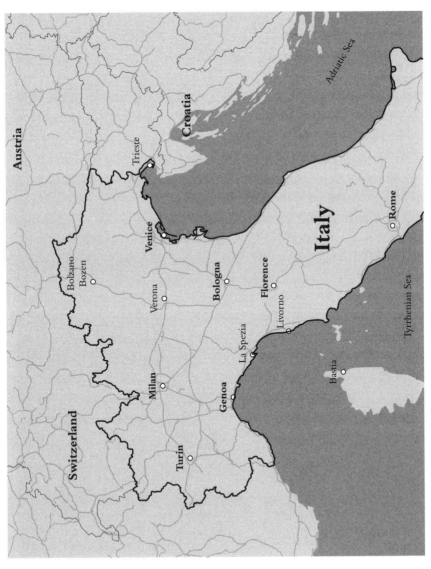

Central and Northern Italy.

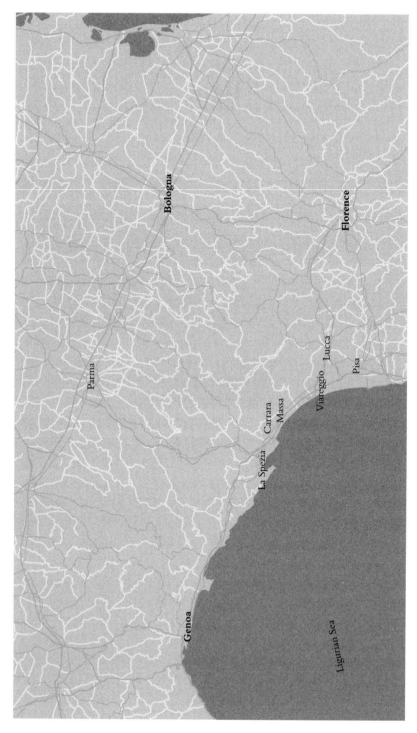

Florence, Bologna and the Tuscan coast.

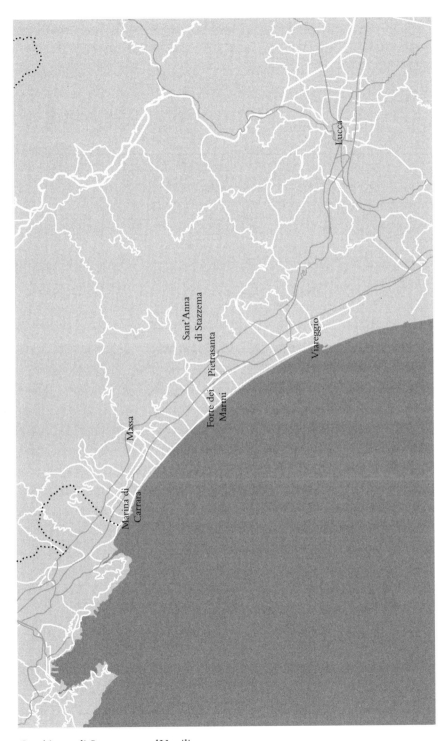

Sant'Anna di Stazzema and Versilia.

Marzabotto and the Monte Sole plateau.

The Rank Structure of the Waffen-SS

Reichsführer-SS	The equivalent of field marshal, this rank was held by one man alone, Heinrich Himmler
Obergruppenführer	Lieutenant General
Gruppenführer	Major General
Brigadeführer	Brigadier General
Standartenführer	Colonel
Obersturmbannführer	Lieutenant Colonel
Sturmbannführer	Major
Hauptsturmführer	Captain
Obersturmführer	First Lieutenant
Sturmführer	Second Lieutenant
Obertruppführer	Sergeant Major
Oberscharführer	Staff Sergeant
Scharführer	Sergeant
Rottenführer	Corporal
Sturmmann	Lance Corporal
SS Mann	Trooper

Prologue

Virtual Remembrance

On Saturday, 25 April 2020, three men stood in front of a war memorial at a mountain village in central Tuscany. Heads bowed, hands clasped, one of them placed a large green wreath of laurel leaves on the stone in front of them. The men came here every year on 25 April, which in Italy is the day that commemorates the liberation of their country from the Germans, the Fascist regime of Benito Mussolini, and the establishment of the new Italian republic. Across the country on this day, old partisans donned red and green neck scarves, their colours of political allegiance from the days of the Second World War. They stood in front of statues, memorials and commemoration sites across the length and breadth of the country, remembering. In the Tuscan mountain village of Sant'Anna di Stazzema, the three men were offering their respects to hundreds of civilians who died there in August 1944, massacred by German troops in a savage reprisal operation. In a normal year, the village and its surroundings would have been thronged with government officials, the mayors of neighbouring towns and villages, politicians from Rome, parties of school children, some old partisans who fought in the war, their children and grandchildren. For Sant'Anna di Stazzema, which sits on an isolated hillside in central Tuscany, is the site of the best-known of all the mass killings carried out by the Germans and their Fascist allies between 1943 and 1945. Simply put, on 25 April, it should have been crowded. But it was deserted. And the reason it was deserted was the reason why the three men laying the wreath were wearing face masks.

Italy, its former partisans and its people, refused to be bowed, however. Covid-19 would not cancel the spirit of 25 April and the celebrations of Liberation Day, pledged the National Association of Former Partisans on its website. Never had there been a commemoration day with such a rich menu of virtual events to attend, it proclaimed proudly. Virtual remembrance was the order of the day. Where former partisans, relatives of fallen soldiers, government officials and onlookers did gather in person, then the draconian rulings of social distancing would be in force, in keeping with the worldwide situation of emergency. The president of the Italian National Partisans' Association said that although the respective authorities would, of course, be laying wreaths and depositing flowers at statues and monuments, most Italians would celebrate in a different way, confined as they were to their homes by lockdown.

They would feel their hearts beat to a rhythm of anti-Fascism, but they'd have to do it online, by posting photographs, thoughts, music and letters, or gathered on their balconies, to sing the eternal partisan hymn that became the anthem of resistance to the Germans and Mussolini's Fascists. At a co-ordinated time, the country could gather on their terraces, at the windows of their houses, on balconies, and together sing the stirring words of the protest song 'Bella Ciao'.

The song originated in the paddy fields of the Po valley in the first half of the twentieth century. Italy's cultivation of rice is centred on the western stretch of land that runs alongside this vast, serpentine river, which creeps dark, slow and bottle green from its rising above Turin to its estuary on the Adriatic. Between Milan and Turin the Po ambles sluggishly, alongside it fields that in the rice-growing season are flooded. To plant, pick, weed and tend the rice, poor migrant workers from southern Italy, mostly women, would trek north every year. The rice estates were owned by big landowners, and the poorly paid female workers, known as mondinas, or weeders, were constantly exploited by them. 'Bella Ciao' – the words simply mean 'hello beautiful' – became their protest song. Once the Second World War erupted, the words of the song were quickly adopted by partisans, industrial workers and anybody who stood up to the Germans and Mussolini. And so on the evening of 25 April this year, the balconies of the country erupted in song. Confined to their homes for weeks, the country's population came out, defiant, resilient, singing, playing instruments, cheering, for a moment united in remembrance and a refusal to be beaten. On a day when their political leaders had donned the tricolour sash of the national flag, and stood, face-masked and solemn, in front of statues and memorial sites across the country, the people remembered what had come before them in another time, seventy-five years before, when another enemy had stormed across their land.

After the laying of the wreath in the village of Sant'Anna di Stazzema, one of the three men took some moments to talk. As a child, he survived the massacre that devastated the village in August 1944, and now Enrico Pieri is the President of the Martyrs of Sant'Anna Association. He said:

> April 25th 1945 was not a party for us. We were still full of pain. And after 75 years we are still here. Since then we left [the village] and went back up. Our houses were destroyed, slowly we were able to rebuild them. I would like to tell young people not to lose heart. We must have a little optimism. There will be suffering, however we will be able to overcome this crisis that is now gripping us. We will come to a rebirth, to have a better future for everyone. And a better, united Europe that gave us peace after the war.[1]

The Second World War, the Covid-19 pandemic, commemoration, past and present, had all seemed to come together in an idiosyncratic mix of crisis, protest, and commemoration. It was backed up by an Italian resilience in the face of hardship that surfaces so frequently across a country that, since 1945, has been no stranger to dysfunctional politics, uncertain economics and social unrest. The Mayor of Florence, Dario Nardella, said the best way of combating what he euphemistically called 'the current crisis' would come from Italians' roots, values and identities:

> Celebrating April 25th in this moment of emergency for the country has even more value because the best resources to overcome this crisis come from our roots, from our values, from our identity. When we

celebrate April 25th we celebrate the deepest value of freedom, our country, our history. That freedom which is the fruit of the sacrifice of the lives of women and men and never as today we need to feel at home. The coming months will be very complex, it will be the most difficult challenge for my generation and for all those born after the Second World War.[2]

Liberated by the Allies in mid–August 1944, the city of Florence and the region of Tuscany was, in the war, the epicentre of partisan and civilian resistance to the German occupation and the Fascist regime of Il Duce, the dictator Benito Mussolini. It was in Tuscany that both carried out the largest number of war crimes against the Italian civilian population, trapped as it was between the advancing Allies and the partisans on one side, and the retreating Germans and Fascists on the other.

In the Tuscan town of Pistoia on 25 April, the mayor said that the fight today was against what he called 'an invisible enemy', and again called on Italians to find the spirit and strength that had animated the men and women who rebuilt Italy after the war.[3] As the country entered its seventh week of lockdown, he said that parallels between the Second World War and the Covid-19 virus were everywhere, especially on 25 April. The war, however, was massively more destructive and more frightening, with Italians armed against each other. And once again he, and other politicians and municipal leaders, chose to highlight what was taking place at Sant'Anna di Stazzema that day as something that epitomised what was taking place across the country, and something that linked the present with the years of the Second World War.

There were no children gathered at Sant'Anna that day, he said, none of the usual crowds, no voices, no women, no men, none of the usual commotion that accompanied the celebration of Liberation Day at Sant'Anna di Stazzema. Just the surreal laying of a wreath in silence, by only three people: the mayor, the President of the Regional Council of Tuscany, Eugenio Giani, and Enrico Pieri, from the Martyrs Association. Sant'Anna di Stazzema doesn't 'close', said Giani, because memory and memorial are a right.[4] And nowhere more so than on the top of the deserted Tuscan hillside at Sant'Anna. And what parallels there were to be drawn between it, Italian history, the war and the twenty-first century. It was a feast day, for Italians, for liberty, and for democracy. And in Tuscany today, like in Tuscany seventy-six years ago, Sant'Anna di Stazzema represented all that is strongest and most relevant when it comes to the wartime resistance.

On the most important day of commemoration in the Italian calendar, at a time of national and world crisis in the face of a global pandemic, many Italian leaders – particularly in the centre of the country – chose to draw parallels between present and past by focusing on this small but highly significant village: what was happening there this 25 April 2020 and what had taken place there in 1944. Why? What is it and what was it about this Tuscan mountain village that evokes such strength of thought, reflection, concern, importance and reverence?

In Italy, memories of war are everywhere. Seventy-five years after 2 million German, Italian, British, American and Commonwealth soldiers fought across the mountains, plains and cities of the country, memorials, commemorations and memories – physical and abstract – are at every turn. No more so than in the evidence of the huge number of war crimes that the Germans committed during their twenty-month occupation of the country. Of the estimated 22,000 Italian civilians killed in persecutions, war crimes and deportations from September 1943 to May 1945, 8,000 of them were Italian Jews, and 14,000 non-Jews.[5] Those who weren't Jews were shot, beaten, burned or starved to death in some 5,300 separate instances, and the Jews deported, mainly to the concentration camp complexes at Auschwitz and Mauthausen. The SS, and the SD (its intelligence arm) and the Gestapo were responsible for several thousands of these deaths and operated within an infrastructure of violence, which they saw as being legitimised by draconian anti-partisan rulings from their commanders. They were overseen by senior SS and Wehrmacht officers in Italy, and were accompanied by an orchestra of lesser units that also played their part.

The old and historically independent city of Turin lies in the north-west of the country, the capital of the region of Piemonte. To the west, north and south-west, the Alps stretch in a snow-capped semicircle around it. South of the city stretches the wine country of the Langhe and then the mountains, which rise like a barrier before the shimmering turquoise of the Ligurian Sea. Across the elegant streets and sweeping boulevards of Turin, some of the houses or schools or shops seem to have one or more small, square, brass plaques set into the pavement in front of the door. These are the memorials to those who used to live there, but who were deported in the Holocaust. The project started in 1992 at the initiative of a German artist called Gunter Demnig, and the brass plaques are set on top of a small cube of concrete; in German they are called *Stolpersteine* or 'stumbling stones'. They can be found in their thousands and thousands across villages, towns and cities in the former German Reich, particularly in Germany, Austria and Poland. There are also many in Turin, which had a large Jewish community targeted for deportation between 1943 and 1945. Italy's Jews were marginally less unfortunate than those in the other three countries mentioned. In Italy, around 38,000–40,000 Jews managed to escape, partly because the operations to hunt them down only began after September 1943, when Italy surrendered to the Allies and Germany occupied the country. But some 8,000 of Italy's Jews were arrested and deported to their death. Many of the brass plaques tell a familiar tale.

Piazza Castello in central Turin is the site of the former royal palaces of the Duchy of Savoy. One of these former royal buildings now houses the tourism board for the region of Piemonte. In front of its swing doors there are three of the small bronze plaques, commemorating the three members of the Colombo family, arrested on 27 October 1943, six weeks after the Germans occupied Italy. Mario was 29, Benvenuto 61 and Enrico 63. The 'stumbling stones' record the details: they were all deported to Auschwitz on 6 December 1943, with the two older family members killed almost immediately, on 11 December. Mario lasted longer, and was killed on 30 March 1944.

Yet for all these plaques, all these deaths, all these deportations of Italian Jews, very few Germans served even an hour of prison time after the war. The senior SS and police commander in Italy, General Karl Wolff, reportedly made a secret deal with the American OSS that he would be immune from prosecution for crimes committed in Italy by the SS and Gestapo if he agreed to appear as a prosecution witness at Nuremberg. When he was ultimately imprisoned in the new Federal Germany, it was for Holocaust crimes committed in Poland, not for any atrocity in Italy. Nobody was ever really certain if he did make a deal, or whether it was honoured, but it certainly appeared so to the British, Italians, Americans, and even some Germans, too. It was one example of the ways – sometimes complex and duplicitous, sometimes simple and bureaucratic – of how many Germans wanted for crimes escaped justice.

One man who should have faced muscular justice for the deportation and persecution of Italian Jews was SS-Sturmbannführer Friedrich Bosshammer, a colleague of Adolf Eichmann's, who was responsible for the deportation of Italian Jews from January 1944 onwards. Yet he lived in freedom in post-war Germany for twenty-three years, working as a lawyer, and allegedly protected by former SS colleagues serving in the new Federal German government. He was only arrested in 1968, went through a four-year trial, during which the Italian writer Primo Levi testified, and then died before serving a single day in prison. What happened to him after the war was, extraordinarily, too often the judicial rule, not the exception, for SS men wanted for war crimes committed in Italy.

The road and railway line that leads south from Turin heads towards the coastal region of Liguria; in early summer, the road snakes alongside a turquoise sea and passes, via tunnels dug out of solid rock, through the mountains that rise sharp and high above the waters of the Italian Riviera. One of these tunnels is at a place called Turchino, and in May 1944 the Waffen-SS shot 246 Italian civilians, in a series of reprisals for the deaths of five German sailors killed by Italian partisans in an attack at a nearby cinema. SS-Obersturmbannführer Friedrich Engel, who commanded the German execution squad, got away with murder. He was sentenced by an Italian court, in 1969, to life imprisonment *in absentia*. Germany refused to extradite him. He was investigated in Germany in 1969, but prosecutors said they could not find enough evidence, despite dozens of Italians who stated that they were prepared to appear as witnesses. A Hamburg court then tried him in 2002, but despite being convicted, he was allowed to walk free on a technicality. Germany's highest constitutional court, the Bundesgerichtshof, then quashed this conviction and formally pardoned him.

The majority of German war crimes committed in Italy happened in Tuscany and Emilia-Romagna, two provinces south of Liguria. The coast road goes south-east from the port of Genoa, following the curve of the sea, through La Spezia, Massa, Carrara and Pietrasanta, the towns and cities that lie on the Mediterranean. Above the littoral, the mountains of the Apuan Alps rise high and forested in the interior. It was in this region in summer 1944, around Bologna, Florence and Arezzo, that the Germans faced down the Allies in constant, heavy combat, as they fought a slogging withdrawal to their pre-prepared defensive positions on the Gothic Line further north. As they retreated, and as the Allies advanced, so Italian partisan activity increased behind the ever-retreating German front line. Emboldened by the Allies' advance, and pushed into armed conflict by the Germans' scorched earth policy of reprisals against the Italian civilian population, the partisans attacked German units with increased regularity and increased daring the further the Germans retreated. The Germans, for their part, responded with ever more savage reprisals.

But it was one unit, the 16th SS Panzergrenadier Division, the 'Reichsführer-SS', that went far further, more brutally, with greater numbers of victims than any other German unit in Italy. The unit had already established a reputation for brutality while fighting in the Ukraine and Russia after Operation Barbarossa, and in addition to noted combat capabilities, it showed the utterly routine disregard for taking prisoners, or looking after any Russian PoWs, that was common to many SS units fighting on the Eastern Front. It brought this operational approach to Italy, and added to it a special barbarity, an imaginative twist of violence evident in every mass killing the unit perpetrated. It was responsible for the killings at Sant'Anna di Stazzema, in which at least 390 people were killed.[6] What happened there remains the highest profile of the massacres carried out not just by the 16th SS, but by all German units in Italy. Partly because of the extreme brutality and the number of people who were burned alive; partly because over sixty of the victims were children, one only three weeks old; partly because as the village and the corpses of the victims were still burning after the massacre, the SS men sat down in the shade of the village and very calmly ate their lunch.

And the other reason why the killings at Sant'Anna resonate so strongly today is because the incident has come to epitomise the enormous failures of justice for war crimes committed by the Germans in Italy. Nobody has been brought to trial in Germany for the Sant'Anna killings, either immediately after the war, or since. Investigations were opened, cases filed by prosecutors, but all the SS men responsible escaped justice to live and die in freedom in Germany. When Italy finally found ten of them guilty, *in absentia*, in 2005, many Italians were appalled to discover that not only were all of these guilty men living in freedom in Germany, but that their native country refused to extradite them back to Italy. For Italians, as well as for many others who know about, or have followed or lived the experience of the Second World War, the denial of proper justice stands as a massive affront. Especially from a fellow EU member state like Germany that so often – and so rightly – stresses the vital importance of confronting the past and dealing with history. Germans respect the law: yet the ways in which they do so, especially in complex war crimes cases like this, sometimes appear baffling and contradictory. Especially to those who have been on the receiving end of atrocities, like those survivors of the killings at Sant'Anna di Stazzema and elsewhere. In the end, only two SS officers served prison terms for any of the 16th SS' atrocities across Tuscany, and one of these men – the division's commanding officer – was released and pardoned after only eight years.

But, in Germany's defence, confronting the past and dealing with history is a very long way away from being simple or straightforward. Each modern successive German government can say it has made a substantially significant effort in doing so, within the obvious provisions of regional, federal and international law. The difficulties sometimes arise when a current administration applies the legal and judicial obligations and absolutism of the present to try and rectify the omissions and errors of the past. Too often the past creeps back to waylay the best intentions of the present. For victims, survivors and relatives of survivors of past war crimes, the apparent lack of sufficient and concrete judicial results shouldn't be able to be explained away by a mix of legal, historical, political and economic pragmatism and realpolitik, by one country or another. But sometimes they are; sometimes, very gratifyingly, they're not.

Today the hills, olive groves, apricot orchards and vineyards of central Tuscany look very similar, in many places, to how they were in that wartime summer seventy-five years ago. At the Carthusian monastery at Farneta, north of Lucca, a memorial plaque reminds visitors of what happened in early September 1944, when soldiers from the 16th SS arrived and took away twelve monks and thirty-two people hiding in the monastery. They tied them to trees with barbed wire and shot them. Nearly four decades after the event, in January 1985, the Italian Prime Minister unveiled the plaque, which reads:

> Forty years after the Liberation, the Association of the Resistance Fighters in Lucchesia and the Municipal Authorities of Lucca remember the martyrdom of six Carthusian fathers, six Carthusian brothers and thirty-two civilians in September of 1944. Nazi savagery imposed the same death both on the monks and on those who at the darkest hour had found brotherly hospitality in these sacred precincts. The presence of the Prime Minister at the inauguration of this memorial stone ensures the entry into the history of the Italian people of the witness of these victims.

The memorial stone might have ensured that the event enters into Italian history, but justice certainly hasn't.

In 2005, a court in the Tuscan town of La Spezia tried, *in absentia*, former SS-Lieutenant Helmut Langer. He had led the half-company of SS men who abducted and then killed the monks and civilians from the monastery. Despite numerous witnesses, the court found Langer innocent. The Rome Court of Appeal, however, found him guilty and sentenced him to life imprisonment. The Germans refused to extradite him. Langer died in 2016, free.

German President Frank-Walter Steinmeier visited the town of Fivizzano in Tuscany in summer 2019, and apologised for German atrocities that had taken place there in 1944.[7] He admitted that his country had not lived up to its legal responsibilities. It was the closest a German head of state had come to admitting that his country had failed in dealing with the aftermath of war crimes committed in Italy in 1944. But as the President spoke, the last SS men who had been in Tuscany in 1944 were dead, or nearing the end of their lives in Germany in freedom. This book tells the story of what they did in Tuscany in 1944, how, where and why. It's the story, too, of those Italians who survived their rampage of massacres.

It tells how for seventy-five years some men of the 16th SS Panzergrenadier Division got away, literally, with mass murder. This unit committed more war crimes than any other in the entire German armed forces infrastructure in Italy in the whole war. The division, whose nominative cuff title was 'Reichsführer-SS', tore across the central Italian heartland of Tuscany in the boiling summer of 1944, massacring hundreds of innocent people at a time in a string of major killings, carried out under the guise of reprisal actions against Italian partisans. It was the officers and men of this unit who, to a large extent, were most guilty of the most war crimes, and who, to a large extent, most escaped justice. This book sets out to find out what happened, what they did, and how many of them escaped.

1

Italy Surrenders

In the early hours of the morning of 10 June 1943, Luftwaffe signals interception stations across the Adriatic, Aegean and eastern Mediterranean began to pick up an abnormally high volume of American and British radio traffic. The German air force had assigned responsibility for this sector of the European front to the 352nd Signals Intelligence Regiment, one of eight such units in the Luftwaffe's *Chiffrestelle,* or cryptanalytical department.[1] To help them intercept Allied VHF signals traffic from North Africa and the Mediterranean, the regiment had installed listening posts on the islands of Crete, Rhodes and Kos, as well as on the Loutsa plateau north-west of Athens. The Luftwaffe intercept teams saw immediately that many of the signals they were picking up that night, transmitted by the Allies in Morse code, began with the same two letters of the alphabet. In turn, these were set in two groups of five letters each. The German air force men knew that the first letters of a coded message, known as the 'indicator', designated the intended recipient of the signal. They were also well aware that an indicator made up of two repeated letters and two five-letter groups meant the messages were being encoded on the American M-209 Hagelin encryption device. The men on the islands and on the high, windswept Loutsa plateau wasted no time. Details of the signals were transmitted to Luftwaffe intelligence headquarters in Athens, and thence to decryption stations at Potsdam and Berlin. Operation Husky, the Allied invasion of Sicily, had just begun. The first signals were coming in from units of the American 82nd Airborne Division, transmitted just after landing on their parachute drop zones.

The United States armed forces had developed the M-209 in answer to the Enigma machine used by the Germans. Named after its Swedish inventor, Boris Hagelin, the M-209 was a lightweight, man-portable device that weighed only 7lb, was versatile and easy to use, meaning US airborne troops could parachute with it. Message encryption was based upon six adjustable rotary wheels inside the machine, each of which contained a different number of letters of the alphabet, from seventeen to twenty-six. When the operator pressed the different letters on the keyboard that he needed to compose the 'plain text' of a message, a corresponding number of alternative letters would be selected by the device from the six rotor wheels, each of which turned every time a letter on the keyboard was pressed. This arrangement gave 101 million possible permutations of letters that could form the plain text of an original message.

Some 140,000 M-209s were made, and American infantry and artillery units in North Africa began to use it in action in late 1942. Cryptanalysts from the Wehrmacht High Command's code-breaking agency broke into their first M-209 messages in early spring 1943. German army units in Tunisia had overrun the headquarters of an American infantry company, and captured parts of signals books containing lists of daily, weekly and monthly settings for the units' encryption devices. Radio operators had tried to burn these books, but had only partially succeeded. Despite this intelligence compromise, for weeks afterwards the Americans did not change the M-209 code settings used by each unit in the same division. This gave German cryptanalysts from the Luftwaffe and Wehrmacht High Command time to decode and compare thousands of messages sent by them.

During the invasion of Sicily, the Germans then captured more Hagelin codebooks, this time completely intact. This meant that for three vital weeks they could read American radio traffic at exactly the same time as Field Marshal Kesselring was withdrawing his troops across the island to the Straits of Messina. From here they could evacuate safely to the Italian mainland. It also meant the Germans could intercept messages sent between the Americans, British and Italians. The

Luftwaffe had a unique advantage in this as they had been intercepting, decrypting and reading signals sent by the Italian navy, army and air force since 1941. The Italian and Allied messages deciphered and read in Potsdam and Berlin also confirmed the Germans' worst fears about their allies: the Italians were trying to negotiate a surrender with the British and the Americans.

Before the Allies were ashore in Sicily, they had begun to negotiate a secret armistice with the Italian King, Victor Emmanuel III, Prime Minister Pietro Badoglio, and senior Fascist officials. The latter were exhausted by Mussolini's autocratic twenty-year rule. It had bankrupted the country, reduced hundreds of thousands of its inhabitants to near-starvation, forced a murderous, terrifying allegiance with the Third Reich, and sent divisions of its finest troops off to die in wars in Russia, Africa and Greece. Il Bel Paese was on its knees, Italians wanted peace, and Fascism's hollow promises that it would reward them with the glory of a lost empire were exactly that. Empty. So on 25 July, Mussolini was deposed at a meeting of the Grand Council of Fascism in Rome: control of the Italian armed forces, he was told, would be handed over to the king and prime minister. Police officers arrested Il Duce after the meeting. Then 200 carabinieri, paramilitary policemen loyal to the royal family, took the deposed dictator and his mistress Clara Petacci first to the small Mediterranean island of Ponza, off Naples, then to an isolated villa on La Maddalena, off the north-east coast of Sardinia. But the Germans managed to sneak an Italian-speaking German agent on to the island, and then flew over it in a Heinkel 111 taking photographs, searching for their ally. So the carabinieri hurriedly moved Mussolini to the Hotel Campo Imperatore, a skiing resort in the Apennines that was built high on the plateau of the Gran Sasso mountain.

During August, Italian and British generals and diplomats met in secret in Lisbon, hammering out the terms of the proposed armistice. By the end of the month they had reached an agreement, and both parties in the talks sent telegrams and signals to this effect back to London and Rome from what they assumed were the secure signals systems of their respective Lisbon embassies. German cryptanalysts from Department-Z of their Foreign Service – shortened to Pers-Z – intercepted and read some of both. The Allies and the Italians then met formally to discuss the terms of the armistice in the village of Cassibile, outside Syracuse.

Much of the negotiation between the Italians and the British was, however, handled in secret, without the Germans' knowledge. A British agent from the Special Operations Executive had parachuted into Lake Como, outside Milan, in July. Lieutenant Cecil Richard Mallaby was equipped with a rubber raft, and his plan was to paddle ashore, link up with Italian resistance groups, and co-ordinate sabotage operations with them. The RAF would parachute explosives, weapons and signalling equipment to him once he had landed and made contact with partisan units. However, his parachute jump over Lake Como coincided with a British bombing raid on Milan. Refugees were pouring northwards en route to safety in Como, the lights of buildings on the side of the lake all lit up. 'Dick' Mallaby floated down towards the water in full view of Italian soldiers. Captured immediately, the young, bilingual officer, who had grown up in Tuscany, was handed over to officers of the SIM, the Servizio Informazione Militare. They, in turn, assumed that his arrival over Lake Como was part of a wider, more cunning plan. They believed he was there to help co-ordinate the terms of the forthcoming armistice with Italy. Being loyal to the king and the prime minister, and opposed to Mussolini, the SIM officers who captured him took him straight to Rome. They provided him with an Italian signals expert and wireless set, and directed him to contact his British superiors, who were simultaneously negotiating with the Italians on Sicily. Mallaby did. Using a series of signal settings code-named 'Monkey', he relayed transmissions backwards and forwards between Rome and Cassibile.

Both sides put their signatures on the armistice on 3 September. However, the Germans had also managed to intercept messages sent by the Americans during the negotiations. Seeing that their duplicitous allies had made a secret deal with the Allies without consulting Berlin, Hitler and his generals were livid. But they moved fast. They were most afraid that Italy's capitulation and the disintegration of its armed forces would mean that the Allies could now occupy Italy without facing significant resistance.

The Germans were saved by British diplomatic dithering. Their Foreign Secretary, Anthony Eden, had been an undersecretary at the

British Foreign and Commonwealth Office during the Abyssinian crisis in 1935; Mussolini had consistently belittled and patronised him during conferences, meetings and in interviews, describing him on one occasion as 'the best-dressed fool in Europe'. Eden was a man who bore a grudge, and he wanted nothing less than a full and unconditional surrender from the Italians. So as the armistice was being signed under the Sicilian sun, the Germans seized the moment. They launched Operation Achse, and dispatched nine extra divisions straight down to Italy as fast as possible; units based in southern France, Austria, Yugoslavia and Hungary. One of these was the 16th SS Panzergrenadier Division, which had been refitting, and on anti-partisan operations in Hungary and Slovenia. Their objective was to reinforce German troops already in Italy, seize tactical and strategic control of the country, and disarm the Italian armed forces.

At half-past six on the evening of 8 September 1943, American General Dwight D. Eisenhower made an announcement on Allied Forces Radio; just over an hour later Italian Field Marshal Pietro Badoglio broadcast an almost identical one. The news spread like an electrical current across the country: Italy had signed an armistice with the Allies. Immediately after his broadcast, both Badoglio and King Victor Emmanuel fled by car north-east from Rome to the port of Pescara, where they boarded a destroyer that took them southwards again to the port of Bari, on the eastern Adriatic. Their flight from Rome left chaos behind it. In the resultant power vacuum, a group of anti-Fascist political organisations immediately met in secret. Outside, on the streets of the centre of the capital, German paratroopers and armoured units accompanied by Italian soldiers loyal to Mussolini fought scrappy, running battles with Italians in turn loyal to their king and to the Allies.

The anti-Fascists immediately announced the formation of the Committee of National Liberation, or Comitato di Liberazione Nazionale, known as the CLN. It was made up of the Italian Communist and Socialist parties, the Catholic Christian Democrats, as well as the Liberal and Labour groupings, and smaller parties like the liberal Action Party. Out of this, three main partisan groups were formed: the communist Garibaldi brigades, the socialist Matteotti brigades, and the

Justice and Liberty units from the Action Party. At dawn on the 9th, they released an unequivocal first communiqué:

> It's necessary to act immediately and as widely and decisively as possible, because only if the Italian People actively contribute to push out Germans from Italy and to defeat Nazism and Fascism, it will be really able [*sic*] to get independence and freedom. We cannot and must not passively expect freedom from the British and the Americans.[2]

South of the island of Capri, the Germans had sighted thirty-six American and British troopships at 4 p.m. on the afternoon of the 8th, two hours before Eisenhower's broadcast. They could see this was an invasion force headed for the Italian mainland at Salerno, so they hurriedly disarmed the Italian army units guarding the beaches outside the town and took over their positions. When Operation Avalanche – the landings at Salerno – began, the Germans were waiting. In the capital, Italian units who had remained loyal to the king, and the Allies, surrounded key buildings and occupied the main roads leading into Rome. That evening, paratroopers of the American 82nd Airborne Division were already embarked in their C-47 Skytrain troop carriers, waiting on Sicilian air bases for the order to take off. Operation Giant II was the code name for a highly risky airborne strike that would see the 82nd parachute on to three Italian airfields north-west of Rome, link up with loyal Italian units, and march on the capital. The signal to launch the operation depended on the decision of the American Brigadier General Maxwell D. Taylor, who had sneaked into Rome through enemy lines along with Italian partisans, his mission to assess the viability of the operation. He discovered that not only were the Italians unlikely to guarantee the support necessary, but in and outside the city the Germans had deployed two full Panzergrenadier divisions, along with 150 tanks. The paratroopers of the 82nd would have been massacred. Maxwell Taylor sent a signal saying the operation was impossible. The Allies stayed put.

Then, in thirty-six hours of hot, confused, contradictory fighting along Rome's cobbled boulevards, under the umbrella pine trees that lined its roads, German tanks and fighting experience won the day. The Italian army contingent in the city surrendered, and its two commanding officers, Raffaele Cadorna and Colonel Lanza di Montezemolo, went into hiding with the partisans. The CLN proclaimed itself the new, anti-Fascist coalition, partisan operations against the Germans and Italian Fascists exploded, and the country fissured down the political and military middle. German divisions poured in from France, Austria and Yugoslavia.

In Tuscany, one of the first battles after the announcement of the armistice took place in the small port of Piombino, which sits opposite the island of Elba. It characterised the chaotic, fluid nature of the fighting after Italy's surrender, involving every faction of its armed forces and civilian population. On 10 September, a group of German torpedo boats tried to enter the harbour in Piombino; the Italian port authorities, convinced they were trying to occupy the town, prevented them approaching. The local Italian army commander – a Fascist – then countermanded this order given by the naval commander – a royalist sympathiser – and the E-boats docked. Civilians, backed by small partisan groups, tried to prevent the German sailors from leaving the jetties; Italian tanks manned by Fascist supporters opened fire on them, until a group of junior army and navy officers united the civilians, soldiers, sailors and port workers against the Germans and the Fascist senior officers. Pitched battle broke out. Italian tanks and artillery sank or damaged nineteen German vessels, while the armed groups of civilians, sailors, soldiers and partisans killed 120 Germans, wounded 150 and took 200 prisoners. Two Italian sailors, a corporal working in the customs post and a civilian were the only Italian casualties. On 12 September, German infantry and naval units retook Piombino, and the mixed groups of Italian defenders, military and civilian, naval and partisan, fled into the hills above the port. And so was formed the first Tuscan partisan group.

Around them across the whole of Italy, the situation was equally confused and contradictory. German soldiers were arriving from the north by road and air and sea; the 16th SS Division was among them. Italian Fascists loyal to Mussolini were heading north. On 11 September, the Germans declared martial law in all areas of the country occupied by their forces. German measures for *Bandenbekampfung*, or anti-partisan activity, had originally been covered in a general directive from Hitler in 1942, primarily referring to operations on the Eastern Front. It described the fight against partisans as nothing to do with soldierly gallantry or the principles of the Geneva Convention. All troops, said the Führer, should use all means, without restriction, to ensure success, and it stated specifically that, 'No German employed against partisans will be held accountable for his actions in the fighting against them or their followers, either by disciplinary action or by Court Martial.'[3]

The German commander in Italy, Field Marshal Albert Kesselring, would update these directives with orders of his own, mainly from May to July 1944, specifically related to anti-partisan warfare in Italy. Initially, responsibility for the latter was assigned to the SS and police units who operated in rear areas behind the German front line, but increasingly whichever German unit of the Wehrmacht or SS was deployed in any particular area oversaw anti-partisan operations. The first large-scale killings of civilians took place within days of the German arrival in Italy, and involved a unit from the Waffen-SS.

The Killings at Boves and on Lake Maggiore

One of the first German units to arrive in northern Italy was the 1st SS Panzer Division, whose official title was the Liebstandarte SS Adolf Hitler. It drew its name from its original role providing troops to be Hitler's bodyguards. When Operation Achse began, and German troops poured into Italy to disarm the Italian armed forces, the SS division had just been transferred from Russia to Hungary. By 19 September, one of its battalions had advanced all the way across north-western Italy, arriving in the town of Cuneo. The city is situated in the foothills of the Alps, near the French border. The SS men were trying to intercept groups of Italian soldiers returning to their country from the Italian-occupied zone of south-eastern France; the Germans were afraid they would try and join partisan groups already operating in the border area. The battalion from the Liebstandarte was commanded by SS-Sturmbannführer Joachim Peiper, a highly decorated panzer commander who had previously served as one of Himmler's personal adjutants. He then won notoriety on the Eastern Front as a capable but sometimes over-aggressive combat leader, one whose men earned a reputation for killing civilians and Red Army prisoners. Peiper's unit was nicknamed 'the Blowtorch Battalion' by other SS officers for its record in burning villages and shooting their inhabitants. It shows the levels of excesses reportedly carried out by Peiper's unit that other SS units, themselves no strangers to atrocities, would coin this nickname. Outside Cuneo, it wasn't just returning Italian soldiers they were looking for – they were also tracking an estimated 1,000 Italian Jews returning home across the border from France. This was an unorthodox practice, frowned upon by the SS divisional commander, who stressed that operations to detain and deport Italian Jews, and seize their property, assets and valuables, were to remain the operational preserve of the SD and the German security police. German units at that point were also under strict orders not to attack Italian civilians, or deploy any form of violence against them: Hitler still had firm hopes that the Italian civilian population, if not the army, could somehow be persuaded to be sympathetic to and co-operative with their new German occupiers. What was to happen in Boves firmly destroyed any chance this policy had of proving effective.

On 19 September, a company of soldiers from the Liebstandarte intervened to try and rescue two of their colleagues. They had been captured by Italian soldiers and partisans in the small town of Boves, which sits on the southern outskirts of Cuneo. In the botched rescue attempt, the Italians killed a German soldier and wounded several others: Peiper surrounded the town, and threatened to burn it down and kill all of its inhabitants unless the German prisoners were released. The Italians complied. Two negotiators, the parish priest and a local businessman, managed to get the German soldiers released, and to get the body of the German soldier returned to his comrades. But in return for respecting their side of the bargain, Peiper's men poured petrol over the two Italian men and set them on fire. The SS commander then gave orders to open fire on the small town and its inhabitants. Many of these had already fled before the shooting began, leaving only the old or those too ill or infirm to move.

Regardless, the Germans killed twenty-three people, including an 87-year-old invalided woman, who couldn't move from her bedroom, and so was burned alive when the SS set fire to her house. The SS men also killed the deputy parish priest as he tried to give the last rites to a dying old man who had been shot in the street. In addition to the killings, they destroyed or damaged more than 100 houses, partly through artillery fire deployed after the German troops had pulled out of the town. There were no partisans in Boves that day – they had withdrawn to the surrounding mountains, along with the Italian soldiers crossing back from France. Relations between the German armed forces and their former allies, and their civilian population, had soured fast and brutally.[4]

On the same day, 170 miles north-eas of Cuneo, another unit from the same SS division carried out a further attack on Italian civilians. Men from the Liebstandarte were carrying out operations along the shores of Lago di Maggiore, a vast lake that stretches between Milan and the Swiss border. They were disarming units of the Italian army, but also carrying out extrajudicial operations of their own. Knowing that the arrival of the Germans would coincide with arrests and deportations of their communities, families of Italian Jews had fled northwards from Milan and hidden out near the lake, both with relatives and with sympathetic opponents of Mussolini. On arrival they discovered that refugees from Greece, also Jews, had been living secretly there since fleeing their country before the German invasion in 1941. Unbeknown to them, their existence, and their hiding places were known to local Italian Fascists. They tipped off the SS men as soon as they arrived.

They then proceeded to arrest the Jews and incarcerate them in a string of hotels along the edge of the lake. They were held in small groups ranging in size from two to sixteen. The Germans held this largest group of them in Meina, a small, elegant lakeside town of nineteenth-century villas and botanical gardens. On 19 September, a small group of SS officers met there at the Hotel Meina to decide what to do with their prisoners. Shoot them, was the decision, then dump their bodies in Lake Maggiore. So on the night of 22 September, and the day of the 23rd, in small groups, the Germans took the Jews from the hotels, drove them to a nearby forest, and executed them. They bundled the corpses into hessian sacks, filled these with rocks, and loaded them into boats, which they had forcibly commandeered from their

Italian owners. In some places the water in Lake Maggiore is between 500 and 1,100ft deep; the bodies in the weighted sacks sunk, out of sight, dumped in the darkness. Except not all of them did. The northern quarter of the lake lies in Swiss territory, and some of the bodies floated or were swept north, and washed up on lakeside beaches in Switzerland. Police in that country opened an investigation.

By 16 September 1943 the Allies had broken out of the bridgehead at Salerno, and Royalist Italians were either deserting from the armed forces in tens of thousands, or being interned and shipped north to PoW camps in Germany and Austria. Many of the 70,000 Allied PoWs imprisoned in camps in Italy also broke out, or were released as their guards switched sides. In Greece, Albania and Yugoslavia, Italians fought the Germans. On the Greek island of Cephalonia the Italian Acqui division initially resisted their former allies for a week, but then surrendered to them. At first, German mountain troops from the 1st Gebirgs Division had tried to persuade them to join forces, and dropped leaflets on their positions informing them that if they surrendered they would receive good treatment and be repatriated back to Italy. Nothing of the sort took place. The Italians refused the ultimatums, and the subsequent fighting lasted a week until, out of ammunition and outfought, they surrendered.

On 18 September the German High Command issued an order that, due to their treason, none of them would be taken prisoner. A total of 1,315 Italians had died in battle. Most of the German mountain troops were in fact Austrians, who then proceeded to execute around 5,000 of their former allies. In walled gardens, under the trees in olive groves, pushed into quarries, up against the whitewashed walls of small houses in backstreets, in groups of four, five, eight and twenty, the Italian soldiers died screaming prayers, throwing rocks at their executioners, or repeating their mothers' name over and over again before they were shot in the head. The Austrians burned their bodies on pyres, left them to rot on the cobbles, or threw them in the turquoise sea. When some of their Bavarian colleagues refused to shoot the Italians, they themselves were nearly shot by the Austrian mountain troopers. Packed on cargo ships, 3,000 more Italian prisoners were then shipped off to the port of Trieste, en route to concentration camps in Germany. The Allies got there first: the RAF bombed the German ships, not knowing they were carrying the Italians. The remainder of the vessels hit mines laid in the waters of the Adriatic.

On the islands of Kos and Corfu, the Germans executed another 400 Italian officers. The effects of these killings were felt immediately, both in Italy and further away. It sent a clear message to the Italian military and the country's civilian population: you are now the enemy of Germany. By the time the American, Russian, Chinese and British foreign ministers had convened in Moscow a month later, they had heard the news about what had happened in the Ionian and Dodecanese islands. So when Stalin, Roosevelt and Churchill signed the Declaration on Atrocities at the end of the conference in mid-October 1943, its wording was direct:

> We note the evidence of atrocities, massacres and cold-blooded mass executions which are being perpetrated by Hitlerite forces in many of the countries they have overrun and from which they are now being steadily expelled. Germans will be sent back to the countries where they have committed their crimes and be judged on the spot by the peoples whom they have outraged.

The cards of a number of high-ranking SS and Wehrmacht commanders were now very firmly marked.

The Italian army in Italy had by now surrendered, and its soldiers had done one of three things: some switched their allegiance to the Allies, and became partisans; a large number discarded their uniforms and simply went back to their homes, as newly self-appointed civilians; the remainder, loyal Fascists, headed north into German-occupied territory and swore allegiance to Benito Mussolini. The former dictator was still on the Gran Sasso by 12 September, when SS colonel Otto Skorzeny launched Operation Eiche, or Oak. An audacious commando coup de main, it involved a group of Luftwaffe paratroopers and SS special forces from the Sonderverband Friedenthal landing on the mountain in gliders. They freed their captive, took him back to Berlin, and then returned him to Rome. Around the town of Salo in northern Italy, the Germans then carved a mini-state out of the territory they occupied,

called it the Italian Social Republic, or the 'Salo' Republic, and gave
Mussolini free rein to run it as his own puppet Fascist enclave.

Sturmbannführer Karl Gesele and the 16th SS in Corsica

As the Italian army was collapsing, one brigade of the 16th SS
Panzergrenadier Division was stationed in Corsica. It watched as,
overnight, its former allies became new enemies. The Sturmbrigade
Reichsführer-SS had been moved from the south of France to Corsica
as soon as the Germans realised the Italians had betrayed them. Corsica
was tactically important: it was one potential landing site for the Allies
once they had occupied Sicily, and it would bring them operational
air bases in the northern Mediterranean from where their fighters and
bombers could reach Austria, northern Italy and southern Germany.
They could even attempt amphibious landings at least half the distance up mainland Italy. The Germans, planning to evacuate their
garrison from Sardinia on to Corsica, knew this. The SS commander
on Corsica was a Sturmbannführer, or major, called Karl Gesele. He
was 43 years old in September 1944. He came from Riedlingen in
Baden-Württemberg, a small and pretty town on the Danube in
south-western Germany. It was the home town of one of the men
who in the nineteenth century had invented the Black Forest gateau.[5]
   Gesele joined the SS in 1931; he rose fast through the ranks, and
by 1938 was a company commander in the SS Standarte Deutschland
regiment. Poland and the invasion of France saw the bespectacled,
determined and tactically astute officer awarded both First and Second
Class Iron Crosses. The first winter in Russia after Operation Barbarossa
saw the coveted German Cross in Gold added to his gallantry awards.
Obedient, disciplined, brave and devoted to the National Socialist
Party, he was SS to the tips of his fingers. When the Allies landed at
Salerno in September 1943, Gesele was in command of his SS brigade, sitting in isolated barracks near the small town of Aullene in the
middle of southern Corsica. Although they were one of the German
units that had been moved from the south of France on to Italian soil
when their former allies capitulated, they were technically still part of

an Italian division. It was commanded by a general who was opposed to Mussolini, and loyal to King Victor Emmanuel, the soldier monarch who was known as *sciaboletta*, or 'little sabre', as he stood only 5ft tall.

He wanted the tough, no-nonsense SS brigade isolated as far away as possible from him and his men while they tried to take over the island. However, the Italian liaison officer attached to the SS headquarters had remained loyal to Mussolini and his German allies. As soon as he heard the news about his commanding officer's intentions, he told Gesele immediately. The SS brigade's half-tracks, self-propelled guns and trucks then roared south through the pine and oak forests of central Corsica, raising dust on the tight mountain roads, driving hard for the port of Bonifacio. Through towns full of grey stone houses, pine forests that balmed warm with the ubiquitous smell of the myrtle that flourishes in Corsica, the SS thundered south. Bonifacio lies on the bottom tip of the island, facing Sardinia, and it was the port where German units evacuating from Sardinia would come ashore. The rocky coastline of southern Corsica made amphibious landings impossible anywhere else: any Allied invasion force would have to come ashore at Bonifacio. So Gesele knew it was vital to hold it. He ordered his men to occupy the harbour and dig into a defensive bridgehead around the town. Within three days the 90th Panzergrenadier Division, evacuated from Sardinia, relieved them.

Gesele then took his men diagonally all the way back across Corsica, from south-west to north-east. The port of Bastia, and the vital airfield at Borgo, lay on the northerly tip of the island. Italians loyal to the King had reinforced the town and the airstrip with a division of infantry, fifteen batteries of artillery and a regiment of tanks. Although outnumbered, the SS turned the situation to their own advantage. Most of the Italian artillery was on the slopes of the mountains that lie to the west of Bastia, separating it from the centre of the island. Yet most of the Italian infantry and tanks were down on the narrow coastal plan around Borgo airfield. When the Germans attacked these units, the artillery wouldn't open fire in case they hit their own men. It took a week of heavy fighting for the SS brigade to destroy them, establish a bridgehead around Bastia, and start to co-ordinate the German evacuation from Corsica.

In autumn, the vineyards outside Borgo hang heavy with light-red grapes that produce a rosé wine. SS men skirmished through the trellises of vines, taking cover where they could, lying on top of fallen bunches of grapes, rocks and the dust of the dry brown soil. The sweet sticky bloom of squashed fruit stained the fronts of their fawn tropical uniforms as they prowled into battle in the 90° heat. At dawn on 3 October 1943, it was over. Karl Gesele stood on the rear deck of the last German ship to leave the island, heading for Italy. For his command of the SS unit in action, he was awarded the Knight's Cross of the Iron Cross. The principal sentiments he took with him back to Italy were of a profound, disgusted distrust of the duplicitous Italians, and a deep loathing of retreat.

While he and his men had been in action on Corsica, the Allies had pushed north out of the Salerno bridgehead. Self-propelled guns and anti-aircraft units from another unit of the 16th SS had dug into positions in the pine trees overlooking the invasion beaches, fighting back at the Allies as they struggled ashore. The Americans, British, French and their vast multinational armies, which included Poles, Indians, Canadians and Rhodesians, then slogged through some of the heaviest fighting of the whole war, as combat roared around Monte Cassino in winter 1943 and spring 1944. Then in January that year came the Allies' disastrous decision to stage a landing at Anzio, a small fishing port 30 miles south of Rome. Initially, their amphibious force was able to exploit off the beaches, but then timid, hesitant generalship saw the invasion force fail to capitalise on their landings and strike north fast, hard and decisively for Rome. Anzio turned into an operational debacle that lasted five months. In places, conditions resembled the Western Front; one German officer said it was even worse than Stalingrad. But by early June the Allies had broken out and were racing northwards from western and central Italy. On 5 June, twenty-four hours before D-Day, Rome had fallen, just as Operation Overlord was about to be launched across the English Channel. The American general Mark Clark drove in triumph through a liberated capital city. His American 5th Army had then advanced up the west coast of Italy, with the British, Canadians, Indians and Poles pushing up along the central spine of the country, and up the Adriatic seaboard to the east.

2

REPRISALS

The Massacre at the Ardeatine Caves

The first mainstream, country-wide demonstration against the Germans came on 1 March 1944, when Communist Party partisan groups co-ordinated with the CLN, and at exactly the same time of the day, every factory in Milan, Turin, Genoa and the surrounding industrial area stopped work at precisely the same time. On the surface, the demonstration was against German mass deportations of Italian workers to provide labour, often in appalling conditions, in German and Austrian factories, or to help build civil defences. The wider implications of the mass wildcat strike were to make a strong statement to the Germans: regardless of political orientation, Italy is united against you. The harsher operational tempo of German reprisal actions in Italy was decided three weeks later.

On 23 March 1944, a unit of German policemen staged a march through the centre of Rome, en route back to their barracks after training at a firing range. But the march also had a second purpose: to intimidate the civilian population of the capital with a physical reminder of martial law. The soldiers' boots slammed in unison on to the cobbles as they marched along Via Rasella, a residential street of nineteenth-century apartment buildings that leads uphill from Via delle Quattro Fontane, set next to the baroque glory of the Palazzo Barberini. The unit was recruited from Bolzano, in the north-eastern Alto Adige region of Italy, and was made up of ethnic Germans. They were singing as they marched. Halfway up the hill, they went past a street-sweeper's cart sitting on the opposite side of the road from them. Hidden inside it, under a cover of rubbish and ash, was a bomb made from 38lb of TNT. Agents from the American Office for Strategic Services had supplied the plastic explosive to a group of communist partisans from a Patriotic Action Group, led by two fighters code-named Spartacus and Cola. They had smuggled it into a nearby flat, attached a forty-second fuse, and left it in the wheeled rubbish barrow. As three other partisans opened fire with a small mortar, and threw hand grenades at the patrol, the bomb exploded. The force of the explosion burst through the steel sides of the cart, across the cobbles and into the police patrol. It killed twenty-eight Germans and two Italian civilians, wounded 110, and blew pieces of the cobbles 3in deep into the masonry of the block of flats opposite it.

The German leadership in both Berlin and Rome ordered an immediate reprisal. Directions for this came straight from Hitler to Field Marshal Kesselring, commanding German forces in Italy, who passed them on to the military commander of Rome, Luftwaffe General Kurt Mälzer, and to the SD, the SS' intelligence arm. They arrived with Obersturmbannführer Herbert Kappler. The former electrician from Stuttgart was the head of the Geheime Staatspolizei, or Gestapo, in Rome.[1] He had joined the SS in 1933, starting his career in 1935 in the SS Security Police. He had never seen front-line duty, and as the war in Russia lengthened and worsened, he was increasingly desperate to avoid it. Almost none of his Gestapo colleagues in the Italian capital had seen active service either. All of Kappler's work with the SS had been either with an Einsatzkommando in Poland in 1939, deporting Austria's Jews after the Anschluss, or as a Gestapo officer in Belgium and then Italy. Speaking fluent Italian, he had worked as a liaison officer with Mussolini, and brought to bear a ruthless cunning in his three main tasks. These included overseeing anti-partisan operations and counter-intelligence against the Allies, liaising with and spying on the Vatican, and tracking down, arresting and deporting Rome's Jews. Kappler's police headquarters was in an apartment block in Via Tasso, in the San Giovanni quarter of central Rome. It was part of the German embassy, and he and his Gestapo colleagues had converted its four floors and basement into an ad hoc prison and detention centre. It was here his men had questioned Colonel Giuseppe Lanza di Montezemolo, one of the two most senior Italian officers who had remained loyal to the King. In return for money, Italian informers told the Gestapo where he was hiding. Kappler's men tried to pull out his teeth with pliars, and managed to extract several fingernails.[2] They reportedly used a blowtorch to torture one of his military colleagues.

On the walls of the tiny cells in the building prisoners had scratched messages into the plaster. *Facile saper vivere, grande saper morire,* said one. ('It's easy to know how to live, but a fine thing to know how to die.') 'Beware of the Rabbit,' said another, scratched next to a small drawing of a rabbit (*coniglio*) sitting on its hindquarters, ear aloft. Il Coniglio was the Italian code name of a partisan double agent known to be working for the Germans.[3] In the basement interrogation room, Kappler's savage methods on an Italian captive had yielded part of the information that Mussolini was being held on the Gran Sasso. The remainder of the intelligence came from wiretaps of Italian carabinieri sympathetic to the King.

In October 1943, after the Germans occupied Rome, one of Kappler's priorities had been to round up Rome's Jews, for deportation into the concentration camp system. To make them believe that they had an option to buy their freedom, he also demanded 120lb in gold. Bullion, coins, jewellery and religious artefacts were all acceptable, he said. Kappler was not being choosy. Gold was gold. So the Jewish community asked Pope Pius XII if the Vatican could provide this ransom payment. Yes, with no interest or fixed repayment date, came the answer. But before it could be paid the Jewish community themselves had found the required amount, and given it to the Gestapo. Yet when the round-up operation began on 16 October, Kappler and his men managed to detain only a fifth of the people they wanted. A total of 1,015 were rounded up in *la razzia*, 900 of whom were women and children. An estimated 5,615 of the capital's Jewish community escaped, after a huge variety of locations including convents, churches and the Vatican itself provided hiding places. Kappler put the remaining people into railway wagons at Rome's Tiburtina station and deported them northwards to

Auschwitz. Only sixteen of them would survive. Reinhard Heydrich, who was the head of the Reich Main Security Office, or RSHA, looked down favourably on his protégé in Rome, and made sure to keep Kappler where he was.

He ran a network of agents inside the Vatican too, both Catholic priests and administrative and lay staff. What was the Vatican's position on the Holocaust, Kappler wanted to know. Would they publicly denounce it? How many Jews and Allied PoWs were hidden not only in the Vatican's sprawling corridors and palaces, but in other churches and nunneries across Rome, and where were they? Was it true that Pope Pius XII was so keen not to see a post-war government centred around former leaders of communist partisan groups that he and his archbishops were feeding information about armed communist cells to the Germans? The Germans were performing a vast, but fragile, balancing act in Italy, trying to keep the country from erupting into open civil war against them as they fought textbook combat against the Allies and a vicious counter-insurgency campaign against the partisans. The bombing in Via Rasella was the biggest challenge to their authority in Italy since they had occupied the country the previous September. How would they react, wondered Allied intelligence chiefs, as well as the Italian partisan and civilian population? Crucially, what would be the nature and severity of the German reprisal? The answer was disproportionate, fast and brutal. One Wehrmacht commander in Rome wanted to torch an entire neighbourhood of the city centre. Hitler finally decided that ten Italians would die for each German killed.

Kappler and his subordinates then made a list of 330 people who would face a firing squad. Kesselring wanted him to round up prisoners who had already been sentenced to death. So Kappler did his best – they were a mix of prisoners from Via Tasso who had been questioned and then condemned to die: these included Colonel di Montezemolo. There were communists and inmates on death row in Rome's Regina Coeli prison, but innocent civilians too, such as Italian residents of Via Rasella who had been at home at the time of the bombing, and any Jews they could find. So on the night after the attack, Kappler and his men made their death list, drinking brandy in a Rome apartment. Once the list of 330 men was complete, the Germans loaded the prisoners on to lorries at dawn, and drove them down the old Via Appia, the ancient Roman highway that leads from the capital all the way to the Adriatic. The lorries drove under the stretching umbrella pines in the early spring sun, to a series of caves and tunnels in southern Rome. The Ardeatine network was a centuries-old mine for *pozzolana*, a type of volcanic ash that, mixed with cement, made a particularly durable kind of concrete.

As the prisoners were being led out of the trucks, Kappler discovered a mistake: there were 335 of them, five too many. But he gave orders that these extra men be shot too, fearing that if they were released, they would be able to give precise details of what had happened to partisans and the Allies, and tell relatives exactly where the victims were buried. This simple error in numbers was to hang over Kappler's head for the rest of his life. In groups of five, Kappler and his SS cohorts lined the prisoners up outside the cave; then led them inside and shot them in the head. The Gestapo chief knew many of his subordinates had never killed anybody before, so he distributed bottles of brandy to encourage them. Half-drunk, nervous SS subalterns then blew the backs off the heads of dozens of prisoners, or, in some cases, missed. Army engineers then blew up the ceilings of the caves, burying the bodies. Dynamite sealed the entrance. The Italians considered the attack in Via Rasella an act of war, and now the Germans had cast the dice of reprisal, telling the partisans very clearly that from now on, they and the civilian population could expect no mercy for any attacks against their troops. The repercussions of the Via Rasella attack, and the subsequent reprisals, ricocheted and shuddered northwards. Across Italy, on both sides, the gloves came off.

German Reprisal and Deportation Operations

Across the areas of Italy occupied by the Germans, they carried out reprisal and deportation operations against the Italian civilian population for four principal reasons. The first was to deter them from helping partisans. One way they did this was to select a prominent figure from the local community, such as a priest or a politician, and make an example of them. One such incident took place in the early summer of 1944.

The small hamlet of Melezet is the most westerly inhabited settlement in Italy, sitting high in the Italian Alps on the border with France. In that wartime summer, its pretty, solid stone houses sat under the blazing blue of the Alpine sky, shaded by the swirling, brilliant green of pine, lime and oak trees. The interior of the small village church of San Antonio Abate, even in those warm months, was chilly, heavy with the smell of centuries-old incense, candlewax, polished wood pews and old stone. A local parish priest was sheltering and assisting Italian partisans. With the help of the British Special Operations Executive, and the American Office for Strategic Services, they were operating in the mountains above the village. They crossed in and out of France to stage hit-and-run raids on German patrols. The Germans arrested the priest outside his church and took him to a local headquarters. They tortured him and took him eastwards to the city of Turin, the capital of the region of Piemonte.[4] Along with dozens of others, they loaded him on to a train made up of cattle cars at Porta Nuova station, Turin being one of the main centres for the deportation of Italian Jews in northern Italy. Father Giovanni joined them, and the wagons headed for Auschwitz. Worked almost to death in the camp, one day the priest offered himself to be executed in place of a Jewish inmate condemned to death. The German guards shot him instead.

The next two principal targets for the Germans were partisans and Jews, the first normally shot, the second deported to concentration camps. Another example took place in the ski resort of Bardonecchia, which lies adjacent to Melezet: there the Germans captured a local partisan commander called Alberto Mallen. He was also deported, this time to Mauthausen.[5] The operation to capture and deport Italy's Jews was the remit of the SD and the Gestapo, and in north-western Italy in 1944 this meant SS-Sturmbannführer Friederich Bosshammer. The fourth type of action carried out against the Italian civilian population was reprisal killings in response to attacks by partisans. The Germans carried out the majority of these operations in Tuscany and Emilia-Romagna, the two provinces that sit astride the coast and the Apennine mountains in central Italy.

On 10 May 1944, Field Marshal Kesselring's headquarters issued his 'anti-bandit' orders designed to combat the particular tactical and strategic situation in Italy as it concerned partisan attacks on German military personnel. These were posted up in barracks, alongside photographs of known local partisan commanders and the aftermath of their attacks on German troops, and maps showing villages, mountains or forested areas where partisans were reportedly operating:[6]

1. The partisan situation in the Italian theatre, particularly in Central Italy, has recently deteriorated to such an extent that it constitutes a serious danger to the fighting troops and their supply lines as well as to the war industry and economic potential.

2. The fight against the partisans must be carried on with all means at our disposal and with the utmost severity. I will protect any commander who exceeds our usual restraint in the choice of severity of the methods he adopts against partisans. In this connection the old principle holds good, that a mistake in the choice of methods in executing one's orders, is better than failure or neglect to act. Only the most prompt and severe handling is good enough as punitive and deterrent measures to nip in the bud other outrages on a greater scale. All civilians implicated in partisan operations who are apprehended in the course of reprisals, are to be brought up to the Assembly Camps which are being erected for this purpose by the Quartermaster General C in C South-West for ultimate despatch to the Reich as workers.

3. The combat against Partisans consists of passive and active operations with centre of gravity on the latter. The passive combat consists of protection of important buildings of historic or artistic value, railways, and roads, as well as essential installations such as power stations, factories, etc. Active operations will be conducted especially in Partisan overrun districts where it is vital to maintain the lifeline of the Armed Forces. These Partisans will have to be attacked and wiped out. Propaganda amongst Partisans (as well as use of agents) is of utmost importance.

On 14 July, an addendum was added, giving German troops further carte blanche to behave as they saw fit with the Italian civilian population:

In my appeal to the Italians I announced that severe measures are to be taken against the Partisans. This announcement must not represent an empty threat. It is the duty of all troops and police in my command to adopt the severest measures. Every act of violence committed by partisans must be punished immediately. Reports submitted must also give details of countermeasures taken. Wherever there is evidence of considerable numbers of partisans groups [*sic*], a proportion of the male population of the area will be arrested and in the event of an act of violence being committed, these men will be shot. The population must be informed of this. Should troops etc. be fired at from any village, the village will be burnt down. Perpetrators or the ring leaders will be hanged in public. Nearby villages to be held responsible for any sabotage to cables and damage inflicted to tyres. The most effective countermeasure is to recruit local patrols. Members of the Fascist party will not be included in any of the reprisals. Suspects will be handed over to the prefects and a report sent to me. Every soldier will protect himself outside villages by carrying a firearm. District Commanders will decide in which towns it will also be necessary to carry firearms. Every type of plunder is forbidden and will be punished severely. All countermeasures must be hard but just. The dignity of the German soldier demands it.

After the Allies liberated Rome on 5 June and advanced northwards, the first large German reprisals came on the 29th. In retaliation for the killing of two German soldiers, men from the Parachute-Panzer Division 'Hermann Goring' executed 224 Italian civilians at the village of Civitella in Val di Chiana, south of Arezzo in Tuscany. They then proceeded to massacre another 177 civilians at Cavriglia, also in Tuscany, and 130 more near Palagnano in the neighbouring province of Emilia-Romagna. They followed this up a few days later with another mass killing of 107 people at Vallucciole, nearby. A template of German actions was being established. Partisans would attack a German position, normally causing very small numbers of dead or wounded, often in single figures. The German unit that had taken casualties would then retaliate with a massively disproportionate reprisal. Given that many of the fitter and healthier Italian men between the ages of 14 and 60 were often fighting with the partisans, the reprisals then hit the elderly, the women and the children left behind. So it was in the Tuscan village of Padule di Fucecchio, which is situated in a low-lying area of marshes and canals 15 miles west of Florence. Italian partisans wounded two German soldiers from the 26th Panzer Division in an attack on a small outpost. The response was immediate. The Germans rounded up 174 Italian civilians and machine-gunned them on the edge of a marsh. And as the Germans started to retreat northwards towards the positions of the Gothic Line, a new phase in their war began. On 1 June General Harold Alexander, the Supreme Allied Commander Mediterranean, had issued a communiqué on Allied Forces radio – all partisans, he said, should do their utmost to slow down, impede and destroy the enemy. In Tuscany, several small partisan groups took this as their cue to join forces.

3

Partisans

In May 1944, the Fascist military headquarters in the Salo Republic made an estimate of how many partisans there were operating in Italy: approximately 80,000 was their answer. The tempo of German reprisals and the Allied advance meant that this figure grew by about 5,000 a month. Some 16,000 of these partisans, they said, were in Tuscany and in the neighbouring province of Emilia-Romagna. Field Marshal Kesselring, however, thought that this number was too high, and made an estimate of around 60,000. He and his staff officers reckoned that, of these, the Germans had probably killed about 5,000, wounded 8,000, and dispersed another 7,000. But with each partisan casualty, another three seemed to arrive to fill their ranks. The Allies marched north, partisan actions increased, German reprisals were ever larger and more frequent, more men joined the partisans, the Allies supplied them, they attacked more German troops … the cycle of action repeated itself entropically.

By early summer 1944, about 80 per cent of the partisans were men, and the remainder women, or teenage girls and boys working on an occasional, ad hoc basis from village to village. The women's role was enshrined in the word *staffetta*, which literally meant 'relay'. *Staffette* were the couriers, used to carry guns, grenades, messages, food, medical supplies and clothes, to and from towns and villages to the mountains, across cities, anywhere the partisans operated. The rationale behind their actions was that Germans and Italian Fascists were far less likely to search women. Women were everywhere in Italy, often running the lives of their families, their absent husbands, providing an economic and material backbone to family and daily life, as their menfolk were away with the resistance, so they made excellent couriers. They could be almost invisible.

The partisans' equipment came from everywhere. They took their weapons from the Germans, from Italian military armouries, and from Allied air drops. Every time they clashed with a German unit they would collect the weapons left behind by the dead or wounded enemy. If a group of thirty partisans ambushed a German patrol containing the same number of men, and succeeded in winning the firefight, and killing or capturing the SS or Wehrmacht men, the weapons haul could be substantial. As many as three MG 42 belt-fed machine guns, fifteen Mauser K98 rifles, ten Schmeisser MP 40 sub-machine guns, hand grenades, medical supplies, Luger or Walther pistols, 60mm mortars, and thousands of rounds of 9mm and 7.92mm ammunition could be added to the Italian weapons they already possessed. These came from Italian soldiers who, after the armistice, joined partisan groups, and from raids on armouries controlled by Italian Fascist soldiers. These would include Beretta M34 and M35 pistols, and the standard 6.5mm Carcano rifle issued to the Italian armed forces. Then there was the Breda M37 machine gun, and the Italian weapon most prized by the military, the partisans, the Allies and the Germans alike: the MAS-38 9mm sub-machine gun, which was considered by all sides as one of the best manufactured and most reliable weapons of the war. Sturdy, accurate and firing a heavier cartridge than the Schmeisser, it also had an effective range of 200yd, triple that of the British Sten gun, and double that of the American .45 Thompson.

In 1943 partisans started to divert the supply of Beretta weapons directly from the factories where they were made: huge consignments of guns that were destined for the armed forces of the Salo Republic, or the Wehrmacht, never got to them. The trucks carrying the deliveries of weapons would be diverted through an area controlled by partisans, who would hijack them. Workers in the Beretta factory would be cooperating with the resistance fighters; machine guns and sub-machine guns for the Germans or Fascists would be tampered with, or misassembled. The partisans also received large supplies of firearms from

Allied air drops co-ordinated by the SOE or OSS. Principal among these were the 9mm Sten gun, the Bren light machine gun, and some Lee Enfield rifles. When the American OSS began air-dropping weapons to partisan groups, there would be .45 Thompson sub-machine guns, and the M3 'Grease-Gun', which replaced it in late 1942. The folding-stock M1 carbine, and tens of thousands of rounds of .30 ammunition, came too. Lightweight, accurate at ranges up to 300yd, with a folding stock, it could be concealed easily, and it didn't jam.

Along with these weapons, both the SOE and the OSS dropped explosives, medical supplies such as bandages and penicillin, radios and industrial clothing such as dungarees and boiler suits that the partisans could wear. There was food as well; ration packs of British and American supplies, with cigarettes, chocolate, jam and biscuits. Boots were prized. A British SOE officer operating with partisans in the mountains on the French and Italian borders noted in his diary that some of the men didn't have any shoes, and almost all of them were subsisting on a diet of boiled mutton, which gave them constant upset stomachs. Yet another SOE agent, parachuted into the mountains above Milan, reported that the partisans were well fed: milk, polenta, wild fruit, lamb meat, vegetables and pasta made up their diet. An American OSS officer was fighting with partisans in the delta of the River Po estuary, on the Adriatic seaboard. Polenta and fried eels were the staple diet of the resistance there, he found. Above the city of Cuneo near the French border, goat stew, goat milk and apples kept one partisan band on its feet.[1]

The resistance groups were heavily reliant on the Italian communities among which they operated. As they were regionally based, the towns and villages and countryside where they operated tended to be the places they came from. They were fighting for political recognition, they were fighting to defeat the Germans and Italian Fascists, they were fighting out of principle, but they were in many cases fighting to protect their families and communities from German reprisals and attacks. These actions inevitably fed into a circular motion of attack and reprisal and scorched earth operation upon these communities, prompting the partisans to fight harder against the Germans. Until the Allies arrived to liberate a particular area of territory, this cycle of attack and revenge exacerbated itself, and only liberation could break it, and defuse it.

The partisans were by no means all Italians: there were more foreign nationalities in their ranks than there were different types of weapons. There were, firstly, escaped British, American, Canadian and French prisoners of war. One partisan group even included an Indian soldier. There were Yugoslavs who had crossed the border into north-eastern Italy, there were Ukrainians and Czechs who, press-ganged into fighting with the Germans, had been captured by partisans. There were deserters from the 162nd Infantry Division of the German army, which was comprised of Turkmens and Azerbaijanis: the Apuan Hunters partisan group on the Tuscan coast included several of them.

There were also hundreds of deserters from the Wehrmacht, mostly Dutch, Poles, Ukrainians, Austrians and Czechs. Operating near Udine, in far north-eastern Italy on the Austrian border, there was an entire partisan brigade made up of Wehrmacht deserters. Across Tuscany, by early summer 1944, the list of foreign fighters was extensive: one municipality near Arezzo kept a count of those operating with Italian groups. There were 1,284 different Soviets, seventy Yugoslavs, forty-nine Poles, twenty-three Czechs, fourteen English, 122 Germans, thirty-three Austrians, twenty-three French, seven Dutch, eight Greeks, two Turks, a Dane, an Australian, an American, two men from Luxembourg, and two from New Zealand, one of whom was a Maori. German intelligence reports were filled with questions trying to ascertain who these men were, and from where they came. Every ambush, every partisan attack, every raid on an armoury, every time the Germans took prisoners for questioning, the presence of dozens of unexplained foreigners in the partisan ranks took them by surprise. The more reprisals they committed, the more priests and Jews they killed or deported, the more civilians they massacred, the partisan groups seemed to expand exponentially.

The German operations against partisans and the Italian civilian population were also aimed at destroying their livelihoods, their logistical and professional infrastructures, their factories, farms, food and way of life. In the Tuscan mountain town of Niccioletta, the workers from the local iron ore mine decided to start hiding their equipment, tools, explosives and mining survey equipment. In early June 1944, partisans arrived to help them guard the mine, and took as hostages some local Fascist officials. Their wives, however, escaped, trekked across the mountains to the next village, raised the alarm, and told the Fascist police there exactly what had happened. The response was swift. On 13 June, 300 German and Italian troops surrounded Niccioletta, and arrested seventy-seven miners and another seventy they accused of being partisans, or of helping the partisans. They pushed 150 men into lorries and drove them north to the town of Castelnuovo, and locked them in a theatre. They split them into three groups: the miners and alleged partisans would be shot; the younger men would be deported to Germany as forced labour; and the older ones would be allowed home. The following morning, a unit of Italian Fascists who had volunteered for an SS police regiment formed firing squads. Seventy-seven of the men from Niccioletta died. Hundreds of square kilometres of Tuscan hills became no-go areas for the Germans as a result. The vicious cycle of revenge turned faster.

Three weeks after the execution of the miners, a partisan group operating south-east of Florence captured thirty German prisoners. One of the commanders of this group, called Pio Borri, was from Pisa and his family were Sephardic Jews who had originally fled from Spain and France and taken refuge in Italy in the sixteenth century. The Germans had already deported Carolina, Borri's wife, to Auschwitz in late spring 1944. When she was arrested, she was pregnant with her fourth child, to whom she gave birth in a cattle car en route to Poland. Commander Pio, of course, knew nothing of this, only that his wife had been arrested, and that he would certainly never see her or his children again. So for a man who had no lack of reasons to take revenge on the Germans, Pio Borri insisted, however, on behaving humanely when possible. He resisted his colleagues' demands to execute the German prisoners they had taken, and instead said that he would take them across the front line, to the nearest Allied unit. When they got there, the Americans asked if two men could volunteer to carry messages back to a partisan unit fighting near the Tuscan city of Arezzo.

The US 5th Army was advancing towards it and wanted to co-ordinate their attack, and arrival, with the partisans. Borri and one other man volunteered. They crossed the front line again, but hiding out for the night near the village of San Polo di Arezzo, they were discovered. They tried to fight their way out, at the same time as another partisan unit attacked the German unit surrounding them. Borri and his colleague were captured and, along with the other partisan survivors, taken to a villa in San Polo. The Germans were not from a Waffen-SS unit, but from the 274 Panzergrenadier Regiment, a unit of the army. Its battalion commander, Hauptmann Wolf Ewert, and a second lieutenant, Klaus Konrad, oversaw the torture of the captured partisans. Then, along with forty-eight other prisoners, the Germans took them outside the villa, made them dig three large graves, and attached explosives to their bodies. The Wehrmacht soldiers shot some of them, and then detonated the charges. They shovelled sand and earth over the corpses, and drove away. Two days later, the front line moved again, and they fled north in retreat. The first Allied unit into San Polo was British, the 1st Derbyshire Yeomanry, from the South African 6th Armoured Division. This, in turn, formed part of the US 5th Army. Corporal Leslie Newman was one of the first to see what the Germans had done:

4 Troop on the North-Eastern road, penetrated beyond San Polo to the first main feature where they were machine-gunned and shelled and were ordered to withdraw to San Polo, where the story of the German massacre of 47 civilians was discovered and some data for the proper investigation of the affair by the Field Security Section Intelligence Corps obtained.

It was at that time, the 16th July, which I and my comrades, members of the 55 Field Security Section Intelligence Corps, arrived in Arezzo. Shells from the retreating Germans were still landing in the town.

My comrades established base in a town centre hotel and prepared to spend the night on the floor of the lobby. Having recently 'liberated' a very comfortable mattress and installed it in my 15cwt Bedford truck I decided that I would spend the night in my vehicle. However, as the hours passed, the shelling became more intensive. It was somewhat disconcerting as one could hear the crack of the mortars being fired, followed by the whistle of the incoming shells and then the explosions. Each blast appeared nearer and nearer. Finally my courage deserted me and I joined the others in the hotel lobby!

The next day the above report from the Derbyshire Yeomanry came through and I and a colleague were sent to the village of San Polo, several miles to the north of Arezzo, to investigate.

We arrived at the village to be greeted by several partisans. We were shown a mass grave which the villagers had been forced to dig. They had then been executed in cold blood. There was no disguising the horror that had taken place. Scraps of cloth hung on trees and there was the indescribable stench of death in the air.

The partisans led us through the deserted village to a house that had been used by the German troops. We searched in the litter and debris but failed to find anything that could identify the unit responsible for these dreadful murders. However, with Teutonic thoroughness, all evidence had been destroyed or removed.

The partisans explained that they had ambushed and killed several Germans and that the unit involved had exacted a terrible retribution on the villagers.

Deeply saddened, we took leave of the partisans to rejoin our section, frustrated to the extreme that our efforts had been in vain, and no one would be brought to justice for this horrific deed.[2]

As a result of the battle with partisans at San Polo, and because of the defiant miners at Niccioletta, in mid-July the Germans issued a compulsory evacuation order against the inhabitants of every town and village in a large rectangle across central Tuscany. Every single person, young, old, healthy, ill, infirm or otherwise, had to move northwards, across the Apennine mountains, to the city of Parma, 150 miles away. It was an impossible order to obey, so thousands of Tuscan families packed what belongings they could carry, disobeyed the ruling, and walked due westwards across fields and mountains, towards the coast. Over the following days, several hundred of these displaced people arrived in the hills surrounding the village of Sant'Anna di Stazzema, which overlooks the coastal town of Pietrasanta. On 29 July, the partisans handed out leaflets and put up posters in and around Sant'Anna and the surrounding towns and villages:

PEOPLE OF VERSILIA!

After turning Italy into a horrible battleground, the Nazis want to complete their destructive task by deporting all the men and boys to forced labour camps in Germany.

Never satisfied, the Nazi[s] are now persecuting women children and the old, making horrific demands on them of all kinds.

People of Versilia, do not obey the Germans! Women, children and old people, do not leave your homes. Offer passive resistance. All men, arm yourselves with breech-loading shotguns if nothing else is available. The Allies are only a few kilometres away, the partisans are ready for action, and they will treat a reprisal with our own reprisal.

People of Versilia, arm yourselves! Your liberty and your salvation are in your own hands! Death to the German oppressor!

Signed; the commander of the Garibaldi Partisan Assault Brigade
29th July 1944

On 30 July, there was a battle between the partisans and the Germans, and on 5 August the SS posted up evacuation orders as well, also in and around Sant'Anna. Everybody had to move. Twenty-four hours later, the partisans then repasted their own posters over those of the Germans. Stay where you are, these told the civilians in the area. We will protect you.

4

THE SS DIVISION

Tuscany, August 1944

With their backs to sea, and enemies on all three sides, Max Simon and his men were surrounded. It was the boiling Italian midsummer of the fifth year of the Second World War, and he and his Waffen-SS division were staging a fighting retreat northwards up the coast of Tuscany. As the fighting moved northwards, so did the SS' headquarters – for a week it had been in the small town of Nozzano, outside the walled medieval city of Lucca. Then the unit had moved to Camaiore, and then, in early August of 1944, they found themselves headquartered at Marina di Carrara, a seaside town 60 miles north-west of Florence. In the requisitioned villa that served as the SS headquarters, one of Simon's officers had pinned a hand-drawn diagram of western Italy on to the wall. The German unit was not just short of its complement of self-propelled guns, half-tracks, lorries, fuel and experienced fighting men, it did not even have enough maps. Yet this did not stop the division's officers from making idiosyncratic gestures of defiance both to the advancing Allies, and to the Italian civilians living around them.

In late June they had pulled out of the town of San Vincenzo, 100 miles south of Carrara. There they had established an ad hoc divisional headquarters in an empty apartment, whose Italian owners had fled the fighting. The oncoming American advance had been fast. But when Max Simon's officers tore out of their apartment, heading for the trucks and jeeps that would take them north, they'd left a present on the table of the sitting room in the flat. It was a large, leather-bound edition of an old German atlas, and one of the unit's officers had taken the time to sign it with a fountain pen, thanking the owners for their hospitality.

The Allies were approaching directly up the coastline from the south, and pushing across country from the east, from the direction of Pisa and Florence. For the SS men the only escape route was to take the road north that led back into German-occupied territory, and to the comparative safety of Austria and Germany.

While his men had been fighting the Allies south of Rome, the German commander in Italy, Field Marshal Albert Kesselring, had used the time to build a strong series of defensive positions that stretched right across the north of the country. The network of bunkers, trenches, pillboxes, dug-in tanks and artillery pieces extended from Pescara on the Adriatic to La Spezia on the Mediterranean. Kesselring had named it the Gotenstellung, or the Gothic Line. The 16th SS was one unit that would help defend it, and try to slow the Allied advance. But the route back to these positions was also blocked by large formations of marauding Italian partisans: Germany and Austria seemed a long way away. Sitting in Marina di Carrara, the 16th SS Panzergrenadier Division was effectively surrounded in a semicircular enclave, and had no choice but to fight its way out.

The unit had been based on the west coast of Italy since May 1944, guarding a 100-mile coastal strip on the Tyrrhenian Sea. This stretched from the ports of Livorno in the south to La Spezia in the north, and then went 30 miles inland as far as the medieval city of Siena. After the Americans had liberated Rome on 5 June, they fought their way north. They ran straight into SS-Gruppenführer Simon's 12,000-strong division north of the little port of Piombino, which serves as a transport link to the island of Elba. The Waffen-SS men and the GIs then fought a series of battles that raged up the coast through a string of seaside towns: from Cecina up to Livorno, and then to Viareggio.

The defenders clung fiercely to each of these, taking heavy casualties, and also inflicting them on the advancing American GIs of the 'Red Bulls', their 34th Infantry Division. The beauty of the Tuscan littoral, the towns sprinkled up its winding length, and the Apuan Alps that rose behind seemed in brutal contrast to the savage fighting. Nature's beauty, the entrancing weather of the Mediterranean, and the elegantly designed sleight-of-hand that was the Italian seaside infrastructure faced off against the worst that man could do. The turquoise of the Tyrrhenian Sea lay off the summer shimmer of the wide, white-grey sandy beaches of each holiday town that stretched up the coast.

Back from the sea, olive, apricot, pear and walnut orchards inter-laced around the houses and their gardens; vineyards of dark-purple grapes criss-crossed the land outside the towns. The woods and fields on mountains behind the coast loomed bright green in the summer heat. Many of the hillsides surrounding Carrara contained a lot of marble: Michelangelo's preferred stone had come from the mountains above the Tuscan town. On the slopes where the quarries were situated, huge sections of the hillsides had been sheared off in blocks where the stone had been removed over the years. White marble dust spread over the surrounding trees and fields. One of the American formations that fought against the Germans in these mountains was the 92nd US Infantry Division, nicknamed 'The Buffalo Soldiers', after the image of a buffalo stitched on their unit shoulder patch. Despite their lack of combat experience, they quickly proved themselves in battle. They were the first entirely segregated African-American unit to be deployed from the mainland United States into combat in Europe, consisting almost entirely of African-American officers, NCOs and other ranks.[1]

Down on the Tuscan coast, the towns were made up of old white seaside villas, solid stone apartment buildings from the nineteenth cen-tury, and piazzas with fountains and umbrella pine trees situated at the intersections of graceful streets. Each town had a station, like a knot tied in the string of the railway line that wound up the coast.

The fighting was as violent as mankind's wars had ever been. The advancing Americans battered up the coast: the SS men stood in their way like Roman phalanxes. Artillery from both sides rocketed overhead through the bright-blue sky; dusty roads, lined with apricot and cypress trees, were carefully mined. American Mustang and Thunderbolt fighter-bombers, flying off Corsican airstrips, power-dived on con-voys of German vehicles wherever they found them. From the air the tanks, half-tracks and trucks were easily visible, especially with the dust trails they left behind them. The aircraft would dive at right angles to the convoys, or attack them from behind, their .50 calibre Browning machine guns stitching explosive threads of fire down and across the roads, blowing some of the vehicles to pieces, knocking others sideways off the road, and sending any accompanying infantrymen leaping into ditches for cover.

Wary platoons of GIs marched up dusty, boiling tracks, Garand semi-automatic rifles at their shoulder, eyes peeled for signs of the enemy. Sometimes the patrols only discovered that the green carpet of the roadside vineyards concealed German anti-aircraft weapons or MG 42 machine guns when the explosive hiss of 7.92mm rounds or 20mm cannon shells, travelling at 1,000yd per second, tore into their ranks. And when both sides closed with each other in the fields, ditches and back alleys, fighting room-to-room in the red-roofed Tuscan houses, it was hand-to-hand combat, with bayonets, sharpened entrenching tools, Walther P-38 pistols, Bowie knives and .45 Colt automatics. Some of the SS men who'd served south of Leningrad in the black mud swamps and frozen trenches of the Demyansk pocket had taken lessons from the Russians. With the outer rubber coating stripped away with a pocket knife, military signals wire made an excellent homemade garrotte. Some of the 'Red Bulls' were tough farmhands and ranchers from South Dakota and Minnesota who had grown up in the vast outdoors of the Midwest, riding trail and carrying guns; they had made a name for themselves in Italy in the fighting around Monte Cassino, where some of their infantry battalions had lost up to 80 per cent of their strength. They and the 16th SS Panzergrenadier Division were a brutal and bloody match for each other. Tuscany boiled beautiful and bruised in the summer of that fifth year of conflict. The world was at war.

SS Major General Max Simon and the 16th SS Panzergrenadier Division

As Max Simon sat in a requisitioned seaside villa in Marina di Carrara at the end of July 1944, he had approximately 12,000 men under his command. He had come a long way since joining the SS in 1933, and his personal story had run in a close parallel to the development of Hitler's personal bodyguard corps. A veteran of the First World War, Simon was inducted into the Waffen-SS in 1933, being given the five-figure officer's serial number of 83086, with the capital letter 'A' of his blood group, in Germanic script, tattooed along the underside of his left biceps. Unlike many of the SS recruits, Simon was not a beery, brawny street-fighter who liked to go head-to-head on the cobbles with the communists or dock workers, or with the SS' original allies, but increasingly new enemies, from Ernst Rohm's SA. He was a pragmatic, bespectacled thinker, who saw order, a sense of direction and great purpose in Hitler's National Socialist Party.

He was a second lieutenant, or Untersturmführer, in autumn 1934, and then was promoted very fast indeed. He made full colonel the following year, when he took on two new responsibilities that would profoundly shape his professional career and his approach to both regular and irregular warfare. In the bloodthirsty, breakneck rise of the Nazi party, the corridors of the new Germany were crammed with ambitious men, all a mix of soldiery, criminality and the bigoted politics of ascendant ultra-nationalism. Everybody seemed to be elbowing each other in the face in the scramble for advancement, and survival. Simon saw he needed a powerful, more senior protector, mentor and master. He found one in SS Major General Theodor Eicke, who by the mid-1930s was setting up the country's system of concentration camps.

By June 1934, Hitler and his coterie of senior officers had decided to eliminate the leadership of the SA Brown Shirts, whom they saw as determined, lethal rivals threatening to stage a coup against Hitler's party. It was Eicke and his deputy, Michael Lippert, who had personally shot the Führer's arch rival, Ernst Rohm, after he was captured during the Night of the Long Knives. Eicke was deeply antisemitic and anti-Bolshevist, and utterly ruthless. His personal motto, which he brought to all of the operations under his command, was 'No Pity'. 'Any SS man with a soft heart should retire to a monastery,' he once reportedly said.[2] It was he who introduced the striped blue and grey pyjamas for camp inmates, brought in a harsher disciplinary procedure at Dachau, and then at the next camps established in the Konzentrationslager, or KL network. He instituted the Totenkopfverbande, the SS units with their silver death's head collar insignia, who provided the guards and the power structure to run a string of economically productive labour camps that both isolated, and imprisoned, the new Reich's myriad enemies in appalling conditions, while squeezing them for every ounce of work they could provide.

He was allowed to recruit ideologically promising teenagers from the Hitler Youth into his death's head units, and oversaw, from the mid-1930s onwards, a regime of ideological and military training for them. By 1935 Eicke was the new Inspector General of Germany's camp system, beneath him the four main centres of his domain: Dachau, Ravensbrück, Buchenwald, and, in an old Prussian military barracks just north of Berlin, Sachsenhausen. He had closely followed Max Simon's SS career and recommended to Himmler that the owlish Nazi ideologue should be fast-tracked for promotion to full colonel. He then told Simon to form a new regiment of camp guards, called the 1st SS Totenkopfstandarte Oberbayern. Then he gave him command of Sachsenhausen. Afterwards, Simon took his SS men into the Austrian Anschluss, the takeover of the Sudetenland, and the invasion of France. He and his men pushed diagonally across the country, by June 1940 arriving at the foot of the Pyrenees.

Next came Operation Barbarossa, where he and his regiment, now part of the 3rd SS Totenkopf division, struck north towards Leningrad. But a Red Army counter-offensive in early 1942 encircled them, bogging them down to the south of the besieged city in the black mud, swamps and snow-covered pine forests of the Demyansk Pocket. Resupplied by the Luftwaffe, fighting and dying desperately in temperatures that dropped below -20°, Simon and his men held out for ten weeks. There was the smell of wood smoke, meat from horse carcasses and grimy skin that stuck to the metal of frozen weapons. And when the snow started to thaw in the spring, clouds of new mosquitoes rose from the swamps. Hitler proclaimed the siege a triumph. After all, hadn't 89,000 Red Army soldiers been killed, or gone missing, to the Wehrmacht and SS's 14,000? Luftwaffe and Wehrmacht chiefs replied to the contrary: they had lost 106 of their precious Junkers Ju 52 transport planes, and 387 pilots. Camouflaged with whitewash, these aircraft flew a vital airbridge into the pocket. To resupply only 113,000 men in a strategically unimportant enclave was a gross waste of lives and equipment, said the Luftwaffe. Regardless, Himmler approved as well: when Simon emerged, it was as a brigadier general, and holder of the Knight's Cross of the Iron Cross.

Yet by now, even among the draconian ranks of the SS, the Totenkopf Division was being looked on disparagingly for their ruthless treatment of prisoners. Other Waffen-SS combat divisions, such as the Liebstandarte Adolf Hitler and the Das Reich, sneered at the collection of sadistic, combat-incompetent concentration camp guards – swollen by recruits from the Hitler Youth – that had comprised the Totenkopf division at the outbreak of war. Theodor Eicke was loathed as an autocratic bully by many senior SS officers, including Reinhard Heydrich, the head of the SS's intelligence service, the SD. What had happened in May 1940 at a small French farm in the village of Le Paradis had confirmed many of these prejudices. Eicke took the Totenkopf division into combat during the invasion of France: eager to prove itself in battle, the unit often sacrificed tactical caution, leading to abnormally heavy casualties. In one attack alone, against 250 dug-in British infantrymen, four SS officers and 150 men were killed, with eighteen officers and 480 men wounded. The unit twice found itself retreating, humiliated in front of other German units, after being outflanked by superior British tactics and superior British soldiering. Fighting the British Regular Army in real war was a bit different from guarding Jews and political prisoners, jabbed both Wehrmacht and SS officers to Eicke. So on occasions the Totenkopf took out its frustration by killing its prisoners.

On 20 May 1940, when soldiers from the division captured 200 French colonial soldiers from Morocco, they were not even allowed to formally surrender: the SS machine-gunned them on the spot. On the outskirts of the village of Le Paradis, two companies of the British Royal Norfolk Regiment then held off a unit of the SS division for an entire day, surrendering at last light as their ammunition ran out. Despite their white flag, the SS marched ninety-seven of the captured soldiers, many of whom were wounded, into a nearby field, raked them with machine-gun fire, and then finished off the survivors with bayonets. News of the killing quickly reached other Waffen-SS combat units serving in France, who reacted with disdain. The SS officer who commanded the company that had murdered the prisoners was called Hauptsturmführer Fritz Knoechlein: a number of outraged SS officers from others units reportedly challenged him to a duel, with sabres. So once unleashed in Russia, Theodor Eicke's division again exceeded itself in the number of Red Army prisoners who disappeared, starved to death or were killed.

One report from the NKVD, or People's Commissariat for Internal Affairs – the de facto Interior Ministry of the Soviet Union – claimed that 23,000 Red Army prisoners of war, Russian, Ukrainian and Byelorussian civilians died illegally at the hands of the 3rd SS Totenkopf Division between July 1941 and summer 1944. Figures from another SS unit's operations help give some perspective to the number of Russian soldiers killed in battle, and those who were allowed to surrender. On 5 and 6 December 1943, parts of the SS division Liebstandarte Adolf Hitler went into action in the Ukraine. In one battle alone, it killed 2,280 Red Army soldiers in action, and took three prisoners. The difference between the LSAH's battlefield statistics and those of the Totenkopf is that the latter's tally of dead PoWs and civilians occurred as the result of actions taken *after* they were captured, not in battle itself.

In December 1942 Max Simon moved south to Hungary, taking core parts of his old SS Totenkopf regiment with him.[3] This contained substantial numbers of men who had served under him at Sachsenhausen, in France and in the Demyansk Pocket, as well as officers who had served on Einsatzkommando operations in Ukraine and Byelorussia. This regiment had cut its teeth guarding concentration camps, committed multiple war crimes in France and against the Red Army, and been forced to retreat by enemies it considered inferior, simultaneously being belittled by its peers for its treatment of prisoners, and lacklustre combat performance; all this before being nearly wiped out in the Demyansk Pocket, only to redeem itself through exemplary performance in battle. The collective unit psychology in Simon's Totenkopf regiment produced by the experiences from Sachsenhausen to Demyansk, was a mixture of paranoia and inferiority, coupled with pride at its own successes and a ferocious ability to feel misunderstood. All of these factors produced the operational basis of a 'perfect storm' for potential war crimes that could be perpetrated by the division.

Into this volatile mix came new recruits from three equally contentious sources. The first was from the Hitler Youth, who combined National Socialist belief with the fanaticism characteristic of elite units composed partly or mostly of volunteers. They looked up to, modelled themselves on and took orders from NCOs and officers with experience on the Eastern Front. Some unit commanders down to company level had progressed from the Hitler Youth to Waffen-SS via the concentration camp guard system and 3rd SS-Panzerdivision Totenkopf, under the tutelage of the bull-necked Theodor Eicke. They were young, too, the troops fresh from the Hitler Youth, and impressionable; over four-fifths of the 16th SS' armoured reconnaissance battalion were aged between 17 and 20.

The new unit also took into its ranks a large number of Volkdeutsche recruits, ethnic Germans living outside the Reich, many from the Balkans and central Europe, keen to prove themselves to their combat-hardened officers from the Fatherland. The Volksdeutsche in Yugoslavia, Hungary and Poland had often been victimised as ethnic minorities, and had seen the rise of Hitler's Reich as an opportunity to escape this oppression.

When the 16th SS was formed, they also were joined by hundreds of Hilfswilliger, or 'Hiwis', auxiliary troops recruited from Red Army PoWs, or Soviet soldiers who had deserted to join their invaders. The deal for these men was simple: fight on the side of the Germans, or be left in one of a series of German PoW 'camps', in reality barbed-wire cages, where the death toll from hunger and disease was over 50 per cent. For the Hiwis, there was no going back. Distrusted by their German masters, they knew the NKVD would imprison them in the Gulag system and shoot them once captured. The Hiwis also worked both as soldiers and police officers: one estimate is that 25 per cent of the troops fighting in the German 6th Army at Stalingrad were local auxiliaries captured after Operation Barbarossa.[4] Both the Hiwis and the Volksdeutsche were to compete with each other to catch the eye of the cadre of veteran officers in the 16th Division who commanded them, in an effort to prove their loyalty to the Waffen-SS.

When Karl Gesele's brigade arrived back in Italy in October 1943, it and the Totenkopf regiment in Hungary became the 16th SS Panzergrenadier Division. After Corsica, Salerno and Anzio, operations against partisans in Slovenia and participating in the invasion of Hungary, the two different brigades were now put together in one unit under Simon's command, and sent to Italy. The unit wore the nominative cuff-title of 'Reichsführer-SS', as the division was being named after Heinrich Himmler, having been part of the personal bodyguard division of the head of the SS, the 'Schutzstaffel' or 'protection corps'. So in May 1944, as the Allies massed south of Rome, they were sent back to the port of Livorno, and given their 100-mile stretch of the Tuscan coast to defend. And thus in July of that year, Major General Max Simon and his men found themselves in Marina di Carrara.

They were based in the middle of war, surrounded by Italians, including Fascists, partisans and civilian villagers and townspeople. There were the Americans approaching, Allied aircraft screamed overhead, and the Wehrmacht was alongside them. Yet it was an isolated existence for the SS, a long way from home, in a country full of enemies that most of the men knew nothing about, and often could only despise, after the 1943 Italian Armistice was signed with the British and Americans, which most Germans took as an enormous, traitorous betrayal by their former allies. This was one reason behind the deployment of the SS' operational policy of scorched earth, as they withdrew up Italy. Destroy the beauty and the people that have let you down. Yet despite its operational tempo of fighting, and reprisal massacres, life for the 16th SS in Tuscany was not always a daily menu of death and killing, or being killed. Photographs from albums, and official records, show men grouped together in tropical fawn uniforms, smiling in the sun, enjoying the weather, and the Italian food. There was occasional swimming in the Mediterranean, set against barrack duties, military discipline under the burning summer sun of a country almost none of them had ever visited, nor would again. It was a schizophrenic existence.

The division was centred on Panzer Grenadier Regiments 35 and 36, each about 2,000 strong, along with regiments of flak, self-propelled guns, reconnaissance and artillery. SS-Panzergrenadier Regiment 35 was commanded by Karl Gesele, now an SS-Obersturmbannführer, or lieutenant colonel, and was divided into three battalions. The second of these was commanded by SS-Hauptsturmführer, or Captain, Anton Galler.

Galler's father worked for the Reichsbahn, the German railway system. The family came from Amstetten in Lower Austria, near the Danube. Anton was brought up not just in a religious environment, but one that adhered to the tenets of National Socialism. He became a baker's apprentice, but then decided to switch it for full-time gymnastics, which led him to the SS, via the Hitler Youth. He saw in the newly emergent National Socialist military a chance to better himself: the baker's apprentice could move up from his working-class background, and become an officer. In 1933, the Austrian Nazi Party and the Austrian SS were banned in his home country, and he took refuge in Bavaria.

He started officer candidate school, became a lieutenant, and was posted to the Upper Silesia Protection Police, which operated in the region that straddled Germany, Poland and Czech territory. A cross between being a soldier and a paramilitary police officer, Galler's posting saw him in action in Poland, in the Sudetenland and in Silesia itself. He became adept at displacing and containing groups of people whom the Third Reich considered its enemies: night-time arrest operations, herding thousands of people to detention camps or train stations, running ad hoc camps, knowing how to use small unit attacks to make large numbers of inhabitants flee a town or village. Reprisals were involved as well, and random destruction and appropriation of property. In 1941 he joined an SS police battalion, and was sent to the front line south of Leningrad. In winter 1943 he moved to the 16th SS, and in July 1944 took over command of the 2nd Battalion of the 35th Regiment in Italy.

One of Galler's deputy company commanders was a young SS-Oberleutnant, or lieutenant, called Gerhard Sommer. He was just 23, that summer in Tuscany, and he came from a suburb of Hamburg where his father had a small company that made tools, such as spanners and wrenches. Herr Sommer had served in the First World War, and like millions of other patriotic Germans who had fought, felt betrayed and let down by what the Treaty of Versailles had done to Germany. So when Gerhard was only 12, his father enrolled him in swift order first in the Hitler Youth, then in the Nazi Party, after which the impetus of National Socialism took him into the SS. He joined up in October 1939, a month after the invasion of Poland, and found his direction.

After finishing basic training, he was posted to Hitler's personal bodyguard unit, known as the Liebstandarte SS Adolf Hitler, or LSSAH. In 1940 Benito Mussolini, eager to imitate Adolf Hitler's successes in invading Western Europe, decided to try to invade Greece, via Albania. The expedition was a disaster; the Greeks outfought the Italians in the mountains on the Albanian border, and the pride of Il Duce's army found itself bogged down and trapped. Hitler saw two things – his impetuous and liable ally in trouble, and the southern flank of Europe, on the shores of the Mediterranean, dangerously exposed. So he invaded Greece, via Yugoslavia, and in the ranks of the Liebstandarte who poured south-west towards Athens, was Gerhard Sommer.

He was wounded between Yugoslavia and Greece, but recuperated before July 1941, when it was time for his SS unit to participate in another invasion. Operation Barbarossa took Sommer and the LSSAH burning across the western Russian and Ukrainian steppes, where he was wounded for a second time, and given the Iron Cross Second Class. He was proving himself fast. Increasingly desperate and harder-fought battles on the Eastern Front followed, before he was moved to the 16th SS Panzergrenadier Division, at that point forming up in Hungary. By January 1944 he was headed for Italy as a second lieutenant, or Sturmführer. By July he was a full lieutenant, and second-in-command of a company of the division's Panzergrenadier Regiment 35.[5] The regimental commander was an SS diehard called Major Walter Reder, who'd lost an arm and won the Knights' Cross in Russia, and who was revered by his men.

Many of the SS men who served under them had been through the same pattern of service – at a lower rank – as their commanding general, Max Simon. In the different companies of the Second Battalion of the 35th Regiment, the SS career patterns and experience of combat – and committing atrocities – of some of the non-commissioned officers was uniform. These were men who saw National Socialism and entry into the SS as a way of bettering themselves socially and professionally, and advancing themselves. The crossover between military operations, ethnic cleansing and occasional mass killings the unit were, and had been, involved in became a form of operational norm for it. There was a mutual parallelism of behaviour between almost all the officers, and many of the men.

By 1944, the average age in the reconnaissance regiment of the 16th SS was just 18, and more than 80 per cent of the German men had been in the Hitler Youth. Almost all of the senior NCOs and junior officers had served with an SS police unit, a Totenkopf regiment, a concentration camp detachment or an Einsatzkommando on operations behind the front lines in Russia, Byelorussia, the Ukraine or the Baltic regions.[6] Their anti-partisan experience had been forged in Russia, and when they arrived in Italy, all ranks of the 16th SS were mutually aware that they were fighting in a doubly hostile country: Italy had been their ally, and then had double-crossed the Germans. And here were the men in Tuscany, fighting not just against Allied soldiers but also against the Italian civilian population and its support structure. The SS men felt strongly that they were surrounded by enemies on all sides, there were no allies, no friends, and no point at which they could let their guard down or operationally relax, except when they were with each other. The different companies of the 2nd Battalion of the 35th Regiment thus had a very representative cross-section of those men who, by 1944, after five years of war and violent anti-civilian operations in Western and Eastern Europe, found themselves on anti-partisan duties in Tuscany.

Werner Bruss was born in Saarbrucken in the west of Germany in 1920, and joined the SS in 1940. In his own words, 'not out of any ideological motives but to get away from a father who was an alcoholic'.[7] He served in Poland, and then in Byelorussia and the Ukraine with an Einsatzkommando, carrying out mass killings behind the front lines of advancing German units. He was involved in massacres of partisan prisoners on the Eastern Front, and by 1943 was an SS-Unterscharführer, or sergeant, and transferred to serve in Hungary with the 5th Company, 2nd Battalion, of the 35th Regiment.

Alfred Concina was from Oelsnitz in Saxony, a member of the Nazi Party from his teens, who joined the air force and transferred to the Waffen-SS. As a sergeant, he was wounded by a hand grenade on the

Eastern Front in July 1943, and then sent to the SS-Totenkopf Division in Prague, and then to the 16th SS Division. He came under the command of Gerhard Sommer in the 7th Company of the 2nd Battalion.

Ludwig Goring was born in Ittersbach, a small town in Baden-Württemberg near the French border. He served as a sergeant in the 6th Company, under the command of SS-Hauptsturmführer Anton Galler. He had joined the SS in 1941 and served with the 16th SS in Russia, then in Holland with a reserve battalion. In May 1944 was transferred to Italy.

Karl Gropler was an agricultural worker from Wollin, near Potsdam, who joined the Hitler Youth in 1937 and the SS in 1942. He saw service in France and Holland, and then with the SS-Totenkopf Division, he fought in Russia, Poland and Hungary. Wounded in the head during the battle for Kharkov in 1943, he was a junior sergeant by the time he was posted to the 16th SS in Italy.

Georg Rauch, meanwhile, was the son of a miner from the Ore mountains in Saxony. He joined the Hitler Youth when he was only 12, in 1933. He took a furlough from National Socialist militarism to start an apprenticeship as a baker and cake-maker, before joining the SS. Assigned to an SS-Totenkopfverbande, or concentration camp guard unit, he first saw action aged 19 fighting with the Totenkopf in Russia. Then came officer training. When he passed out he was still a sergeant, then returned to the Eastern Front, was wounded, and then sent to Poland to fight against partisans in the Warsaw Ghetto. Promotion then came fast to second lieutenant and then lieutenant. In September 1943, fifty-nine officers from the Totenkopf were transferred to the 16th SS, making the leadership backbone of the unit one that was mainly composed of Death's Head regiment junior leaders. It was akin to an injection of pure SS ethos into the mainstream of the new division. Rauch was a proficient organiser and combat soldier, and he became the adjutant to Anton Galler in the 2nd Battalion in June 1944, co-ordinating logistics, administration and operations within the unit.

Fighting in Tuscany and retreating northwards to the prepared defensive positions of the Gothic Line, the SS were adhering closely to Field Marshal Albert Kesselring's orders as laid out in his 'Anti-Partisan Activity' or Anti-Bandenbekampfung ruling. As explained, this was instituted in German–occupied areas of Italy in September 1943 and updated several times. The Allies were aware of it: in autumn 1943 code-breakers at Bletchley Park in England had intercepted the signals announcing Kesselring's initiative. It specified that, firstly, all partisans were to be shot if captured, and that if any German commander whose actions against partisans exceeded 'standard levels of severity', he would be protected by Kesselring. Even the terminology fit: the Army Group command in Tuscany described one of the 16th SS' deployments against partisans and civilians as a Vernichtungsunternehmen, or annihilation operation. Its aim was to physically exterminate all resistance: the officers running this and other operations were backed up by a framework of orders and standard operating procedures that covered them for almost any eventuality. In addition, the 'Hitler Directive' of December 1942 had forbidden any military legal proceedings against German soldiers for any crimes committed against civilians. This had been drafted with the German armies on the Eastern Front in mind, after Hitler's legal advisers counselled him that were it to be possible for any persons or organisations or governments to charge Wehrmacht or SS men with crimes committed against civilians, then the numerical equivalent of a whole Army's-worth of men could find themselves facing courts martial.

This ruling was adopted from September 1943 by all SS commanders in the Mediterranean, demanding as it did use of 'any means, without limitation even against women and children, so long as it leads to success'. For the men of the Reichsführer-SS, on operations against partisans and the Italian civilian population that harboured them, it was to provide a highly permissive environment, a breeding ground for a perfect storm of large-scale war crimes and serial atrocities. One British officer described the German approach to the Italian civilian population as 'a systematic policy of extermination, looting, piracy and terrorism'.[8]

And so on the night of 11–12 August 1944, the 5th, 6th, 7th and 8th Companies of the 2nd Battalion left their barracks in Pietrasanta and Marina di Carrara, and boarded trucks and half-tracks. They drove eastwards towards the foothills of the Apuan Alps. The men were hefting light mortars, MG 42 machine guns, boxes and belts of 7.92mm ammunition, ration packs, jerrycans of water and petrol, signals rockets, hand grenades, and their personal weapons. For some of the men these were K98 Mauser rifles, MP 38 and MP 40 Schmeisser machine pistols; officers carried 9mm Walther and Luger automatics. A number of the men of the unit had equipped themselves with Italian Beretta MAS-38 sub-machine guns: firing a heavier 9mm round than the Schmeissers, they were more accurate at longer ranges, sturdier, and benefited from the attention to detail of the Italian engineering system.

The SS men drove in three different directions towards their target: the 5th Company approached from the west, disembarking from their trucks in the olive groves and chestnut trees that lay on the slopes surrounding the village that was their target. Officers had given detailed orders before the men left their barracks: this was an anti-partisan operation. Enemy fighters would be in the operational area. The 6th, 7th and 8th Companies were respectively deployed to the east and the north.

So at about six o'clock in the morning of 12 August, Ludwig Goring and some thirty-five to forty men from Anton Galler's company lined up and started walking up the mountain from their positions. Goring was on the left flank with his MG 42, there to provide fire support if the section came into contact with partisans. Other men in his section carried belts or boxes of ammunition for the automatic weapon. The night was dark, but the sky was clear and full of stars. Sweating under the weight of their equipment, they manoeuvred up the ridge and over the hill, until they came in sight of the first house below them. One of the men in Galler's headquarters section loaded a rocket into a small mortar launcher, and fired it into the air, where it ignited and lit up with a soft, glowing whump, that lit up the sky with a green glare. The signal to the other units was clear: 5th Company crossing the start line, moving into contact. Below the Germans on the slope in front of them, the village of Sant'Anna di Stazzema was still asleep.[9]

5

The Children of Sant'Anna di Stazzema

Sant'Anna di Stazzema was a village that preferred to hide away from the world. It sat at the top of a dirt road that climbed up from the Tuscan coast, and led nowhere. The village, with its red-roofed houses, was the last stop before the towering mountains of the Apuan Alps. Sant'Anna had never done anything wrong, had certainly never hurt anybody, and was noticeable only for its complete anonymity. It was a village like dozens of others sprinkled across the mountains and foothills of rural central Italy. The people were *contadini*, smallholders, while some were subsistence farmers. They grew olives, kept a few cattle, and every year in autumn harvested the thousands of chestnut trees that grew around the village. The soft yellow nuts went to make *farina dolce*, a sweet flour prized in the making of cakes and unleavened bread. By the fifth year of the Second World War, as Rome fell and the Allies advanced northwards, the village stayed isolated from the outside world. There was no radio, no newspapers, no running water and no electricity.

Word of the outside world came from the inhabitants of the village who travelled by donkey and the occasional car down to Pietrasanta, a small town lying 2,000ft below on the Tuscan coast. Dictated to by its geography, Sant'Anna di Stazzema seemed cut off from the outside. The children only wore shoes to go down the mountainside, or to visit neighbouring villages. The small clutches of red-roofed houses stood in copses of chestnut, plane and olive trees, surrounded by small fields of maize that sloped steeply across the side of the mountain.

It overlooked the glimmering cobalt of the Tyrrhenian Sea. Looking down and directly westwards from the village, the seaside towns of Viareggio, Pietrasanta, Massa and Carrara lay spread along the Tuscan littoral.[1] The livelihood of Sant'Anna was its chestnut and olive trees, and they seemed not to look up at the mountains behind them but down to the shimmering waters of the coast. The eternal light and the seasons decided the colour of this sea: turquoise in spring, cobalt in summer, thundering dark blue in autumn. Many of the children in the village had never been far enough down the mountain to visit the sandy coastline, nor even dipped a toe into the warm waves. Sant'Anna stood happy where it was, away from the world.

Enrico Pieri was 10 in August 1944, and lived with his grandparents, his parents and his two sisters in a house a few yards from the village square. Shy yet determined, when not at the village school he helped his father look after their sheep.[2] Everybody knew everybody in and around Sant'Anna, and one of Enrico's friends had a little brother, called Enio Mancini, who was 5. He lived with his grandmother, his brother and his mother and father, who worked in a nearby iron ore mine. Further up the hillside in Sant'Anna lived one of the largest families in the village. There were nine Pardini children, the oldest an 18-year-old girl, the youngest a 3-week-old baby. Through the village school, through working in the fields together, through coexisting in an isolated mountainside community, everybody seemed to know the heartbeat of everybody else's lives. By the summer of 1944, each time the children's parents left the village, they would come back in the evenings. They'd bring word of what was happening down on the coast, and how close to them the war was coming as the Allies advanced northwards from Rome.[3]

But, like the other adults who went down to the coast, the parents of Enrico Pieri, Enio Mancini and Adele Pardini had already seen the German posters. They were plastered outside the town hall down in Pietrasanta, at the bottom of the mountain. They were outside the local cinema in the nearby town of Lucca. And at the beginning of August, the children saw them, too. On the 8th of that month, with the summer sun blazing at its brightest, German soldiers arrived in Sant'Anna in a truck, winding slowly up the steep mountain track. They came with posters, hammers and nails. They put up posters that bore a simple message: anybody who harbours partisans will have their house burned down. Finally, it seemed, the war had arrived in Sant'Anna. That summer, every Italian everywhere was following the Allies' plodding advance up Italy. They tuned in illicitly to the BBC where possible, they learned to pick their way through the propaganda broadcast on the German-controlled local radio, and even picked up Allied forces broadcasts from Algiers, Rome or Monopoli on the Adriatic coast. In early June they heard that the Americans had liberated their capital, and from then on Italian radio stations could pick up the American dance music broadcast on the GIs' channel.

As the Allies moved up Italy, from Salerno to Monte Cassino, and then to Rome, so the Germans retreated, and so the Italian partisans waged an increasingly intense guerrilla war behind their lines. The clashes and skirmishes between them and the Germans were normally short, fast and intense: the partisans would ambush a convoy, attack an outpost in the night, or open fire on a German patrol spreading through the orchards and olive groves, and then the Italian guerrilla fighters would evaporate into the countryside. These attacks would normally leave small numbers of Germans wounded or killed, yet all the more determined to hit back at the partisans and take revenge on their support structure of civilian families living in the small villages dotted across the Tuscan countryside.

To warn Italian civilians of the dangers of helping the partisans, the Germans had put up the posters everywhere. They showed a picture of the German commander in Italy, Field Marshal Albert Kesselring, alongside photographs of German soldiers, partisan prisoners, and a background of lightning flashes and explosions. The German field marshal's message, written on the poster in German and Italian, was to the point, and warned the Italian civilian population of the dangers of harbouring or helping partisans in any way. Italians who worked for the Germans, partisans who had been on the wrong end of German custody, and the never-ending, humming buzz of the wartime gossip and rumour mill said that on other posters outside German barracks, in prisons and wherever German soldiers circulated, there was also another message. In it the German commander urged his men to be as tough as possible on the Italian civilians who looked after and harboured any partisans.

By late July and early August 1944, Enio and Enrico's parents had told the children that, although the Allies were approaching and would soon arrive in their region of Tuscany, and although there would be fierce fighting, they would probably be spared from the worst of it.[4] After all, Sant'Anna was a mountaintop village and the only road into it led nowhere. Also, almost all of the younger men in the village had left earlier in August, either looking for any form of paid employment in the towns on the coast, or to join partisan groups. The population of Sant'Anna normally consisted of some thirty extended families comprising around 250 people, but this number had been increased that summer by another 2,000 people who had arrived as refugees. They were fleeing fighting elsewhere, from as far away as Naples, and as close as Viareggio down on the seaside, where the fighting between the Americans and the Germans was expected to come.

The families from the coastal towns had moved in with the families from the village. There wasn't much space, nobody had much food, but in rural Tuscany in summer you could drop a pebble into the earth and it would grow and bear fruit. The village lived off the land. For the children it was all rather new, and sometimes exciting, and life seemed untouched by the war that was creeping inexorably northwards towards them. This didn't seem to matter much to the children like Enio and Enrico, because by the end of July their parents told them that the partisans had moved away, and so the village of Sant'Anna would be safer. For Enio, the war just seemed to be noise from far away. It seemed to be like a game. There had been a small battle that spring between partisans and Germans on a neighbouring mountain, and Enio and the other children had opened the windows in their house to listen to the crack-cracking of weapons, the soft boom of the hand grenades exploding.

Life in the village carried on regardless, with lessons in the church and red-roofed schoolhouse, and games under the plane trees in the little piazza, the young children dancing in circles, holding hands, first this way, then the other. On the night of 11 August they all went to bed as normal in the little stone houses, three or four children tucked up in a line under one blanket, while outside the Tuscan night was warm, midnight blue and ricocheting with the noises of cicadas. It was the night of the feast day of San Lorenzo. Before they went to sleep some of the children looked up into the sky, hoping to see lucky shooting stars, dispatched across the heavens by the saint. Instead, at dawn the following day, they got the Waffen-SS.

Enio's father shook him awake before sunrise. He said almost nothing to his 5-year-old son, just that he had to leave the village that minute. But Enio should not be afraid, he added, because nothing bad would happen. Fifteen minutes later the other children in the family were wide awake too, as were the eleven Italian refugees living in the Mancini's house. From their windows, all the people in the household saw and heard the soft thump, the airborne whoosh, and then the vast glare of white and coloured lights that lit up the sky. Somebody was coming. It was the Germans, firing magnesium signal flares further down the hill. Still half asleep, nobody in the Mancini house could work out what was happening. The grown-ups were now awake too: the young men in the houses around them burst out of the doors, shouldering knapsacks, shouting and pulling on their clothes. They hared off through the chestnut trees, running as fast as they could towards the far end of the village. Unlike the children, they knew exactly what was coming.

The children hadn't even got dressed when the first soldiers arrived at seven. They were terrifying to look at. Some had pulled hessian sacks over their heads, eye slits cut in them. It wasn't clear who these men were. But the Germans all had bare faces, sweating from their climb up the mountain. As Enio and the other children stood there, terrified, the German soldiers screamed three words again and again: '*Raus, Schnell! Raus, Schnell! Valdicastello …*'

To force everybody to start moving down the mountainside towards the neighbouring town of Valdicastello, the Germans opened fire with flame-throwers, engulfing some of the village houses in sheets of burning petrol. The most precious asset the Mancini family possessed was their cow, who provided milk that the family could barter for food. For Italian civilians in wartime Italy, having enough to eat was all of their life's priorities rolled into one. The roiling smoke from the burning houses swept up behind the Mancini's house towards the tethered cow, engulfing her in grey, oily smoke. Neither the Mancini children nor the refugees had shoes on, and only two or three of them had even had time to step into the wooden clogs they normally wore. Then another group of German soldiers suddenly appeared in front of their house.

The children were motionless with fear; the Germans grabbed the eldest child, and half-pulling, half-pushing, forced him to lead a group of the children down a narrow dirt path that led in front of the house. Enio was one of them. They stumbled down through the chestnut trees towards the clearing in the trees that was the village square. Two earth roads criss-crossed through the village houses, several dirt tracks led further into the trees, and myriad small paths flicked their way through the chestnuts and olive groves towards the sloping fields.

A teenage German soldier with blond hair was pushing Enio and the group of children. They were terrified, but all that came into Enio's mind was that with his blond hair under his helmet, the soldier looked exactly like what the children's parents said Germans looked like. He was so young he was almost a teenager. Along with a group of half-a-dozen other children, this soldier pushed Enio down the narrow track, dark earth and stones slipping under their feet. They were coming towards the open grass space by the small village church. Suddenly, behind some trees, the German soldier stopped them. The children stood huddled, too frightened to move. Then the young trooper with blond hair waved his arm, and hissed at them, trying to be quiet. Go, he said, get lost, go back home, get out of here …

He waved his arm, gesturing urgently at them to walk back up the hill, and disappear. Enio and the others hesitated. Then the soldier raised his sub-machine gun and fired a bullet into the air. The children took to their heels, and started running for their lives back up the slope. Then below them, they heard the shooting start.

Meanwhile, 10-year-old Enrico Pieri had been up early, with his parents and family around their kitchen table. Suddenly a group of German soldiers crashed through the four pomegranate trees that stood outside the kitchen door. The Germans burst in, squeezing to get through the door, burdened down with guns and equipment. As the men negotiated the cramped space inside the house, a small girl from the refugee family grabbed Enrico. She was called Grazia

Pierotti. The Germans dragged the Pieri and Pierotti families out of
the kitchen, into the garden, and towards a neighbouring house. Then
they turned a flame-thrower on the Pieri's house, and threw stick grenades in afterwards.

Grazia Pierotti had managed to hide in a small triangular cupboard
underneath the stairs. As the Germans forced the adults out of the
house, she opened the small door of the cupboard, and saw Enrico
standing by himself in the kitchen, frozen, almost paralysed, as his house
began to burn down. She dashed out from her hiding place, grabbed
him by the arm, and they ran into the garden. They dashed behind their
house, into the vegetable patch, and tumbled down on to the damp
earth between rows of runner beans. The wooden canes that supported
the plants were curled round with big green leaves and bean pods, and
by lying flat on the ground Enrico and Grazia could make themselves
almost invisible. They stayed there; nobody came past. They didn't see
any soldiers' boots from their hiding place, so pressed their faces into
the earth and waited. Then they listened. It took minutes. They heard
ripping, stammering bursts of machine-gun fire. They could also hear
shooting coming from the rest of the village. They stayed under the
bean stalks, too terrified to move.

Enio, meanwhile, ran back up the slope towards his parents' house.
It was on fire, and their cow was on her side on the grass, suffocated by
smoke. Along with the other children whose lives had been saved by
the young German soldier, Enio turned and ran. Meanwhile, the noise
of the Germans arriving had also woken up 4-year-old Adele Pardini,
three of her five sisters and her mother Bruna. They had dressed as fast
as they could and gathered in the kitchen of their house, their mother
carrying the baby sister Anna, only 3 weeks old.[5] Two of the other
sisters were already outside, walking their way to work in the nearby
fields as the sun came up. The Germans arrived, along with an Italian
who was wearing a black triangular mask across the lower part of his
face. They ordered Bruna, Adele and the other two girls to get out of
the house and join a large group of people gathering on the dirt track
outside. Within minutes, the number of people in the group had grown
to about fifty, and then more. By the time they stumbled down the
slope towards the village square, there were more than 100 of them.

The Germans had set up a machine gun in the small grassy space, and had crowded a large number of old people, women and children in front of it. The women were pleading that the war had nothing to do with them, and the children were crying. A German officer arrived, saw that there were no men in the group except elderly people, and turned to the village priest. He demanded to know where the men were hiding. The priest said that there were no men in the village. The German officer asked him again. The reply was the same. The German lifted his pistol, and shot him in the head. Then he gave the order to the machine-gun crew to open fire.

Adele and her sister stood completely terrified beside her mother, who was carrying the baby Anna in her arms. The Germans beat them with rifle butts and forced them up against the wall of a house. Alongside her was her mother, carrying the tiny baby, and three of her sisters, Cesira, Lilia and Maria. Standing with the stones behind her, Adele's mind grasped on to something familiar. She remembered that it was at this exact spot that a photographer had taken a picture of their family, on the day of the First Holy Communion of one of her sisters.

Then four Germans and a masked man approached them. The Germans stood back. The man wearing the black triangular mask shot Bruna, and another woman standing beside her, with a single shot each. Then they stood back, running clear as the other Germans opened fire. As Adele's mother fell, her body collapsed against the little 4-year-old, standing diagonally behind her. The weight of her mother's body pushed Adele backwards against a small door set in the wall of the house behind her, which fell open. Adele crawled in, with Lilia and Maria. It was the last time she saw her mother. Her baby sister Anna was beside her on the ground, splattered with blood.

In the runner beans where he was hiding, Enrico Pieri could hear the machine guns beginning to shoot. He and the little girl, Grazia, got up and went back towards his house. It was half burning, and all they could see was the bodies of some members of their families lying on the floor, dead. Blood was splattered everywhere. The two children ran away from the house, through the pomegranates, and towards a stand of plane and chestnut trees that overlooked the empty space in the front of the village church. It was full of bodies. Both Enrico and Enio Mancini

arrived almost simultaneously, looking at the scene from different positions on the slopes above it; Enio, from where he was standing, could
see the village square, too. He saw bodies without heads, and without
legs, and already, as the sun started to come up, the corpses started to
attract a swarm of flies. A lot of bodies were now burning inside the
houses, and the village was wreathed through with blankets of grey and
black smoke. From his position in the trees, Enio started looking, trying
desperately to identify the bodies of the children with whom he had
played the night before. All he could smell was the thick, sweet, meaty
stink of burning flesh. And all he could hear was the soft, harmonious
chant of the German soldiers below him, as they sung their way slowly
and gently through the lines of 'Lili Marlene'. They had piled some of
the pews from the church in front of the building, and used it to start a
fire with which to incinerate the corpses of the dead. So as the village
burned, the German troops sat in the shade under the trees, took out
the rations with which they had been issued the night before, and ate
lunch.

The SS left the village around four o'clock in the afternoon. They
were afraid to spend the evening and night in the mountains for fear of
partisan attacks. Enio crept out of hiding again after they left, and along
with all the other people who had survived, helped prepare a mass grave
for around 200 of the bodies, some of them carbonised, some of them
burned down to the skeletons. The air still smelt of the petrol from the
flame-throwers. Enio's father returned to their destroyed house at the
end of the day. Unlike many children in the village, the 5-year-old boy
still had a father. And so, as night fell on 12 August 1944, the children
of Sant'Anna di Stazzema slept out under the stars, curled up under the
chestnut trees that grew all around their village.

6

A TRAIL OF MASSACRES

Five days after the attack on Sant'Anna di Stazzema, a platoon of SS men were given a task: their quartermaster had filed a request for more fresh food for the men of the division. So a unit of men from the 7th Company was sent out to buy, barter, forage or if necessary steal it at gunpoint from the Italian population. Despite the fact that the men had slaughtered over 500 civilians less than a week earlier, and thus could do little to regain any sympathy or trust of the Tuscan populace, the quartermaster insisted that proper procedure be followed, and that if requested the German soldiers should pay for the animals, fruit and vegetables they were trying to buy.

On the morning of 17 August, the platoon of German troops drove into the hamlet of Bardine di San Terenzo. It lies about a mile from the village of San Terenzo Monti, and 8 miles north-east of Marina di Carrara.[1] The men decided to confiscate half a dozen cows and ten sheep, under the pretext of denying them to the local partisan population. The animals were loaded on to the trucks, in one case the men crowded in with the sheep, and the Germans drove back down the hill. The inhabitants of Bardine, short of food, their village filled with 200 displaced people, desperately needed their livestock. So they asked a group of partisans to attack the German trucks, and if possible to not kill the sheep and cattle, only the SS men. So as the German trucks wound down the slope from the village, ripping bursts of fire from Sten guns, Schmeissers and a Bren light machine gun stammered out of the olive groves, vineyards and stands of wellingtonia trees at the side of the road. By the time the trucks crashed into the side of the dusty track, sixteen German soldiers were dead.

On the 19th, the SS sent three platoons up the road to collect the bodies of their dead comrades, and attack both Bardine and San Terenzo Monti. The one-armed commander of the 16th SS' reconnaissance regiment, Major Walter Reder, led the operation. The men from the Aufklarungs-Abteilung 16 had brought with them fifty-three civilian hostages they had arrested a few days earlier. Reder's men took them to the site of the ambush, and marched them into a vineyard by the side of the road. His men tied them to the concrete and wooden posts that supported the grape trellises, and shot them. He then drove up the hill to the two hamlets, forced 159 elderly men, women and children from their houses, and executed them in a small square.

Five days later, the whole of the 2nd Battalion of the 16th SS began a huge anti-partisan sweep, or *rastrellamento*, near the town of Fivizzano, 9 miles north-east of Marina di Carrara. The Italian word literally means 'raking', and was the preferred term for an anti-partisan operation, where lines of German soldiers and Italian Fascist troops – and sometimes coerced civilians – would often criss-cross hills and fields in lines, designed to cut off and flush out any partisans hiding in woods or forests, or isolated buildings. After the operations of spring and summer of 1944 in Tuscany, it became synonymous with forced displacements and shootings of civilians.

The operation carried out near Fivizzano was exactly that. A large number of civilians were killed in a three-day operation that took place between 24 and 27 August, when the SS burned down houses, and rounded up the civilian population who were hiding in the woods surrounding fourteen different villages. The three-day operation finished in and around the mountain village of Vinca: the civilians who had fled the other villages had converged there, thinking they were safe. They weren't. On the 26th, a company of the SS were moving down a hillside when they ran into a group of partisans: engaged in a running firefight, they took casualties before the partisans pulled back towards Vinca. The next day the SS arrived there in force, and rounded up both the partisans they captured there, as well as the civilians who had returned from woods and caves. They shot 162 of them.[2]

A week later, and 15 miles to the south-east, word of the killings had reached the Carthusian monastery at Farneta. The small village sits north of the walled medieval town of Lucca, on a beautiful plain of olive trees, orchards and cypresses, near the Serchio river. Half a mile outside it is the monastery, where an order of Carthusian monks and lay brothers lived – and still live – under a vow of complete silence. Their monks devoted their lives to prayer, and working on a small farm that supplied their food; the monastery seemed cut-off from the war that was criss-crossing Tuscany that summer and autumn of 1944. Of the whole monastic community, only a few of the monks or lay brothers were allowed to converse with strangers from outside the abbey. The monks got their news in dribs and drabs from occasional contact with these outsiders, and that summer these included a partisan who, along with his children, had arrived to hide in the monastery. He was taking refuge from German revenge, from the SS anti-partisan operations that were taking hostages, taking reprisals and killing hundreds of innocent people in and around Lucca, as well as in the towns and villages of the mountainous Tuscan interior.

The partisan fighter also told the Carthusians that he had heard, from fellow partisans, of a large-scale killing of civilians in the village of Sant'Anna di Stazzema. A week before, he said, fifteen villages around Vinca, to the north-west of Farneta, had been set alight by the Germans, and a large number of civilians killed. There were reports coming in as well of an earlier reprisal killing in three villages near Sant'Anna. In all of these incidents, said the partisan, the same German unit of the Waffen-SS was involved. Also taking refuge in a cell in a lodge in the monastery grounds were a police officer from Lucca, who had been helping hide local Jews. Vito Rizzo, and his son Vincenzo, 18, had fled to the monastery when the Germans and Fascist police had discovered how they were helping hide some of Lucca's Jewish community from arrest and deportation.[3]

On 23 August the prior of the monastery had received a letter from a priest in Lucca, warning that a German raid on the Carthusian community was imminent. By this time, a mixed collection of partisans, their families, local Italian Jews, children from a local orphanage and former Italian Fascist soldiers had gathered in the farm and outbuildings of the monastery. The community could not welcome anybody inside the church and monastery itself, but as the numbers of people arriving to take refuge increased, the monks decided to relax this ruling. The prior went down to Lucca and visited the German commander there: the monastery had nothing to fear from the Wehrmacht or the SS, he said, so long as they were not hiding any partisans, Jews or wanted people. On his return, one of the lay brothers told the prior that since late July, three German soldiers, pretending to be deserters, had been coming to mass regularly: they would sit in the pews during the service, he said, staring around them at everybody in the church, assessing points of entry and exit, their faces, said the lay brother, still, grim and as though set in marble.

On 1 September, a Slovenian lay brother called Guido Percic saw Germans blowing up a nearby bridge, as they prepared to withdraw northwards. On the night of 1–2, an SS sergeant called Eduard Florin, who had visited the monastery several times before, bluffed his way into the building. He told the monk who opened the door that as his unit was now withdrawing from Lucca, he had brought a farewell package for the community from his commanding officer in the town. As the monk opened the door, Florin and some twenty of his fellow soldiers forced their way inside.[4] Several SS men then arrived silently in the monastery's chapel while the monks were at prayer. The Germans told the men to keep silent, or they would die. They set a belt-fed machine gun on a tripod in front of the altar. Then the Germans left suddenly. One of the people taking refuge in the monastery was a disbanded Fascist soldier, who had fled Mussolini's army, and was thus liable to execution by the Germans. This 22-year-old, a trainee lawyer called Lorenzo Coturri, said that a German sergeant had been turning up to receive confession several times in preceding days. Coturri suspected it was a trick. It was.

The Germans started retreating from the area around Lucca the following day. Then they arrived outside the monastery gates, forced their way in, and gathered everybody inside into one group. They made the monks go and change out of their habits, and into civilian clothes. Over the next two days, the Germans took the entire monastic community, along with some forty partisans, Jews and civilians, to an olive oil mill in the nearby village of Nocchi where the retreating Germans had set up a temporary command post.

Herded into a room, the Germans questioned the monks. One father was forced to stretch his arms out in front of him, on which a

German soldier placed a heavy plank, making him do leg bends while beating him with a stick. A second German soldier held a flame to a monk's beard. There was almost no food and water. For three days the SS soldiers beat and shouted at the monks and civilians, until they were ordered into one large group and made to march towards a nearby valley. Two priests who couldn't keep up were shot; the Germans set the bodies on fire and then buried them. One of them was not even Italian, but a Venezuelan lay brother. Before the Germans shot him, they accused him of being a member of the American Office of Strategic Services, and the head of the partisan resistance that was supposedly based in the Farneta monastery.

Two days later the group arrived in a village outside the town of Massa, where along with thirty civilians, and seven more of the monks, the Germans lined most of the prisoners up in front of a row of trees. The SS went along the line of men, unrolling a large coil of barbed wire. They used wire-cutters to shear off a length in front of each prisoner, and then tied them to the trees with several turns of wire. Once the prisoners were attached to a tree – in some places two men to one tree – soldiers and NCOs advanced down the line with machine pistols, rifles and handguns, shooting each person. Of the Carthusian contingent, two were Swiss, one was German, and one was French.

The Germans left the bodies attached to the trees, and took the remainder of their prisoners to the town of Massa. The whole SS division was in retreat; the Americans were fighting a few miles south of the town. American soldiers arrived in Lucca the day after the SS took their captives on their death march. African-American infantrymen from the 92nd Division liberated the old Tuscan town, and afterwards, military policemen from the British Intelligence Corps' Field Security Sections went to work.[5] The Allied soldiers knew that what had occurred at Farneta with the SS was by no means an isolated event.

Simultaneously, men from their units were beginning to investigate the other massacres that had occurred at Sant'Anna di Stazzema, Fivizzano and San Terenzo di Monte, and at least fifteen other villages. Hundreds and hundreds of people had been killed, almost all of them civilians, mostly elderly people, children and women. The death toll was between 1,000 and 1,100 by this point. The unit that had carried out these killings? The same one that had arrived outside the monastery at

Farneta in the first days of September; the 16th SS Division, the men whose black and silver cuff titles read 'Reichsführer-SS'.

By mid-1944, as the Allies advanced and the front line crept northwards, so bombing attacks by the RAF and USAAF increased on the German-occupied towns ahead of them. One of these was Massa, situated half a mile down the coast from Marina di Carrara. The prison there sat outside the railway station, and fearing that it could be hit by Allied bombs or air-ground attacks, the Italian police moved the inmates to the medieval Malaspina castle overlooking the city. The prisoners in the castle were a typical mixture of those incarcerated by the Germans and their Italian allies – anybody in the town who had opposed Mussolini, small-time criminals, some black marketeers and desperate, starving civilians who had stolen to try and feed their families. The fitter, healthier men had escaped with the help of sympathetic Italian warders, paid by partisans, and fled into the hills. Inside the castle it was over 90°, full of mosquitoes, with hardly any clean water, single toilets shared between dozens, and hardly anywhere to wash. It was no wonder that the inmates wanted to go and fight with the resistance.

But most of the guards at the prison were not the gently sympathetic Italians, but the military police, the Feldgendarmerie, of the 16th SS. On 2nd September the Germans ordered that by the 15th the entire population of Massa would have to leave the city and head across the Apennines towards the city of Parma. The 16th SS were pulling out, and heading north, to be replaced by regular units of the Wehrmacht. Then in the first week of September the ranks of the prisoners in the castle were increased by the arrival of another eighty inmates: anti-fascist politicians, priests, some Greeks, Albanians and Libyans fighting as partisans, and Italian Jews.

On Sunday, 10 September, seventy-four of the political prisoners were taken out of the castle and shot outside the grounds. They were buried in improvised mass graves dug into the hard, dry soil near the castle's entrance. On 16 September, the rest of the prisoners were put on board lorries and told they were being taken to a prison in northern Italy. They were, in fact, taken only a short distance to some open ground on the banks of a stream called the Frigido, near the church of San Leonardo. Among the prisoners were prison inmates on stretchers, and some who were forced to use crutches. The Germans found three bomb craters in the ground, the result of a recent air strike by the RAF. The prisoners were lined up on the edges of these, and machine-gunned. Only three were spared. The death toll was climbing: another 147 people had just been added to it.[6]

The 16th SS continued its string of reprisal killings on that same day, 16 September. A lone partisan had shot a German soldier on a mountain road near La Foce Pass, which sits above Carrara. The soldier's body lay sprawled in the dusty road, just when a fireman happened to pass by, returning to his home in the nearby village of Bergiola Foscalina. He panicked when he saw the body, immediately assuming that if any German troops found him near the corpse, they would automatically assume he was responsible for killing the SS trooper. So he fled back to his village. Unfortunately, as he was hurrying, he dropped his rucksack in the road.

At four o'clock in the afternoon of the same day, one of the units from the 16th SS' reconnaissance battalion drove up to his village. They had found the body and found the rucksack, and wanted to know where the owner was. Driving into Bergiola in half-tracks and jeeps, the only people they found were women, children and pensioners. The partisans had fled. A young sergeant from the customs police, the Guardia di Finanza, saw immediately what was about to happen, and offered himself to the Germans. Leave the civilians alone, he implored. Shoot me instead. He didn't know that among the hostages were his own wife and daughter. The SS officer present informed him that his understanding of the rules of war forbade him from shooting an enemy combatant in uniform as a reprisal. So the customs officer, who was called Vincenzo Giudice, took off his uniform tunic, telling the Germans that he was now effectively out of uniform, and hence a civilian. The SS shot him. Then they locked thirty of the elderly people and the women and children in the village primary school. They set it alight with flame-throwers. They then set fire to the houses of other villagers who had taken refuge in their homes. By the time a group of partisans arrived on the scene, the SS had left. All that the resistance fighters could do was to help put out the fires, and count the dead. There were sixty-one of them, of whom twenty-four were children and teenagers, and twenty-eight grown-up women.[7] Among them were the wife and child of the courageous customs officer.

SS-Major Walter Reder, from the 16th SS Panzergrenadier Division 'Reichsführer SS'.

SS-Major-General Max Simon, from the 16th SS Panzergrenadier Division 'Reichsführer SS'.

7

THE AMERICANS INVESTIGATE

On 7 September, an SS trooper called Willi Haase deserted. He belonged to the 5th Company of the 2nd Battalion of the 35th Regiment, commanded by Major Karl Gesele. He had decided he wanted to surrender to the nearest Allied unit he could find. In the previous twelve weeks his unit had fought repeated battles as they retreated up the coast. Now the division was on standby to move northwards again: a new Allied offensive was storming up towards them. Behind them lay the pre-prepared positions of the Gothic Line. All that seemed to lie ahead for Haase was fighting, and a greater than average chance of being killed. He had only just arrived in his unit. But in the previous three months before he got there, his new colleagues' lives had been filled with two months of battles, skirmishes and constant movement backwards up the Tuscan coast. In August there had been six anti-partisan operations. But Haase was still alive, and wanted to stay that way. So he just walked away from his platoon's position outside Pietrasanta and headed south-east, keeping the sea on his right. He would have wanted to meet American or British soldiers as they advanced, and not to fall into the hands of partisans or Italian civilians.

After the massacres in August, he knew that both would almost certainly kill him out of hand: pleas that he was a deserter would see him treated as a German spy. Hadn't his fellow SS men just bluffed their way into the monastery outside Lucca by pretending to be faithful churchgoers, or soldiers who wanted the Catholic monks to hear their confessions? The Reichsführer cuff title and the SS death's head on his uniform was enough to see him tied to a tree and shot in the head, or just be killed where he stood, his body thrown into a ditch. He and his colleagues knew that up against them in the line were American, British and Brazilian soldiers, as well as Italian partisans. After the fighting at Suvereto and Belvedere in June, Willi Haase was also aware that there were Japanese soldiers with the Americans, too. Then there were black troops as well, company intelligence briefings said, and behind them and around them, a huge mixture of Canadians, Poles, New Zealanders, South Africans and the so-called Gurkhas, brown-skinned Indian soldiers with their long, curved knives.

So when SS-Sturmmann Willi Haase walked bang into an American patrol, he was very lucky. His captors stripped him of his papers, the contents of his pockets and took him back down to their company headquarters, and handed him to the Military Police. A truck ride with other PoWs took him south of the front line to the port of Livorno, and a makeshift cell set up in one of the buildings the US Army had occupied as their temporary headquarters. There on 16 September, nine days after he had deserted, he found himself in front of his interrogators, who were three American officers.[1]

Allied War Crimes Investigators in Italy

By midsummer 1944, war crimes investigations in Italy were the responsibility of the Allied War Crimes Commission; this in turn was part of the Allied Control Commission, based at the former Royal Palace at Caserta, outside Naples. The Control Commission was the body set up by the Allies in September 1943 as the de facto military administration of those parts of Italy occupied by the British and Americans. The War Crimes Commission was responsible for investigating any such incidents carried out by the Germans and their Italian Fascist allies such as massacres of the Italian civilian population, reprisal shootings, destruction of towns and villages, as well as any crimes committed against Allied soldiers. This commission was split into three parts. At the headquarters in Caserta, the first section of the commission was made up of military policemen and military lawyers who co-ordinated investigations, collated reports of crimes and prepared cases. The Moscow Declaration of October 1943, signed by Stalin, Roosevelt and Churchill, had specified that German perpetrators of war crimes would be sent back for trial to the country in which the crimes had taken place. This meant that any German personnel charged with war crimes carried out in Italy would be tried in that country by the Allies, and potentially by the Italians, after the war had ended.

The second section was the British War Crimes Group, which deployed teams of military policemen from Sections 60 and 78 of the Royal Military Police's Special Investigation Branch; they began investigations after they had received reports from British troops of any war crimes that had taken place in their respective areas of operations. As the Allies advanced northwards, more and more of these crime scenes were being discovered. The third section was the American War Crimes Investigation Unit, which fulfilled exactly the same role as the British, except in those areas liberated by the US Army or other Allied troops under their command.

Because of the organisational structure of the American and British forces in Italy, the two operated alongside each other, with British units frequently attached under the command of their allies. Thus military investigators from both armies increasingly found themselves co-operating with each other, in the same area, on the same incidents of war crimes.

In summer 1944 the American 5th Army, commanded by Lieutenant General Mark W. Clark, consisted of four American divisions and three British. They operated alongside the British 8th Army, itself in turn commanded by Lieutenant General Oliver Leese. Under his command he had Canadians, New Zealanders, Poles, Rhodesians, Free French, and soldiers from India, Greece and South Africa. Leese had succeeded Lieutenant General Bernard Montgomery after the latter was recalled to Britain to prepare for Operation Overlord, the forthcoming invasion of Europe. The 8th and 5th Armies were now moving northwards from Rome, preparing for the coming battles against the Germans on the fortified positions of the Gothic Line. The 5th Army's strength had been diminished by the loss of two key infantry divisions, which had been diverted to take part in Operation Dragoon, the Allied landings in southern France, which took place on 17 August. To fill the gap in its ranks, a wide variety of units, from British anti-aircraft regiments operating as infantry soldiers, to a Brazilian Army Regimental Combat Team, were now serving alongside the Americans of the 5th Army.

General Clark's Chief of Staff was called Alfred M. Gruenther – his fellow officers had nicknamed him 'The Brain' because of his logistical and analytical expertise. In 1942 then-Brigadier General Gruenther had been assigned by American General Eisenhower as one of the senior planning officers for Operation Torch, the combined Anglo-American invasion of French North Africa. A year later, by then a major general, he was in charge of all staff responsibilities for General Clark's forces. He in turn devolved responsibility for war crimes investigations to the headquarters of the Office of the Inspector General of the US 5th Army. And so, on 10 August, this department had assigned a new investigative assignment to three American majors: Edwin S. Booth, Milton R. Wexler and Carl H. Cundiff.

Gruenther and the Office of the Inspector General decided that the three officers would be part of the 5th Army Group War Crimes Commission, operating in areas liberated by his units. They would function under the legal rules both of the US Supreme Military Tribunal, as well as those of the Allied War Crimes Commission. Like most Allied soldiers in Italy, these three American officers knew that as the Allied front line moved northwards, so their colleagues in the infantry would come across evidence of atrocities committed by the Germans. They would also receive information from Italian civilians and partisans, and from Italian and German deserters and prisoners.[2]

But before their questioning of Willi Haase could begin, one of the American majors had an outstanding task to complete. Milton Wexler had a letter to finish, concerning another investigation he had been working on during the month of August. Prior to being commissioned in the American army as an administrative investigative officer, he had been a physicist. He was now carrying out an inquiry in Italy that involved his former professor, to whom he was now drafting a letter. He was writing to Albert Einstein. He had been a student of Einstein's at Princeton, after the university had given a professorship to the Jewish particle physicist when he had fled Germany as a refugee in 1937, and taken up American citizenship.

His first cousin, Wilhelm Robert Einstein, was an engineer, and his wife Caesarina was Italian; the couple had two grown-up children called Luce and Annamaria, and lived in Florence. In summer 1944, as the Allies approached, they moved out to their summer residence at the Villa Il Focardo in the town of Rignano sull'Arno, 10 miles south-east of the city. As the British pushed closer in late July, partisans warned Robert that, as a Jew, he was on a list of those to be arrested for deportation to a concentration camp. They warned him to hide in the forests outside the small town until the Allies arrived. So on 3 August, Robert Einstein left his wife and daughters behind, who hid in the cellar of the villa, believing that if the Germans arrived they would be safe as they were not Jewish. Shortly after fleeing from the villa into a neighbouring wood, Robert heard the sound of shots, and then saw the building begin to burn. He rushed back. The Germans had executed his wife and two daughters, and reportedly left a note saying that the family had been killed as they were Jewish. They weren't. His two nieces survived. Meanwhile, the American war crimes investigator, Major Milton Wexler, was on his way to find out what had happened.

Along with a squad of American soldiers, Wexler arrived at the villa the day after the killings, on the 4th. The Germans had left, and he discovered the crime scene, and found Robert. On his return to headquarters he started composing a letter to Albert Einstein, telling him what had taken place. 'Censorship does not permit me to dwell upon the tragedy which is well known to me,' he wrote.[3] He would send the letter on 17 September, the day after he and his colleagues from the war crimes commission started to interview SS deserter Willi Haase.

When the interrogation began, Haase spoke to the American officers via a translator attached to their team, a Lieutenant William De Wall. The German soldier confirmed that the whole of his unit, the 5th Company of the 2nd Battalion of the 35th Regiment, had been sent to Sant'Anna di Stazzema on what the men had been told was a partisan operation. Haase had not been among his fellow soldiers as the company left for the mountains above the coast: he had just been transferred to the unit, and was still at regimental headquarters waiting to be posted to them. He also told his captors that it was not just the 5th Company that was deployed, but the whole of the 2nd Battalion. This, he said, meant that between 250–300 men, sub-divided into four company groups, the 5th, 6th, 7th and 8th, had been in and around Sant'Anna di Stazzema that day.

When the troops returned afterwards, one of the officers and some of the men had told him that it had been a reprisal operation, and that it had involved killing women and children. Innocent blood had been spilled, said one SS officer. And he'd added that a lot of the men under his command had to be forced to do the killing, because they wouldn't consent to do it otherwise. Could Haase remember any of the names of the men who'd been in the village, asked the Americans? He mentioned the names of an SS sergeant from the 5th Company, Martin Janssen, who had taken part in the massacre. He in turn had told Haase that their unit commander, a lieutenant called Theodor Sasse, had given orders during the operation. And who else, asked the investigators? Well, there was Horst Richter, he was a sniper specially chosen for the operation. Alfred Liebssle would have been there, he was in that unit, and Philip Werthmann.

At this stage the Americans still thought the massacre had taken place on 19, not 12, August. Haase did not correct them. What he did say that was that the operation had to have taken place on any of the days before 20 August, because he only arrived in the 5th Company on the 21st. And yes, it began in the early hours of the morning, and was an operation against partisans. He had spent very little time in the 5th Company, only arriving on 21 August and then deserting on 7 September. Then he confirmed that in fact he remembered Theodor Sasse as his own company commander for his short spell in the unit. And then he mentioned the names of two officers who had been in command on the operation that morning in Sant'Anna di Stazzema. The commander of the 2nd Battalion was a lieutenant colonel whose name was Gesele. And the 7th Company of the battalion? Yes, the officer in charge was a lieutenant called Sommer.

Wexler and Cundiff decided to question other witnesses first and to see if any of them could give a description of some of the SS men who had been at Sant'Anna that day, in particular any of the officers or senior non-commissioned officers who were giving orders. If Haase could then give them a name-by-name breakdown of the command structure of his company, that would mean that the three American majors could begin to focus on those SS men who might have had what they termed 'command and control responsibility'.

The next interviewees to come in front of the American officers were two Italians called Alfredo and Marino Curzi, who were displaced people who had fled south towards Livorno after the killings. They were the first primary witnesses whom the Americans questioned.[4] Alfredo said that around six in the morning of the day in question, he had been in Sant'Anna and that he had been woken up by the sound of gunfire. Running out of his house, he had first hidden in some bushes 70m from the door and watched what had happened. People were taken from their houses, dragged towards the piazza in front of the church, where the Germans pushed everybody together in a group on the edge of the wooded slope leading down into a gulley opposite.

The Germans had pulled the pews out of the church and laid them around the villagers in a circle, piling straw and branches on top of them. They poured petrol on top of this, and set fire to it. As the villagers began to burn, the SS men opened fire on them with a machine gun. Yes, said Curzi to the Americans. They were definitely SS. They had the silver skull on their caps and helmets.

Marino Curzi was also woken up by the sound of gunfire, and he witnessed the events that took place in the village from the entrance of a mine, about 500m distant. The shooting started about half-past six, he said, and continued until about midday. He was desperate to find his sister, who had left the house at about five o'clock that morning, and he had no idea where she was. So he got to within 50 or 60m of the Germans, who were in the village, without being seen. He saw that about ten of them were almost certainly officers, as they had gold and silver markings on their epaulettes. Did he hear any of their names being used, asked the American officers questioning him? No. Nor, from that distance could he read anything on their uniforms, but they were all SS, he said. He didn't find his sister: instead, on the piazza in front of the church he found 200 to 300 carbonised dead bodies, and another 200 strewn around in a number of locations: behind a stable, in the entrance to the church, in their houses. Almost all of them were women and small children, he said. The men had managed to escape in time.

The three American officers realised that the testimony of the German soldier and the two Italians indicated that a substantial reprisal operation had been carried out at Sant'Anna di Stazzema, and that as soon as the Allied front line had advanced as far as the sector of the Apuan Alps where Sant'Anna was situated, they or other investigators should try and reach the village.

As they were questioning Willi Haase and the Curzis, and afterwards as Milton Wexler was finishing his letter to Albert Einstein, Allied soldiers were fighting their way towards the outskirts of the town of Pietrasanta. The men of the 16th SS Division retreated north. The Allied unit attacking the town was a mix of British, American and Brazilian infantry, armoured units and artillery regiments fighting as ground combat troops. Joint Task Force 45 had been put together in early August to plug the gap in the 5th Army's ranks left by the divisions that had been diverted to the invasion of the south of France. It formed part of American Major General Stanley Crittenberger's IV Corps, whose other units included the 1st US Armoured Division, the 6th South African Armoured Division, the racially segregated 92nd US Infantry division – nicknamed the Buffalo Soldiers – and the 1st Brazilian Infantry Division. The British troops in the task force included three light anti-aircraft regiments, who had left their 40mm cannon behind and were deployed as infantry companies. Both the Brazilians and Americans were also deployed on Sherman tanks and light armoured personnel carriers, supported by artillery batteries.

Alongside them were posted a battalion of Japanese-American soldiers from the 442nd Regimental Combat Team. They were recruited from Nisei, second-generation Japanese immigrants to the United States. Initially interned as aliens after Pearl Harbour, they had then been formed into a separate unit that had already distinguished itself in the fighting north of Rome. Within this hybrid mix of fighting men were groups of Italian partisans who attached themselves to Joint Task Force 45 as it fought northwards. By 17 September, these units were advancing on Pietrasanta, and by the morning of the 18th, were on the outskirts of the town.

One of the Italian partisans was a young 20-year-old called Mario Salvatori, who, along with his group, was operating in the hills above the small walled city.[5] During the afternoon of the 16th, he went down into the town itself. Its centre is surrounded by medieval walls, and Salvatori and two colleagues ran through an arch into the central Piazza della Duomo. He spent the night of 16–17 September lying on the paving stones, on alert, waiting, pointing a Bren gun around a street corner. As dawn came up, three British soldiers crept slowly, and with extreme caution, up the street towards the Italian partisans. They were moving slowly because one of them had been wounded by a mortar round in the thigh; so the partisans took him to an empty carabinieri barracks to treat him. As they did so, they saw other Allied soldiers arriving in the town, the first of whom were speaking a language that sounded similar to Spanish. They were soldiers from a Brazilian Regimental Combat Team, in action for the first time on the Italian front.

American troops arrived after them, then more British soldiers, and finally on the 19th a combination from all three nations, accompanied by Italian partisans, out-fought three remaining diehard German machine-gun positions. Hardly had the partisans killed the crews of the MG 42s than German artillery fire started slamming into the town, firing from the surrounding hills. They had bracketed, and were now targeting, their former positions. Italian partisans rushed towards the town square, desperate to raise the Italian tricolour flag on the church tower of the Duomo di San Martino. But at the very moment of the liberation of their city and their country, they were cautious enough to realise that anybody climbing the outside of the building risked falling off and killing themselves. Caution and self-preservation got the better of them, and the flag was raised in front of the town hall instead. As American Sherman tanks rumbled down the road into Pietrasanta, another partisan had run ran out to greet them. Giorgio Giannelli was on his way to the neighbouring seaside town of Forte dei Marmi, a mile away:

I was now running into delirium, and when I reached Viale Apua outside the pine forest, I found myself like a pygmy in front of a wall of giants. A mountain of steel, an endless row of American tanks with the white star painted on their sides, very high, dazed, noisy …

I watched that scene as hypnotised: it was the price of freedom. I embraced the first one I found.[6]

When he got there, he and his colleagues found some bottles of vermouth that had survived the German occupation, and so they laid out thirty glasses on a table in the town hall, ready to greet arriving Allied officers. Before they arrived, Giannelli decided that he should deal with a sandbagged German machine-gun post, still set up on a neighbouring street corner. The partisan leaders from the CLN, the Committee for National Liberation, cheered him on. They filled the pockets of his jacket with 'hand grenades as big as lemons', and he went outside to attack the gun position. He took one look at it, and realised that it would be suicide to make a frontal attack on an MG 42 and five enemy soldiers protected behind sandbags. He looked up at the roofs around him. What if he climbed up to the roof, or simpler, took the stairs inside one of the buildings, and then dropped his grenades on top of them? Gianni's uncle had worked his whole life in an insurance building in one of the streets behind him. He knew the building well. What if he ran indoors and climbed up those familiar stairs, got onto the roof, and just dropped the hand grenades over the balustrade? Then he took another look at the sandbagged machine-gun post. It would be suicide. So, realising that it was better to live to see the liberation of his hometown, he decided to run off and warn the approaching Allies. That night he and other partisans celebrated with Brazilians and the African-American Buffalo soldiers.

The following day, with Pietrasanta liberated by Task Force 45, three Italian families came looking for the British and the Americans. They had been forced to flee from their villages above the town because of the fighting. They wanted to talk to the Allied officers who had just arrived. The 16th SS and other German army units had pulled swiftly out of Pietrasanta, they said, and then waited for the Allies and the partisans to arrive. They were now dug into positions in the hills around the town, and as if to confirm this, on the day after the liberation repeated barrages of artillery fire crashed into Pietrasanta. The Italian civilians also gave second-hand accounts to British and American officers about what had taken place up in the hills in August, information that itself had been passed on to them by survivors. So as a result of this, two days later a British captain from the 110th Battery of the 39th Light Artillery Regiment took two of his non-commissioned officers and a small group of infantrymen as an escort, and then drove eastwards out of Pietrasanta towards the village of Valdicastello.

It was still late summer in Tuscany, with long, warm days, and the apricot orchards and vineyards stood silently as the British jeeps passed. In farmhouses, barns and empty municipal buildings along the road, families of displaced people and survivors from the mountains had taken refuge. Smoke from cooking fires curled in the air, washing hung on makeshift lines, families slept where they could, everybody sharing the well. War had passed through here hours before: a German half-track with its front wheels slewed heavily into the ditch, hit by artillery fire; rumpled, uniformed bodies half in, half out of the green grass by the walnut trees. It wasn't long before the British soldiers found the first group of survivors from Sant'Anna, who told them what had taken place in the days before the massacre.

On 31 July, they said, a patrol of twelve German soldiers had arrived in the small hamlet of Farnocchia, which sits a mile to the east of Sant'Anna on a wooded hillside. Screaming at the Italian civilian inhabitants, the Germans forced them to abandon their homes, which they then set on fire. As the civilians were running down the hill away from the burning houses, a group of partisans appeared, opened fire on the Germans, and killed eight of them. The families from Farnocchia then headed as hard as they could across the valley towards Sant'Anna. A week later, several hundred more people had joined them too, after the Germans forced them from their homes across the valley early in the morning of 7 August. That day, German patrols had appeared in and around Sant'Anna, and on the roads that led to it. They put up posters on trees and the sides of buildings.

The population had a deadline of five days to leave and seek shelter elsewhere. But hardly had the Germans left, said the displaced families interviewed by the British captain, than groups of partisans reappeared. The first thing they did was to reassure the inhabitants of Sant'Anna, and the families taking refuge with them, that they were there to protect them against the Germans. Then in their turn they left as well, vanishing into the trees. And what happened next, asked the British captain? Accounts from the displaced people differed, depending on where they had been, what time it was, whether they had fled immediately, or whether they had hidden and seen what had happened.

On the morning of 12 August, from eight o'clock onwards, a group of about 150 German soldiers had appeared through the woods, rounded up the people they could find, and those trying to escape, and herded them towards the centre of the village. They shot some of them, threw hand grenades into their houses and set them on fire after dousing the outsides of the buildings with petrol. They used flame-throwers too, said other witnesses. One of the survivors to whom the British talked was a 12-year-old boy called Mauro Pieri. He and the other adults and children with him said that about 150 Germans had approached the village between half-past six and seven in the morning; two of them at least, said Mauro, spoke Italian.

Sixteen-year-old Milena Bernabo said she saw the Germans push people up against walls and hit them with rifle butts. After this the Germans formed these people into a line, gave them heavy boxes of ammunition to carry on their shoulders, and forced them to walk downhill. Halfway down the slope was a chapel, with two stables situated next to it. The Germans made Milena and the others push the cows out of the byres in the buildings, and take their places in the straw and mud. Mauro Pieri noticed that one of the soldiers was speaking the dialect of Versilia, the local coastal region. He unslung a small mortar and fired a rocket into the air, as though it was a starting signal. Seconds later another one burst into the sky, further up the slope, as if in reply. By this time there were some thirty people in the two buildings. Then the Germans opened fire into the stables with pistols, and threw in hand grenades, too. The people inside burst outwards trying to escape, but there was a machine gun set up on a tripod in the yard that fired at them as the crowd surged towards it.

Inside the stable, Milena scrambled under some of the bodies of the people who were hit by bullets and fell on top of her. Mauro Pieri pretended to be dead, hiding under bodies as well. Both of them estimated that there might have been twenty people inside the stable, and twenty outside. They told the British soldiers one other thing, too. Other survivors had told them that up in the village of Sant'Anna, once the Germans had rounded up people into the piazza, and burned them, a German soldier had sat down. He had taken out a harmonica, started to play, and then began singing.[7]

When the British detachment returned to Pietrasanta, the captain typed out his report of what the civilians, both adults and children, had said to him and his men that day. When he had finished, he prepared the list of the recipients of the report: the three war crimes sections at Caserta, the commanding officer of Joint Task Force 45, the chief of staff of the British 4th Infantry Division (to whom his unit belonged), and the office of Major General Gruenther, the 5th Army chief of staff. On receiving it, the latter's office passed it on to their Office of the Inspector General, and it was delivered to Major Milton Wexler. After he had read it, he filled out a signal form in plain text, to be sent to the chief of staff of the 2nd US Armoured Group, then part of Joint Task Force 45. His orderly sergeant took the written form to the signals office at Livorno, where the words that Wexler had written were transmitted north.

On 28 September, the Germans were still shelling the town of Pietrasanta, and the coastal area around Forte dei Marmi. In just ninety minutes alone that day, seventy German shells landed. So Major John B. Bergin of the 2nd Armoured Group was wary as he and five other men drove in two jeeps due east of Pietrasanta, up through the olive groves and the chestnut forests that looked down on the dark blue sea, taking the winding road that climbed up the mountain until it arrived in Sant'Anna di Stazzema. With him were three other infantry officers, a captain from the 673rd Medical Collecting Company, and a captain from the US Army's Dental Corps. Donald J. Wolken was from Clayton, Missouri, which was a suburb of the state capital. He had graduated from St Louis University Dental School, and then set up his own practice before he was conscripted in 1940, aged 24. He arrived in North Africa in 1942, just behind the first units to land on Operation Torch, and then in 1943, was ashore on mainland Italy two weeks after his colleagues in the infantry had taken the beaches at Salerno. A year later, he was among the six-man party as they drove up to the village in two Willis Jeeps. The official report that Major Bergin wrote afterwards said:

An investigation party consisting of officers from 2nd Armoured Group and one medical officer from the 673rd Medical Collecting Company visited Sant'Anna on 28 September 44 to confirm an investigation made by elements from the 110th Battery, 39th LAA Regt (British.)

Practically all the houses in the town were burned. Practically all civilians, with a few exceptions who escaped, were either killed or burned to death. A few civilians who escaped are again living in S.Anna.[8]

The group of officers walked through and around the village, into the burned-out houses, looking under the trees, and in the open grass areas:

In many of the burnt out houses there still remain charred remains giving mute evidence of the massacre. Capt. Kessel identified many of the bones as those of women and young children. This was further substantiated by Capt. Wolken who inspected jaw bone structures and the teeth of the remains.

Yet Bergin's very short report told almost nothing of what happened during the visit to Sant'Anna di Stazzema. After the group of officers had been through the village, they walked under some trees towards a slope, on the side of which was a cave. In it was a group of survivors of the massacre, who had been hiding there, terrified the Germans would return. They had been living on runner beans, potatoes and chestnut flour. One of the Italian children among them had never heard another language spoken except his own, and he was not sure what was the nationality of these foreign soldiers. He was also confused as one of them was an African-American, and it was the first time the little boy had ever seen a black person. His life spared by a teenage Waffen-SS trooper, he had been liberated by the Americans. His name was Enio Mancini.[9]

On 8 October, with the area around Pietrasanta and Sant'Anna firmly in Allied hands, and the risk of German counter-attacks diminished, Major Wexler and his team from the War Crimes Commission drove north to the hamlet of Valdicastello. There they interviewed a priest called Father Giuseppe Vangelisti, who told them that he, in turn, had been informed about what had taken place at Sant'Anna by a woman from the village. He was the first person the American team had spoken to who mentioned the date of 12 August: he was sure about this because he remembered clearly that on the 13th he had had to ask permission from the Germans to go up to Sant'Anna to start burying the dead. When he arrived he found the church still smoking, burned bodies on the ground. He counted 130, but knew there were many more, because a lot of the corpses had already been buried. The ones that he counted, he said, were all those of women, children and elderly people. On 11 October, a few days after meeting the Americans, Father Giuseppe then told them that he had started writing a report on 27 August. It contained witness statements he'd collected in and around Sant'Anna, from two eyewitnesses whom he had interviewed.[10]

Vangelisti told the American investigators that he had sent a copy of his report to the Italian military governor in Viareggio, a large seaside town just south of Pietrasanta. The Americans could get hold of it from him. The two witnesses, Angela Bottari and Ettore Salvatori, had both signed the document. When Major Wexler saw the pages, he saw that only the priest's signature was legible, as one, if not both, of the witnesses didn't know how to write. There were no signatures from them, just marks. What else did he have to tell the war crimes commission, asked Wexler, when they talked in Valdicastello. Father Giuseppe knew Sant'Anna di Stazzema very well, he said, as he went there each Sunday to celebrate mass. He mentioned in particular detail the various encounters and clashes that had taken place in the weeks preceding the massacre, between the Germans and the Tuscan partisans. The latter, it seemed, came and went from Sant'Anna as they wanted.

In his statement, the first thing Ettore Salvatori did was to confirm the date of 12 August, the first direct witness to do so. At half-past seven in the morning the SS had arrived, and the moment he heard shooting the first thing he did was to grab his son and two other small children, bolt out of the front door and run into a field of corn and runner beans, where they hid. Meanwhile, another group of men were running as fast as they could for the cover of the trees in the forest. The next thing he knew, the Germans had surrounded the house he had just left, and started shooting at it, and into it. Inside were Salvatori's wife and 5-year-old daughter: from his hiding place he could hear not just their screams, but also those of other women and children. The SS hustled them out of the house and on to the narrow path used by donkeys in front of the house. Salvatori decided to leave his hiding place, and join them, and ran towards the group of nineteen people whom the SS were pushing down the path, towards a ditch beside a corn field. Before he could get to them, the Germans opened fire, and somehow did not appear to see him. A woman broke from the group, trying to run, away but an SS man shot her in the arm: behind them, Salvatori could see houses that were already on fire, burning heavily.

With the Germans there was also was a group of Italian men, one of whom was carrying a box of ammunition, while the other two were empty-handed. The Germans had by now set up a machine gun, and the first burst hit Lofelia Ghelardini as she was pleading for the life of her 5-month-old daughter Maria Sole. More SS men opened fire, joining in with their personal weapons, as the MG 42 machine gun sprayed bursts towards the group by the ditch. Once the Germans had finished shooting, they moved away, leaving the women howling with pain, broken with the appalling realisation that their children were dead. The SS men returned after ten minutes, talking among themselves, discussing what to do. They opened fire again, killing the remaining women and children who were still alive. Salvatori took a bullet that hit his belt, but did not penetrate it. He played dead, lying on the ground near the group of women and children.

The Americans then interviewed another survivor: although not a direct witness, he told them that he had seen the carbonised remains in Sant'Anna, of which he estimated at least thirty were those of children. The next interviewee was more complex. Garibaldi Aleramo was an Italian who claimed that he had been forced to work as a porter for the Germans on the night of 11–12 August, carrying ammunition boxes. In fact, according to the testimony he gave to the investigators, he made it very clear that he had had no choice whatsoever – the Germans had killed his wife and three children the following day, and only spared Aleramo because they needed him to carry heavy metal cases of rifle and machine-gun ammunition. He said that on the morning of the 12th, from about eight o'clock in the morning onwards, the SS unit to which he was attached killed some thirty or forty people.

Many of them were women and children shot near a ditch on the edge of a field. He thought that the SS battalion as a whole had killed some 300 people that day in Sant'Anna, between twenty-five to thirty of whom were children and 120–130 of them women.

To Milton Wexler, his testimony sounded very laboured. If he had been working for the SS on the night before the operation, why had he not managed to somehow pass word to somebody – anybody – in the village that the German troops were on their way? After all, his wife and children's lives were at stake. Aleramo also told Wexler that as a reward for the assistance he had given the Germans, one of the non-commissioned officers from the same unit with which he had worked on 12 August had given him a piece of paper, a *passe partout*. It allowed him to come and go as he pleased in and around Sant'Anna di Stazzema for a fortnight after the operation, without his movements being restricted by the Germans. He showed it to the American major. The German unit registration number on it was FPN01011B, the code of the field post office of the 2nd Battalion of the 16th SS. The authorisation signature on it was clear – it had been signed by the same SS non-commissioned officer who had also confided to the deserter, Willi Haase, that he and his unit had been ordered to participate in the killings. Martin Janssen.

Three more witnesses then confirmed that the date of the attack had been the 12th, that the SS had surrounded Sant'Anna from three sides, that there had been no partisans in the village, and that the dead were almost exclusively women, children and the elderly. After completing these interviews, the three majors from the American War Crimes Commission team decided they had enough material to present a strong case to Washington that both further investigations, and possible court cases, were the next step. Milton Wexler returned to Pietrasanta, and then to Livorno, and typed up his report. Four copies were sent by army postal service: two went to Allied Headquarters at Caserta, to the American War Crimes Section, and one to Major General Gruenther, the chief of staff of the US 5th Army.

The other went to the office of the Combined Chief of Staffs in Washington DC. The US War Crimes team in Caserta waited to hear what Washington wanted to do with the report: the answer, when it came, was straightforward. Leave this to us. So they did. Meanwhile, on the ground in Italy, the American investigative teams were to carry on hunting.

8

On the Plateau at Monte Sole

On 12 September, the Allied Combined Chiefs of Staff met in Canada for the Second Quebec Conference. One of the priorities was to decide the next stages of the war in the Mediterranean. By the summer of 1944, the Italian Front was vital to the Allies for three primary reasons. Defeating the Germans and occupying the Italian peninsula meant that the British, Americans and their multi-national and Commonwealth armies could break through the 'Ljubljana Gap' and advance north-east out of Italy into Austria and Hungary. This would enable them to push into the Third Reich from the rear, and form a buffer zone on the Yugoslav border between the advancing Russians and Italy itself. Control of the Italian seaboard also meant tactical and strategic control of the Mediterranean for the British Royal Navy and the US Navy. The Americans saw the advance through France as a more pressing priority than that up Italy, which was why they had diverted seven divisions away from the US 5th Army to take part in the August landings in southern France, code-named Operation Dragoon.

By the beginning of August, this meant that the on-paper strength of the 5th Army had dropped from 250,000 to 153,000. There were now only eighteen divisions in this army – including the Brazilians, African Americans, Japanese Nisei, South Africans – up against the German 10th and 14th Armies, which had a combined total of fourteen divisions with five or six in reserve. So for the Allies, it was vital to try and push north-wards out of Italy as soon as they could, and to do this they had to break through the Gothic Line. Only then could the American 5th Army and the British 8th Army cross the Apennines into the flat terrain in the valley of the River Po, where they could hopefully deploy their armour. Then both armies could push north-east into Austria and Hungary.

So on 25 September, the British and the American armies launched their long-awaited main assault on the Gothic Line. From La Spezia in the west, to Rimini on the Adriatic, the Allies assaulted this long line of defensive positions that stretched all the way across Italy. The British assault centred on driving up the eastern seaboard of the Adriatic, heading for the seaside resort of Rimini. It saw three different Army Corps go into the assault, as the British, Canadians, New Zealanders, Poles and Greeks attacked across a front that stretched in a vast semicircle around the town. The fighting would last a month, and the commander of the 8th Army, Lieutenant General Oliver Leese, reckoned that it was as tough as any battle they had fought in North Africa or Italy; it was easily as hard as El Alamein, or the Mareth Line.

The attack, code-named Operation Olive, aimed to draw the key German reserves from the centre and west of Italy towards Rimini in the east; this would leave the Apennines sector in the centre exposed, allowing Mark Clark's 5th Army to drive northwards from Florence, heading for Bologna and across the mountains into the Po Valley. On the western flank, on the Tuscan coast, a mixture of units under American and British command would push northwards through La Spezia towards Genoa. The British XIII Corps would be on the American right, moving east of the Apennines, and then flanking right and left into the Po Valley. Such was the plan. The aim was to convince Field Marshal Kesselring that the main attack was at Rimini, so he pulled out reserves leaving his centre exposed for an American attack through Bologna.

More than 1.2 million men would take part in the battle, making it the largest deployment of men and equipment in the entire campaign in Italy. For the Americans, the crucial lynchpin of a successful drive through the Apennines meant taking Bologna. And to take this city, they wanted the vital high ground around it to be controlled by the Italian partisans, so they could thus block control of this important terrain to the Germans. If the latter could establish themselves on the vast Monte Sole plateau and mountain range, which stretched south-west of Bologna, commanding all access roads northwards, their artillery could devastate any forthcoming American attack. The Germans knew this, and it made them determined to control the plateau. And to control it, they had to remove any partisan units from it, who would, inevitably, be hiding out and operating among the civilian population. The same actions against resistance fighters embedded in a compliant local populace that the 16th SS had carried out in Tuscany, with such enormous civilian casualties, looked set to be repeated on the Monte Sole plateau. On 10 September the US 5th Army attack was launched against the mountain bastions south of Bologna, led by the US II Corps: one of their subsidiary units was the 6th South African Armoured Division, which included the British 24th Guards Brigade. This unit contained battalions from each of the different regiments of British Foot Guards. The divisions' order was to advance on Bologna, along Route 64, which led along the south-east side of Monte Sole, through a wide valley. En route they were to capture the twin mountains of Sole and Caprara, both of which form part of the same massif stretching up above Route 64.

On the German side, the task of taking, occupying and holding this high ground that overlooked Bologna was given to Max Simon's division. Field Marshal Kesselring wanted a defensive barrier of high ground south-west of Bologna that stretched at least 10 miles: he would use this to hold the Allies at bay until spring came. Combined with the winter snows and mud, he estimated he could hold the Allied advance south of Bologna until February 1945. So by the end of September Max Simon's men had left their villas and barracks and positions on the coast of Tuscany and were heading north.

The killings at Massa and Bergiola were their blood-stained swansong to the towns and villages of Versilia, and now they were heading north-east towards Bologna, on to an operation that promised to be bigger, bloodier and more strategically vital than those that had preceded it. That the civilian death toll and collateral damage of material promised to be just as high, if not more so, than in Tuscany was not a consideration for the men of the 16th SS Panzergrenadier Division. And to lead the operation on Monte Sole and around Bologna, Simon chose one man, who had already proved himself in the reprisal actions at Vinca, Bardine, San Terenzo Monte and Bergiola. This was the one-armed SS-Sturmbannführer, Walter Reder. More than anybody in the division apart from its commander, Reder epitomised the spirit of the Waffen-SS combat unit to which he belonged.

Major Walter Reder and the Waffen-SS

Walter Reder was born in 1915, a citizen of the Austro-Hungarian Empire. In the economic depression of the 1920s, his father, who ran an industrial company, had managed to lose not just the family enterprise, but his own job and his family's income and wealth. It was to prove a bitterly learned lesson to Reder, who subsequently determined not just to prove himself, but somehow win back the family's previous affluence. He grew up blaming the Jews, Bolsheviks, liberal Germans and Communists for the economic collapse that had impoverished his family. The family moved to Austria, and he went to school in Salzburg, and then Vienna, before joining the Hitler Youth. He spent his time reading Volkisch nationalist literature. In 1934, he ceased to be Austro-Hungarian, and was granted German citizenship. He joined the Allgemeine-SS, its general administrative body, which differed vastly from the two other branches of the organisation, the combat soldiers of the Waffen-SS and the concentration camp guards of the SS-Totenkopfverbande.

He then went to SS officer candidate school at Brunswick, graduated sixtieth in the class – close to the bottom – and was commissioned as an SS lieutenant eager to prove himself. His first posting was in 1936, to command a unit of concentration camp guards at Dachau, which was where he found himself at the time of the invasion of Poland in 1939. By this point, ambition, frustration and a keen sense of perceived grievance – an ability to take offence –was showing through in his character: the Austro-Hungarian citizen whose father had been bankrupted by the Jews and Bolsheviks, who had finished in a lowly place at candidate school, and was then sent to guard a selection of people little better than common political criminals? He not just wanted more, he felt that he deserved and was owed better. His duties in Poland involved commanding a platoon that followed behind the front line, dealing with what he euphemistically termed 'Polish stragglers, Jews and Communists'.

When in 1939, the Totenkopf guards were incorporated into a new SS infantry division, Reder thought his time had finally come, but no. He was given a job as an administrative liaison officer, and then as a divisional staff lieutenant, during the invasion of France. Awarded the Iron Cross Second Class for this, he then also got married. Heinrich Himmler, as head of the Race and Settlement Office, or Rasse Und Siedlungsamt, had personally approved Reder's union, after which he left for the Russian front and the beginning of Operation Barbarossa. It was as he crossed the border into Russian territory in July 1941 that a previously unseen aspect of Reder's character made itself manifest: he was an extremely proficient combat soldier and inspirational leader. Men would follow his orders and follow him into battle. He was given command of a company as an SS captain and then, a month into Operation Barbarossa, the Iron Cross First Class. He was shot in the neck south of Leningrad in September 1941, and spent five months convalescing, before returning to the front line in February 1942. He served as a company commander and leader of a battalion, was awarded the German Cross in Gold, for gallantry, and fought with two different regiments of the Totenkopf Division. His career and combat record prior to Operation Barbarossa was nondescript, but afterwards it soared.

Underneath the proficient combat soldiering, Reder had a profound respect for and admiration of the founding values and attitudes of National Socialism, and what he saw around him in Russia went a long way to confirm this. Like his future commanding officer, Max Simon, he had a healthy respect for the fighting abilities of the Russian infantryman, although a next-to-zero tolerance for the tactical and strategic deficiencies of the Russian officers. Reder, and Simon, had both endured, beaten off, and endured again the Russian infantry attack and counter-attack and subsequent counter-attack too many times not to have a deep but grudging respect for the Red Army. And at the battle of Kharkov in March 1943, leading his men in an assault, the Russians got the better of him. Reder was hit by a Russian rocket and hospitalised, his left lower arm amputated. He was awarded the Knight's Cross of the Iron Cross, and sent to assist in the destruction of the Warsaw Ghetto. The Jewish survivors were sent to Treblinka. Reder was sent to Italy, and command of the 16th SS' reconnaissance regiment.

The Operation on Monte Sole

On 26 September, Max Simon summoned Walter Reder to the head-quarters of the Reichsführer-SS division in the town of Reggio Emilia, north-west of Bologna. Aufklarungsabeitlung 16, Reder's reconnais-sance regiment, would lead the assault on the Monte Sole plateau, accompanied by a battalion of captured east Europeans, a so-called Ostbattalion, alongside of whom would be two regiments of Luftwaffe anti-aircraft troops. A partisan brigade that ran with the nom de guerre of Stella Rossa, or Red Star, controlled the area around Monte Sole, 50 square miles of rocky, scrub-covered mountainside. Its commanders were two former mechanics, both from villages in the area of the moun-tain, who had joined the Italian army in 1940 and then become partisans after the armistice. Mario Musolesi and Gianni Rossi had established a large and successful partisan unit: it had been fighting the Germans since 1943. It specialised in ambushing small units on the roads surrounding Sole and Caprara and sabotaging German trains, the local railway lines and tunnels, and communications infrastructure such as signal boxes and telephone exchanges. On 6 June 1944 they ambushed a German staff car, whose occupants included a German major, captain and two troop-ers. The documents the partisans found in the vehicle included detailed maps for the defence of one particular sector of the Gothic Line: with the maps strapped to his stomach, a resistance fighter was told to head north to Switzerland and deliver them to representatives of the OSS. He succeeded. Meanwhile, at the ambush site, the incriminating evi-dence of the German staff car still had to be disposed of, so Musolesi directed a large group of farmers with shovels to dig a very large hole in a field, in which they buried the car. By 25 September, Musolesi, code-named Comandante Lupo, or Commander Wolf, realised that the

German attack was imminent. He sent two escaped Allied prisoners of war, both pilots, back across the front lines towards Florence, with a message. We need weapons, he said, forty Bren guns, 350 Stens, 200 hand grenades. The Germans are coming.

The Stella Rossa brigade was caught unprepared by the SS operation that lasted from 29 September to 5 October. Mario Musolesi was killed on the first morning; the commander of the unit that killed him was SS-Hauptmann Wilfried Segebrecht of the 1st Company of the reconnaissance regiment, which was in action on the morning of 29 September:

> Around midday there was only one partisan on our right side and he was trying to run away. A dispatch rider, Woelfele, chased him and engaged him in a machine gun duel. Each took shelter, fired, jumped and ran. At the end the partisan fell to the ground. My soldier took the badges and documents and took them to headquarters. The Italian prisoners confirmed unanimously that this partisan was Mario Lupo, commander of the brigade. The partisan commander not only abandoned his people but he also had a large amount of money with him. While his people fought to the last, he wanted to escape. For us, we could not understand why, after his death, he was decorated with the highest Italian honour. [1]

After Musolesi's death the band disbanded, and by the afternoon of the 29th, the Germans reckoned that real armed resistance was effectively finished. Both the partisans and the civilian population were unsure as to what the Germans would do next. At this time, the deputy commander of the Stella Rossa Brigade was Gianni Rossi. The Allies were getting nearer every day, their artillery was getting closer and closer and then the fighting reached partisan territory. Rossi had 800 partisans under his command: knowing where and when the Germans intended to attack would allow him to deploy his forces in the most tactically and strategically important spot. They could see German troops below them, crossing through two valleys each day, and in the distance, Allied units were visible a mile away.

On 25 September, Mario Musolesi had told his men that there would be no more than three days of fighting to be done because by the 28th the Americans would arrive up the road from Florence to Bologna. But then, to the partisans' horror, the front line stopped for six months, and the mountains of Monte Sole were not just on the wrong side of this front line, but also occupied by the men of the 16th SS. The Americans were only a mile away. The night before the German attack, Musolesi and ten other partisans went to Cadotto, one of the houses in Monte Sole, on the slopes of the Setta river, which flows north-east towards Bologna.

They spent the night there and on the morning of the 29th, the SS attacked. The partisans were caught unawares and unprepared by the German troops advancing up from the Setta Valley. There was no reason to go to Cadotto, said another partisan commander, it was outside the partisans' operational area, and away from their command post. The reason why the two unit senior officers were absent from a focal control point during the opening stages of the German attack was simple: they were spending the night with their girlfriends. Adriano Lipparini was a partisan of the Stella Rossa Brigade, who described the night before the German attack:

> Lupo and his brigade never had good relations with the partisan Committee for National Liberation and wanted to be autonomous and didn't like the political commissioner or orders from outside. It is possible that this report might be biased against Stella Rossa.[2]

Other partisans confirm that the brigade split up and disbanded after Musolesi had been killed, leaving the civilian population at the mercy of the advancing Germans. No one was able to organise any type of effective resistance apart from isolated incidents of stiff but tactically pointless action: the partisans were not contributing to the defence of the civilian population and nor were they pinning down the SS, enabling the Americans to advance. Nevertheless, as Lipparini says, it is difficult to explain why 800 partisans, even badly armed, were not able at least to reduce the threat to the population and why only ten to twenty partisans died in the fighting:

In my opinion, together with the absolute deficiency of the information service, I add a fact that was crucial for the destiny of the brigade. At the time of the attack, Lupo and his deputy commander Gianni were not in the brigade headquarters but in a farmers' house on the edge of our action area. In this house there were their lovers, in whose house they spent many nights, including the night of the attack. They didn't have the capability to command any actions from there. On the contrary, that house was one of the first to be surrounded and attacked.[3]

At the headquarters of the SS division, Walter Reder came up with a plan for the attack. His approach was to make a two-pronged assault up the southern and western slopes of the mountain complex, which was dotted with small villages both on the summit and on its lower slopes. At the top was a windblown hamlet, with the church of San Martino. It was called Marzabotto. There was another church in the village of Casaglia, and the hamlet of Caprara lay between the two, the site of the village shop. The small local school was in nearby Cerpiano. At dawn on 29 September, the SS regiment left their headquarters in Carrara, their half-tracks, armoured vehicles and jeeps covered and camouflaged with branches the men had cut from olive, orange and cypress trees. They drove first to Reggio Emilia, and then southwards to the bottom of the Monte Sole plateau: the first attack went up the slopes at ten o'clock. Reder ordered his troops to 'kill all cattle and civilians, regardless whether they are men, women, or children, and to set all buildings on fire'.[4]

SS-Sturmmann Julien Legoli, a student and volunteer from Alsace-Lorraine, served in the machine-gun platoon of the 5th Company of Walter Reder's reconnaissance regiment. He deserted from the unit on 29 September and was captured by the Americans four days later. Picked on and bullied for being Alsation, NCOs had made his life hell. At first the Americans didn't trust him and assumed that he was an intelligence plant. After all, a Frenchman deserting from a German unit and confiding in his American captors? But what Legoli was to say when questioned made perfect sense, and was to fit in with the testimony of numerous other witnesses and participants in the operation:

Ammunition was then distributed and we were marched off at about 0600 hours, 29th September 1944. We proceeded, after crossing a road … up hill for one hour. We came upon a group of three farmhouses; from the cellar of one of which a burst of tommy-gun shots was fired, without any casualties resulting. One of the farmhouses was about fifty to seventy yards away from the other two, which were close together and the shot came from the solitary farmhouse. No. 1 Company of (16th) Recce (Regt) attacked the other two farmhouses, meeting with no resistance and fetched out the inmates; about thirty civilians in all, two of whom were elderly men and the remainder were women and children. These civilians were stood up in front of a wall and killed by machine gun fire by a private, whose name I cannot remember, on orders of Segebrecht, the Commanding Officer, No. 1 Company.[5]

The bodies were left lying where they fell, and the SS men set the buildings on fire. Legoli's platoon continued marching. After approximately thirty minutes, they witnessed three women and three or four children fleeing from the advancing troops. Orders were given to shoot these civilians, and then the German advance into the hills continued:

Along the way, two males, thirty to forty women, and three or four more children were shot by the Germans. The unit stopped to burn a Catholic church. When the church would not burn, the platoon commander gave the order to destroy the altar.

Some remaining partisans of the Red Star Brigade, however, dug themselves into positions in a series of deserted houses and farms on the lower and middle slopes of the mountain, fighting a rearguard action, retreating up the hillside as the SS opened fire on their positions with mortars and machine guns. By the time Major General Max Simon had arrived in the middle of the morning to make an assessment of how the attack was going, the SS had lost sixty-four men – twenty-four killed and forty wounded – in just four hours. This was double the partisan casualties. Both Simon and Reder realised that they were up against something much larger and stronger than a platoon or two of partisans who had embedded themselves in the villages and hamlets with the civilians. The fighting continued all that day and all through the night, and when the morning came, the Germans estimated that they were up against a force of partisans some 1,000 to 1,500 strong: the Special Operations Executive and the Office for Strategic Services had in fact sent instructions to the partisans to gather in formation on the top of the plateau, so as to deny control of the high ground to the Germans at the crucial moment when the Allies were moving up the roads through the valley below, en route to Bologna.

Early on the 30th, Reder withdrew his command post and some of his units south-west to the small town of Lagaro, which sits at the bottom of the mountain on the main road that leads from Bologna to Florence. Other SS platoons and companies were meanwhile halfway up to the top of the plateau, heading for the village of Marzabotto. They were moving through the hamlets of Sibano and Sperticano, Cerpiano and Caprara, across and through some 50 square miles of massif, covered in woods, barns, clumps of houses and rough, semi-cultivated fields.[6] The partisans retreated further up the slope in the face of each German attack, until they were at the summit, in the small village of Marzabotto, and below it in Casaglia di Monte Sole. The civilian population had taken refuge in and around the churches of Santa Maria Assunta and San Martino. In the small village of Casaglia, the inhabitants gathered in the church, hoping they would be safe until the German soldiers left.

The priest, Don Ubaldi Marchioni, began reciting the rosary to try to calm the people. Among those in the church was a grandmother, Nanni Vittorio, who was paralysed from the waist down; she could not do as she was told by the Germans, and flee the church, as she simply couldn't walk. So the Germans shot her. The rest of the civilians in the chapel were shoved and forced down the path to the cemetery, pushed inside the enclosure, while an SS man opened fire. He and others threw hand grenades on to the bodies to make sure there were no survivors: some 145 people were in the cemetery at that moment. Fifty were babies or very small children. Cornelia Paselli found herself looking straight at a German MG 42 machine gun in the cemetery. She told American and Italian investigators afterwards that:

She felt her legs and her feet rise in the air and her head bump down on the ground. There was a thump-thump as bodies began to fall on her, and she felt a splash of heat on her right side. She pushed her hand through the layers of flesh that surged over her and touched her hip and drew back a handful of blood.[7]

When the German machine gun stopped, Cornelia was under a pile of wounded and dead bodies, and she could hear her mother trying to find out if her children were alive, by calling out to each of them in turn. Her sister Giuseppina was wounded, but Cornelia's 10-year-old twins, a boy and a girl called Gigi and Maria, were dead.

In his after-action report, Walter Reder said that a total of 728 partisans were killed by his men; survivors and partisan groups said that a total of 1,835 civilians and partisans died. Reder asserted, for his part, that the deaths on the mountainside were simply 'the rotten fruits of war'.[8] The truth was that during the seven-day period of the whole operation on Monte Sole from Friday, 29 September to Thursday, 5 October, in eighteen different villages, towns and simple clusters of houses on or around the plateau, a total of 769 people, almost all of them civilians, were killed.[9]

After the massacre at Monte Sole the Fascist Italian party of Bologna denied that it had taken place. In a newspaper article they said that it had only been a police operation against rebels and that only some of the rebel leaders were killed. It is unclear whether, as at Sant'Anna di Stazzema and at Fivizzano, local Italian Fascists were actively engaged in the operation alongside the Germans. What is certain is that they knew about it but denied it publicly. One of the families who died during the operation was surnamed Laffi; on 30 September, a relative of theirs called Giuseppe Foresti came to see them. He worked as a lathe turner in Bologna in a factory making torpedoes for the German Navy. On his way to the village of Colulla di Sotto he was stopped by German soldiers, who warned him not to go any further. In Marzabotto itself, he saw the local head of the Fascist Party arriving in a motorcycle side-car from Bologna.[10]

Il Resto del Carlino was the conservative, pro-Fascist newspaper in Bologna, and one of the oldest papers in Italy. The name originated in the nineteenth century when shopkeepers would often give a small newspaper to buyers, in part exchange as change for a '*carlino*' or small coin. On 1 October the newspaper's editor, Giorgio Pini, wrote an editorial article about what was happening in Marzabotto. The information was given to him by an old friend and colleague, who happened to be the German pro-consul in Milan, Baron Gustav-Adolf von Halem. Pini was extremely pro-Fascist, and was to write an official biography of Mussolini:[11]

> The usual uncontrolled rumours, the typical result of wild fantasies in time of war, were claiming until yesterday that a hundred-and-fifty women, elderly people and children had been shot by German troops combing the town of Marzabotto, during a police operation against a gang of criminals. We are able to deny these macabre rumours and the alleged facts on which they are based. The actual facts were ascertained during an investigation, which has resulted in an official denial. It is true that a police operation against a group of rebels was conducted in the Marzabotto area and this led to the death of several dangerous rebel leaders. However, fortunately it is untrue that the combing resulted in the massacre of more than a hundred-and-fifty civilians. What we are seeing here is the umpteenth, ridiculous manoeuvre by the usual reckless ones. Anyone wanting to interview any honest inhabitant of Marzabotto, or any person coming from the area, would have learnt the true version of the facts.[12]

The Italian Fascist authorities in Bologna then tried to cover up the war crimes committed in Monte Sole and deny any conflicting reports that suggested that a massacre had happened.

The chain of information then reached Benito Mussolini himself. The chief of the Italian Fascist party in Bologna was called Dino Fantozzi, and on 10 October 1944 he was told about the events at Monte Sole by Baron von Halem from Milan. He had also been given a much more accurate version of events by the local town hall secretary from Marzabotto, a man called Agostino Grava, who had managed to escape the Monte Sole fighting and then drive to Bologna. However,

Fantozzi ignored his story and sent a telegram, and then a longer communiqué, to Mussolini, who was then in Milan as well:

> In that area some repressive actions were taken against rebel elements of the Red Brigade, commanded by Lupo. In this actions about 700 bandits were killed, including the commander of the brigade. The General Consul himself does not exclude that during these actions some inhabitants might have been killed, including some women. This is because many of the houses spread across the area have been transformed into fortresses by the bandits. On the other hand, reprisals against the civilian population were not taken. [On this basis] the statements made to me by the Secretary of the Townhall of Marzabotto – Agostino Grava – should be considered as exaggerated.[13]

Within days, news of the massacres outside Bologna had reached the Allies, who began to transmit the information up their chain of command. By 19 October, General Harold Alexander, commanding the Allied Forces in Italy, issued this warning to all German officers and men still fighting in north Italy. It was translated into German, distributed by hand, while thousands of copies of the statement were dropped behind enemy lines by Allied bombers, to warn the Germans of what would happen to those who participated in any form of war crime, including reprisals against the Italian civilian population:

> WARNING
> To German soldiers and officers
> By General Sir H.R. Alexander
> Commander-in-chief of the Allied forces in Italy
> 1. Reports about atrocities – killings, mass reprisals against innocent civilians, torture and other acts – committed by German troops in Northern Italy are coming to our attention each day with increasing frequency. 2. I draw the following to the attention of German officers and soldiers in Northern Italy, who may give or implement orders to commit such atrocities: 3. The fact that, for example, in a certain village, Italian patriots, wearing or not wearing uniforms, bracelets,

or other recognizable badges, have attacked German soldiers, is not, according to any military or moral code, a justification for collective reprisals against the population of that village, nor for the killing of people without proper judgment and proper evidence. 4. Officers or soldiers that have given or implemented orders for such acts, are war criminals. (…) 6. I have given orders to all the Italian patriots and civilians in the occupied territory to take detailed written notes of the names, divisions and other identifying details of the officers and soldiers that gave or implemented orders for such crimes.
H.P. Alexander, Warning to German officers and men,
19th October 1944

The 6th South African Armoured Division, which had been tasked with attacking the positions on the hillsides overlooking Bologna, was immediately south of Monte Sole when the massacre was being carried out. By these first two weeks of October, the division had taken Monte Stanco, which is just south of Grizza Morandi and also just under 4 miles, as the crow flies, from Monte Sole. By 23 October, the 6th Division, including its brigade of British Guardsmen, then captured Monte Salvaro, and was only 2 miles from Monte Sole. The units of the 16th SS withdrew west of the main Florence–Bologna road, and dug in on the mountain. They fortified the hamlets of Cerpiano, Casaglia, and Caprara, now empty of their inhabitants, their dead, ghostly bodies strewn around the surroundings of their villages.

The South Africans knew that the SS were waiting for them. In two days of fighting in pouring rain, they and the British went up against the 36th Regiment of the 16th SS Division, but could not dislodge them from their positions, despite firing an artillery barrage of more than 10,000 shells. The deluge of rain turned to floods, the drenched sky prevented any air support, the steep, muddy tracks became quagmires, and tanks and vehicles could not climb the slope. The 6th Division was withdrawn. A Wehrmacht Panzergrenadier division arrived to reinforce the 16th SS. The autumn mud and rains gave way to snow on Monte Sole, as the SS, the Wehrmacht and the Allies moved into winter.

There were now to be three completely separate investigations, carried out by the British, the Americans and the Italians. The three different nationalities only sometimes consulted each other or shared information. This was at a time when synchronising intelligence-gathering was vital if the Allies were to have any chance of even finding, let alone obtaining convictions for, the SS officers, NCOs and men who had been involved in the massacres, not just at Marzabotto and Sant'Anna di Stazzema but elsewhere in Tuscany and Emilia-Romagna. British and American investigators from the Royal Military Police, and the Counter-Intelligence Corps, as well as additional staff from the two war crimes commissions from Caserta, arrived in Florence in early November 1944. They were looking for any survivors and witnesses, and German prisoners of war, who had been on and around the Monte Sole mountain massif between 26 September and 6 October.

In villages south of Monte Sole, they found no shortage of displaced people from the mountains of Sole and Stanco, who offered them testimony of what had happened.[14] They found SS prisoners of war, and one of the first Germans they found in a makeshift cell in an American military police headquarters was the deserter Julien Legoli, Alsatian, formerly of the 5th Company, 16th Reconnaissance Regiment, 16th SS Panzergrenadier Division. Unlike his fellow SS man and fellow deserter Willi Haase, who had never even been near Sant'Anna di Stazzema, Legoli had been in action on Monte Sole, seen his fellow SS men murder civilians, and listened to the commands being given by officers and NCOs he could see and identify. He was the perfect witness: a participant with a grudge against the unit in which he had served. And there was no shortage of Italians who had information to share, stories to tell, secrets to pass on about the one-armed SS Major, Walter Reder, notorious across Tuscany for his unit's atrocities. One Italian teenager, then living outside the city of Lucca, wrote in his diary that summer of 1944:

On August 9th 1944, the 16th Panzergrenadier Aufklarungsabteilung arrived in Pietrasanta, on the coast near Carrara, Major Walter Reder in command. Reder was twenty-nine, an Austrian, and because he had a partial amputation of his left arm, he was known as Il Monco (the Stump) by the Italians. He had already established a reputation with the Italians: he was regarded as very dangerous and not at all sympathetic towards civilians. His orders: anyone caught helping partisans would be shot on the spot. During that time there were no official newspapers so news travelled by word of mouth, or was printed on sheets of paper that were passed among the people like handbills. We heard that on August 12th just outside the walls of Lucca in Sant'Anna di Stazzema, over 500 civilians were shot and killed by German SS troops …[15]

The Survivors in Tuscany

From Sant'Anna di Stazzema to the villages around Fivizzano, and from the hills above Massa to the slopes below Marzabotto, the survivors of the trail of massacres that had taken place that summer were now displaced from their homes. The families of Enio Mancini, Adele Pardini and Enrico Pieri moved to Pietrasanta. Along with dozens of other families, they were now forced to live in semi-destroyed houses, in church halls, and in tents. They were just three children among hundreds of thousands who, that autumn of 1944 in Tuscany, were in desperate need of assistance. Their parents had not had a moment to rescue any of their possessions from their houses in Sant'Anna before the Germans burned them; the most important possession of the Mancini family, their cow, suffocated. Enio and Enrico had wooden clogs to wear, and the clothes in which they stood up in; after the Americans and British had arrived in Sant'Anna, their parents had returned up the hillside from Valdicastello and Pietrasanta, and had considered rebuilding their houses there and then, and establishing the village as a semi-functioning community again.

Enio's father wanted to live in their burned house, while Enrico's relatives said that if they could only return to their village then it would show that the Germans had not won. The Pardini family hardly existed any more: in the first week of October Adele and one of her sisters were among those who returned to Sant'Anna for a service of mass commemoration. A communal grave sat in front of the church; burned houses, soaked by late summer rain, sat sulphurous and shattered. Carbonised timbers and scorched roof tiles were scattered around. The muddy earth on the village paths was churned up by the feet of those walking to and from the destroyed dwellings. Enio and Enrico's surviving father and uncles and aunts took what there was left to save and packed it on their backs, or on mules they used to trudge belongings and possessions up and down the mountain.

Communal committees were established by the Catholic Church, and with the American army, the fledgling United Nations Relief and Rehabilitation Administration, and the Italian Red Cross, had designated the different categories of people who needed help. These were refugees and homeless people, abandoned elderly people and children, families seriously affected by the misfortunes of war, particularly large families, pregnant women, nursing mothers, the disabled and the unemployed.[16] In Pietrasanta in autumn 1944, this was almost every Italian family there was. The Americans had reinstated the former Fascist mayor of the town, who had been removed by partisans in June as the Allies approached. He categorised the three most needy and vulnerable groups in the area as those needing immediate feeding, assistance and jobs.

Again, this embraced nearly 80 per cent of the Italian population. Food, shelter, money, food, medicine and employment were the priorities. In September 1945, the Tuscan commune of Bucine, outside Arezzo, was given 200 pairs of shoes by the UN Relief and Rehabilitation Administration (UNRRA). The queue of people who asked for these shoes was long: fourteen partisans, seventeen veterans, 146 returned PoWs, 138 PoWs yet to return, twenty-nine unemployed men, 177 widows of political victims, ninety-six orphaned children of whom nineteen were younger than six, and every widow and orphaned child from the village of San Pancrazio.[17] On 29 June German soldiers from the Parachute-Panzer Division 'Hermann Goring' had killed seventy-one people in the hamlet in a reprisal operation. In Pietrasanta, the children who had seen their parents massacred, their houses burned and their villages destroyed were at the top of the list of the most vulnerable.

One UNRRA worker in Italy said that 'needy in Italy in 1944 is a relative term'. It encompassed the phrases 'desperately needy', 'truly needy', and 'absolutely most needy', as well as those 'in conditions of real need'. One small village outside Arezzo was typical of hundreds. In this Tuscan village four widowed women received 2,000 lire to divide among themselves: these included a mother whose son had been killed by the Germans in the massacre at San Polo, a mother who lost three sons in the killings at San Pancrazio, a woman who lost her husband in the massacre at Meliciano and another who lost two sons and a son-in-law at Meliciano.

African-American soldiers from the 92nd Infantry Division had arrived in Pietrasanta in September 1944. The unit's Communal Affairs Team worked with the Italian Red Cross, the UNRRA, the local government agencies – in practice, the mayor – the Catholic Church and two orders of nuns. The displaced people of Pietrasanta found themselves dependent on all of these, none more so than on the American soldiers. They would wait for the GIs to finish eating their meals, and then delve into rubbish bins to rescue the leftovers; the American soldiers gave them sweets, cigarettes, blankets, shoes, medicine, bread, tinned fruit and meat; American army doctors treated sick and injured children, American engineers cleared German mines and booby traps, and American military reconstruction teams tried to rebuild some of the municipal buildings. American and British military police investigators were continuing their hunt for survivors of the different massacres, and trying to make a solid list of names of those German SS men who had participated.

During this period of desperation for much of the Italian civilian population, an Italian actress called Maria Mellato, originally from Carrara, was displaced to Foccette near Barga. She worked during the day in an Italian villa used by soldiers from the 92nd Division as a headquarters, helping to clean and serve food in their dining facility:

> There are many things that with an empty stomach I see passing my eyes, slices of fresh meat, huge loaves of white bread, rice pudding with pineapple, hot chocolate drink and pastries. I see the cook frying innumerable slices of smoked pancetta, that they call bacon, whose aroma fills the kitchen and produces such an effect on me ... We have become friends with these wonderful boys. The Lieutenant, a huge man, always smiling, ordered the cook to bring us food three times a day. It seems like a dream! The stores in our area are all closed, even in nearby villages it is impossible to buy anything ... the only commerce is the exchange of goods. There are a few small stores where

they are beginning to sell vegetables, squash, turnips and chestnuts. But the weather is getting much colder …[18]

On the Monte Sole mountainside, the devastation was complete. One returning family found that there was almost nothing left. Angelo Bertuzzi had been the postman who used to deliver the letters and parcels to the whole area of Monte Sole in the 1940s; when the first troops from the 16th SS Division had started to arrive, he had taken his family and moved towards Bologna as fast as they could. In the second week of October, after the killings and military operations had finished, he and his wife returned to the hamlet of Sperticano:

Angelo, his wife and the children settled there as best they could. The morning after, Angelo took his brown leather post bag and went up the mountain. He didn't go any further than his usual first stop: San Martino. He saw corpses scattered all along the path and beyond the small, half-burnt wood on the hill before San Martino. He looked round as thoroughly as he could. In front of him, where there should have been a church, a village, several big stables and straw bales, there was nothing any more. Everything had been levelled to the ground.[19]

The only thing that remained of their house was the walls, and at the church in the hamlet of San Martino there was nothing left but the font, and some rocks and building stones that had previously been part of the cemetery wall. It was scorched earth indeed. The men of the 16th SS had not just massacred the inhabitants, they had physically destroyed the village:

In the direction of Casaglia he could only see fields with big trenches and barricades. He turned and went quickly down the mountain. His wife asked: 'So? What did you see on your route?' 'My old route,' said Angelo, drying his eyes. 'It's all gone, dear. I no longer have anywhere to deliver the post to.'[20]

9

Getting Away with Murder

Max Simon moved from Italy to Austria to command the XIII SS Army Corps; Karl Gesele would be sent to Hungary, in charge of the 37th SS Cavalry 'Division', in reality only a brigade, whose officers were almost all ethnic Germans from Hungary. Gerhard Sommer spent the autumn of 1944 serving as a training officer with the 4th SS Panzergrenadier Volunteer Brigade Netherlands, almost entirely comprised of Dutch volunteers. He re-joined the unit after it had been evacuated from the Kourland pocket in Latvia, and was posted to fight on the River Oder, on the frontier between Poland and Germany.

After a wartime career that had seen him and his subordinate units execute thousands of Red Army prisoners and Russian, Ukrainian and Italian civilians, Max Simon committed the cardinal error of killing his own countrymen, laying himself open to indictment, trial and imprisonment in Germany. By spring 1945 the XIII SS Army Corps was fighting in southern Germany and Austria against a seemingly unstoppable American enemy. Their 4th Armoured Division went up against the tanks and men of Simon's troops in the wine country of Franconia, heavily laden Sherman tanks crunching through the snowy mud of overgrown vineyards in the fighting that swept between Nuremberg and Wurzburg. Outnumbered, low on fuel, ammunition, medical supplies and food, Simon's men decided to push south into Bavaria and then over the Alps into Austria. Movement during the day was next to impossible, with the skies controlled by the Mustangs and Thunderbolts of the United States Air Force; and always, it seemed to the men, they were retreating, retreating, retreating. They started to destroy some of the lesser bridges over the Rhine, until ordered south towards Munich and the Danube. Simon gathered his company commanders and senior NCOs around him, and together they decided they would head for Berchtesgaden, and the Eagle's Nest of Adolf Hitler.

En route, their vehicles stopped outside Brettheim, a small village 30 miles west of Nuremberg, and equidistant from the town of Schwabisch Hall in Baden-Württemberg. A farmer called Friedrich Hanselmann had taken away the guns of three 15-year-old boys from the Hitler Youth, and thrown the weapons into the muddy water of the village duck pond. The young Hitler Jugende had reported him to their commanding officer, an SS major, who said that Hanselmann should be arrested. A man who taught at the local school was asked to confirm the sentence – he refused, as did another man from the village. So the SS men hanged the teacher, and Freidrich Hanselmann, from a tree at the entrance to the village cemetery. On his arrival there on 13 April, Max Simon ordered that the bodies should be left hanging for four days. A company of American Sherman tanks approached the village and paused, to see if Brettheim could be occupied without a battle, without civilian deaths, without yet more blood and devastation this late in the war. The SS refused to let anybody raise white flags. The Americans opened fire. Seventeen civilians died. The town would not forget the name of SS-Gruppenführer Max Simon.[1]

When Max Simon finally surrendered, it was to paratroopers of the American 101st Airborne Division. He gave himself up on 1 May 1945, a few hundred metres outside the Alpine hamlet of Schwendt in the Austrian Tirol. The village is only 20 miles west of the Eagle's Nest. Leaving most of the XIII SS Army Corps inside Germany, in the last week of April Simon took a handful of fellow officers, drove south and crossed the border into Austria. Some of his officers thought that once he reached Berchtesgaden he would signal for the remainder of his division and corps to join him for a last defensive battle in the mountains. However, the Americans blocked them. Simon, seeing that the end of the war had come, decided to surrender to American paratroopers south-west of the Eagle's Nest. They took him to meet

Major General Maxwell Taylor, the commanding officer of the 101st Airborne Division, with whom he signed a formal surrender of his unit. He asked immediately for a guarantee that none of his men would be handed over to the Russians. Maxwell Taylor agreed, and the remainder of the XIII SS Army Corps, a battered, exhausted and depleted unit, gave up their arms.

At the other end of Austria, meanwhile, the 16th SS Division were a long way from being the force that had rampaged through Tuscany the previous year. Their strength was reduced to around 6,000 men, many lost in the fighting in Hungary, and many detached in urgency to other SS units in the final weeks of the war. The Military Police of the 101st Airborne contacted their British colleagues, operating at the far eastern end of Austria, outside Klagenfurt. Around this border city other elements of the 16th SS, detached from the division's main retreat into Bavaria, were surrendering, too. The British Military Police, who wanted to question Simon about his actions at Marzabotto and around Fivizzano, told the Americans to hold him. The SS general was the only man from the entire 16th SS Division taken into custody, at Klagenfurt, in Bavaria or in the Tirol.[2]

Simon was almost relieved – he was wanted, after all, by the Russians, too. A Russian military tribunal had sentenced Simon to death in 1943 for the killings of an estimated 10,000 civilians outside Kharkov, and anything was preferable to what he could expect at the hands of Stalin's NKVD. He was imprisoned first in a camp for senior SS officers in Austria, and then taken to Berlin, and then England. In the British capital, he was held in a detention centre known as the London District Cage, situated in three large houses in Kensington Palace Gardens.[3] Run by MI19, this was an interrogation facility for senior SS and Nazi Party officials: they were transferred to and from PoW facilities in Great Britain to attend these sessions in London, carried out by officers and NCOs from the British Intelligence Corps. Simon was questioned there, as were other high-ranking German prisoners whom the British and Americans wanted to put on trial after the war had ended.

In between questioning in London, they were held in a camp outside Bridgend in South Wales. Known as Island Camp, or Special PoW Camp XI, it was a collection of drab, damp Nissen huts and concrete accommodation blocks, surrounded by barbed wire, set in open fields. Before the Germans arrived, American troops had been billeted there prior to the invasion of Europe. German field marshals, generals and colonels would pass through Island Camp: the SS and Gestapo hierarchy from Italy was well-represented. SS officials Karl Brunner, Wilhelm Harster, Willy Tensfeld and Karl-Heinz Burger spent time there, as did the senior SS officer in Italy, Karl Wolff.[4] Along with Max Simon, the six senior officers accounted and were responsible for a large proportion of the atrocities committed against civilians in Italy.

SS-Standartenführer Karl-Heinz Burger had arrived in Italy in 1943 from the Ukraine. One of the senior SS police chiefs in the German-occupied north of the country, he was a subordinate of SS-Obergruppenführer Karl Wolff. He was in charge of the fight against partisans in the Veneto, the region around Venice, along the Apennines as far south as the Tuscan city of Arezzo, and in Lombardy, the region around Milan. Einsatzkommando Burger was an SS police unit that had devolved responsibilities from Wolff.

Operating alongside him was SS-Brigadeführer Karl Brunner, who had served with an Einsatzkommando during the invasion of Poland. In Italy, he had been responsible for the arrest and deportation of Jews in the area under his jurisdiction in the Alpine foothills. His headquarters was in Bolzano, in the north-west of the country. Aside from his operations to deport Jews, his actions crossed over in a Venn diagram of security operations with Karl-Heinz Burger's anti-partisan missions. His final crime against civilians had been right at the end of the war, in Bolzano and Merano, just before he was arrested by the Americans. He gave orders to his SS men and to Wehrmacht troops to open fire on Italian civilians celebrating the German surrender. Fifty-two of them were killed. Brunner was arrested in Bolzano on 13 May.

For his part, SS-Brigadefuhrer Willy Tensfeld had served in Russia, and then as the SS' liaison officer with the Italian Fascists from September 1943 onwards. From January 1944 until April 1945 he was the senior SS and police leader in north-western Italy. The last member of this group of SS officials was SS-Standartenführer Wilhelm Harster, who for three years was head of the German Security Police and the SD in the Netherlands. He was responsible for deporting 104,000

Dutch Jews, among whom had been Anne Frank. When he arrived in Italy, Wolff gave him command of the transit and detention camp at Bolzano. Under questioning at the London Cage, Simon was keenly aware of his fate if handed over to the Russians. Yet in an apparent effort to save his subordinates, he told his captors almost nothing about war crimes committed by his division, nor the command structure and names of officers under his control. So the British returned him to Italy, to be prepared for trial in a military court in Padua.

Karl Wolff and the American OSS

On 12 May 1945, two weeks after Max Simon had surrendered, six Germans gathered in the courtyard of the Villa Pistoia at Bolzano in north-western Italy. Five of them were officers of the army and the SS, the last an economist and political scientist. It was early summer, and the war in Europe had been over for five days. On 7 May at Reims in northern France, General Alfred Jodl had signed an unconditional surrender of all German forces on the Eastern and Western Fronts. On 29 April, 800,000 German troops in Italy had also surrendered, seeing an end to two years of fighting in the country. This had happened nine days before the principal surrender in Germany. In a photograph snapped that day at the villa in Bolzano, which froze a moment in time, all the six men were smiling. There was General Hans Rottiger, a veteran panzer commander who had been at Stalingrad with the 4th Army and by mid-1945 was Chief of Staff of Army Group C in Italy under Field Marshal Albert Kesselring. The only man standing in the courtyard wearing civilian clothes was Gero von Schulze-Gaevernitz, an economist from Freiburg who was co-ordinating with Allen Dulles, the head of the American Office of Strategic Services in Switzerland.

Alongside him were two SS officers, Eugen Dollmann, and Eugen Wenner, and two of the most important German generals in the country. One was Heinrich von Vietinghoff, commander of the German 10th Army, the other SS-General Karl Wolff, the Supreme SS and Police commander in Italy. Wolff had sent an emissary who had travelled to Allied Headquarters at Caserta, outside Naples, for him. This officer had formally signed the surrender document on behalf of the German armed forces under Wolff's and Kesselring's command. Yet in the courtyard in Bolzano that day was a seventh man, an OSS agent called T.S. Ryan. He took the photograph, and he was there on the orders of Allen Dulles as an OSS liaison officer to report on another matter that had just taken place in Bolzano and Switzerland between the Germans and the Americans.

For several months Wolff had been involved with Dulles and the OSS in negotiating an early surrender to the war in Italy. The head of both the SS and German security police contingents in the country, he was to become an unexpected obstacle to justice for the survivors of the massacres at Sant'Anna, and elsewhere, that had been carried out by the Waffen-SS. He had official command and control responsibilities for the operational actions of both the SS and Gestapo in Italy; however, the opinions of some of his staff were conflicting as to whether Wolff took orders for such matters as anti-partisan reprisal operations from Himmler or Kesselring. One of his deputies, called Harro With, was to say that Wolff took orders from Kesselring when it came to anti-partisan warfare. His personal secretary, SS-Obersturmbannführer Heinz Joaquim Richnow, reportedly stated that he took his orders from Himmler.[5]

Wolff was then 45 and had joined the SS in 1931, his career ascending as he became first the adjutant, and then the chief of staff, to Heinrich Himmler. By 1945, only one man in the SS was senior to him: Ernst Kaltenbrunner, the head of the Reich Security Main Office, or RSHA. But Wolff had managed to antagonise the notoriously prickly and acerbic Himmler in 1943: he did something as domestically straightforward as get divorced and remarry. But this was the SS, this was 1943, and nothing could really be considered normal. The SS Reichsführer felt betrayed and let down by Wolff's actions – after all, wasn't a senior general of the SS meant to embody decent Aryan values of fidelity and loyalty to his wife? But it went deeper than that, for Wolff had asked Hitler for approval of the divorce, rather than Himmler. The latter saw this as gross disloyalty, and Wolff was dispatched to Italy. There his command overlapped with Field Marshal Kesselring's, and the two men were officially equal in seniority. Wolff was well aware of the Holocaust too – he described accompanying Himmler in August 1941 to witness a mass shooting near Minsk, carried out by Einsatzkommando B.[6]

During this visit, Himmler reportedly felt sick and nauseous, especially after a piece of prisoner's brain matter splattered on to his face or coat as the man was shot. It left him feeling convinced that the execution of prisoners was brutal and obsolete, and it was gassing, rather than shooting, that was the most efficient way to carry out the Final Solution. Wolff also personally oversaw the deportation of Jews from the Warsaw Ghetto to Treblinka, going so far as to thank the head of Germany's railway system, the Reichsbahn, for his efficiency in deporting those he called 'the Chosen People'.[7]

He was focally involved in Operation Sunrise. Brokered by Allen Dulles, the head of the American Office for Strategic Services in Bern, and aided by Swiss military intelligence, in this highly covert operation American and British intelligence were trying to negotiate a secret surrender of all German forces in Italy as early as February 1945. A cunning and duplicitous man, who had survived a decade of internecine SS power struggles between himself, Himmler, Eichmann, Ernst Kaltenbrunner, Walter Schellenberg and Reinhard Heydrich, Wolff knew exactly where the skeletons were buried. And in return for information, to be given as a prosecution witness at Nuremburg, he was asking the Americans for immunity from prosecution for himself. Some of his subordinate officers went further, and claimed that he was bargaining for immunity for *all* the SS fighting men who'd served under him in Italy, whether they were indicted for war crimes or not. Karl Wolff and his claims of his deals with US intelligence were to very seriously impede the determined and clear-sighted war crimes processes against the SS on which the American and British investigators were working so hard.

Operation Sunrise had involved secret meetings between William Donovan and Allen Dulles from the OSS, Wolff and other SS officers, Italian businessmen, partisans and political leaders, British Major General Terence Airey and American Major General Lyman Lemnitzer, as well as British officials from the Special Operations Executive. The two generals had flown from Naples to Switzerland in civilian clothes, disguised as Irish businessmen, with their cover story being that they wanted to buy a German dachshund called Fritzel. Only afterwards did the covert meetings become code-named Operation Sunrise; at the beginning they were called 'Fritzel'. The aim of the planned deal was to secure a surrender of the German forces in Italy as early as February 1945, hopefully triggering a capitulation of Axis troops in northern Europe. The Western Allies wanted to secure the surrender of the 800,000 troops of Army Group C as soon as they could, and not to get savagely bogged down in a battle for the Third Reich's vaunted 'Alpine Fortress'. British and American intelligence officers had been warning for four months that the SS planned to make a last stand in a mountain redoubt somewhere in Austria: Eisenhower took this threat sufficiently seriously to divert his advance on Berlin southwards to Bavaria. Despite the secrecy surrounding the Sunrise meetings, which took place in Lugano on the Swiss–Italian border, the Russians had not been formally invited to the table, but had discovered what was going on. This had caused a major diplomatic rift with the British and Americans. The operation was subsequently dropped like a scalding potato.

Wolff, however, had by then reportedly negotiated a preferential deal between himself and the OSS: in return for his assistance to them with Operation Sunrise, he wanted immunity. The most senior SS officer in Italy, with overarching command and control responsibility for all anti-partisan and security operations, had allegedly made a deal to guarantee himself, and possibly his subordinates, immunity from prosecution for war crimes after the war, in return for appearing as a prosecution witness against his former SS colleagues at the coming Nuremberg Trials. The OSS had supposedly agreed, but not on paper.

Two key Swiss personnel at the meetings, Major Max Waibel and Max Husmann, were to testify that they had been present when Dulles and Wolff made their agreements. Major General Terence Airey, who was assistant chief of staff to British General Harold Alexander, said after personally attending the negotiations he could not rule out the possibility that a deal had been made. Wolff felt safe. In the diary and operational notebook of Wolff's chief of staff and adjutant, Harro With, there is reportedly no information in it that links any order given by Wolff to any SS reprisal operation against civilians.[8] Wolff's personal secretary, meanwhile, SS-Obersturmführer Joaquim Richnow, had served with the 16th SS after January 1944, and could reasonably be argued to be somebody who would stand up for and defend the

SS chain of command. It was he who would say that Wolff took orders from Kesselring.

But the OSS believed that Wolff had been responsible for operations that killed civilians, involved hostage taking and reprisals, and that he had also been responsible for giving orders to kill foreign nationals – i.e. Allied servicemen – captured by men under his command.[9] This could have meant that some OSS officers, believing that it was Wolff who had personally overseen the interrogations and executions of their colleagues in Bolzano, were determined to discredit him. But one of Dulles' colleagues, Colonel Russell B. Livermore, concluded that Wolff was a moderate SS officer, who was a gentleman who should not be prosecuted.[10] It does not seem surprising, therefore, that Wolff was prepared to co-operate with the Americans.

OSS agent T.S. Ryan reported that after the meeting at the Villa Pistoia there was a dinner party. During this, he had felt obliged to bring up the subject of other American agents from the Office of Strategic Services who were being held captive in SS prisons in Italy. One of these was a lieutenant called Roderick Goodspeed Hall. Ryan had reports he was being held in Bolzano itself. His parents, Ray Ovid and Gertrude Goodspeed Hall, were business people and he'd been in China, but came from Massachusetts. Hall had spent time in north-eastern Italy before the war, climbing, skiing and hiking, especially around the Brenner Pass, which joined Italy with Austria. He joined the infantry as a private, was commissioned, and then in 1943 wrote to the Office of Strategic Services saying he had a plan.[11]

Would they supply him with explosives, tools, weapons, and a team of men? Then could they parachute him into the foothills of the Italian Alps so he could link up with partisans, arrange air drops of weapons and radios to them, and then proceed to carry out sabotage missions around the Brenner Pass? Perhaps he could blow up a strategic dam at Cortina d'Ampezzo as well? He sent the letter to the Director-General of the OSS, William 'Wild Bill' Donovan. Back came the reply: yes. Report for training, and then you're going to Algiers – and Italy. Hall arrived in Caserta in July 1944 and joined up with a team of agents from the 2677th OSS Regiment, the same unit to which T.S. Ryan belonged. He and four other agents parachuted on to a mountain plateau south of the

Brenner Pass in late August. Then followed six months of demolition missions with partisans, weapons air drops, hiding in the mountains, and avoiding omnipresent German patrols. In January 1945 Hall made his way north on his own, on skis, towards the Cortina d'Ampezzo dam, intending to blow it up. Frostbite on his feet stopped him in his tracks. Discovered in hiding by a game warden, then betrayed by one of his own partisans who identified him as an American agent, Hall was arrested by Fascist police, who turned him over to the SS. The captured OSS agent, and his fate, then became the subject of intense bargaining, not just at the Operation Sunrise negotiations, but also at the trial of the SS officer who tortured and hanged him at the Bolzano concentration camp. His evidence in turn was to compromise Wolff, and start to expose the immunity deals he had made with Americans that allegedly led to wanted SS men escaping justice.

When T.S. Ryan brought up the subject over dinner at the Villa Pistoia, Wolff felt deeply embarrassed that this part of his deal with the OSS had not been honoured. Furious, he stormed into an ante-room and told his junior SS staff that such lapses of attention to detail could cost him, Wolff, his carefully negotiated special status with the Americans. An SS officer, Eugen Wenner, was ordered to pick up the telephone immediately and find out what had happened to First Lieutenant Goodspeed Hall. In the days following the German surrender in Italy, Wolff and a number of senior officers then behaved in a manner not necessarily befitting a high-ranking general from a defeated regime with a lot of blood on his hands. *Stars & Stripes*, the US Army's newspaper, published pictures of SS officers around Bolzano arranging preferential accommodation for the arriving Americans.

On 13 May, Wolff and his wife were giving a dinner party for Rudolf Rahn, the German ambassador to Italy, at the Villa Pistoia. It was the German general's 45th birthday. He and his guests were relaxed and at ease. So when infantrymen from the US 88th Division arrived in his courtyard to arrest him, he was taken completely by surprise. He was put into a lorry with other SS officers, and then taken to a detention camp near Verona. Shortly after the arrest, the OSS complained to the US Army that they were not respecting the deal they had struck with Wolff. Wolff's former SS comrades who were imprisoned with him saw their general receiving specifically individual treatment. He ate different, individually served and better food, wore full uniform, and was permitted to carry his Walther PPK pistol on his belt. In August, the Americans moved Wolff to a small American PoW camp on Lake Gmunden in Austria. A report in the *New York Herald Tribune* said that the former SS general spent the summer of that year with his family, and had even asked for his private yacht to be brought down to the lake. The story was half-invented, the product of anti-OSS political lobbying in Washington and New York.[12] In September, Wolff was moved to a British-run prison outside Berlin. Unbeknownst to him, the British Combined Services Detailed Interrogations Centre (CSDIC), which was run jointly by the War Office and the British Army with the participation of intelligence agencies MI5 and MI9, was recording German prisoners' conversations. During one recorded conversation, Wolff boasted that his surrender negotiations with Dulles had resulted in the favourable treatment he was currently receiving, and he praised the Americans for keeping all their promises to him.

Not all SS and Gestapo officers in Italy were to prove as loyal to their oath, and to their comrades, as Major General Max Simon, who had plea-bargained rather than appropriate blame on his individual unit commanders. One man who was quick to provide information on his SS colleagues was SS-Sturmbannführer Heinrich Andergassen. An Austrian SS officer who served in northern Italy with the Sicherheitsdienst, or SD, the SS' intelligence police, he also operated with its sister organisation, the Gestapo. He oversaw the Bolzano concentration camp and detention centre, and it was he who had tortured and hanged OSS Lieutenant Roderick Hall, four downed American air force pilots, and two British officers from the Special Air Service. One of his SS colleagues, Arthur Schuster, said that he and others regarded him as a brutal sadist, especially when drinking. In turn, the Americans and British very much wanted him alive. Knowing the war was over, on 30 April Andergassen and two SS colleagues changed into civilian clothes, packed MP 40 machine pistols and magazines, and put their SS uniforms into rucksacks. In a black Mercedes, they headed north-east for the Brenner Pass, and then Austria. Outside Innsbruck an American patrol from the Counter-Intelligence Corps stopped them, pulled them from the vehicle and arrested them.

Under questioning, Andergassen told his interrogators everything. For them, one particular revelation was like a bombshell. It had been an open secret in Wolff's SS headquarters in Bolzano, he said, that their general was involved in secret negotiations with the OSS, the Swiss and the British, partly in return for a guarantee for himself of immunity from prosecution in forthcoming war crimes trials.[13] Andergassen said that it was also common knowledge that Wolff had made a separate deal, whereby attacks by the SS or German security police on the Italian civilian population would not be the subject of future war crimes investigations. For the officers and men of the 16th SS Panzergrenadier Division, including all those who had been at Sant'Anna di Stazzema on 12 August 1944, this would help shape their future.[14] The problem was that Andergassen knew he was going to be executed, and did his best to incriminate his superiors; the British officer who interrogated Wolff described him as an unreliable witness, especially about himself; as stated above, his secretary – an SS major – said that orders to individual SS commanders in the field often came from Heinrich Himmler in Berlin; the result for the Allies War Crimes Commission was that there was hardly enough evidence to prosecute Wolff.

One other German SS man certainly benefited from protection by the Americans. SS-Sturmbannführer Eugen Dollmann was one of Wolff's adjutants, and had worked as an interpreter between Hitler and Mussolini. As the war ended, with Wolff arrested, Dollmann fled south, and tried to get help from a group of Catholic priests and bishops whom he knew. Italian Cardinal Alfredo Schuster had also been involved in the Operation Sunrise negotiations, and at first he hid Dollmann in a mental asylum on Lake Maggiore outside Milan. The former SS officer and diplomat ventured south to Rome, where he was recognised by a member of the audience in a cinema. The Italians arrested him, but James Jesus Angleton, then head of counter-intelligence for the OSS in Italy, managed to negotiate his release from the police, and took him to Switzerland to meet Allen Dulles, with whom he had co-operated during Operation Sunrise. Dulles arranged for him to take refuge in Switzerland under an assumed identity.

10

VICTORS' JUSTICE

In the first springtime of peace for six years, twelve men went home. They were all from the SS, the Gestapo, SD and the Wehrmacht, and were just a handful among the millions of German soldiers, sailors, air force men and civilians returning as best as they could to a half-destroyed Germany. They went by lorry, by car, on foot, or in carts drawn by horses. The roads of central Europe was shuddering to the tramping feet of millions of Europe's displaced: Polish and Russian slave labourers, escaped Allied PoWs, French workers forced to work in factories in the Ruhr, Austrian refugees, Italians imprisoned after their country surrendered, and American and British aircrew who had been in hiding since being shot down. Everybody was moving west, or north towards Germany. Nobody was moving east, towards Russia and the Red Army. And threaded through the convoys of refugees and displaced, were the American, British, Canadian and French tanks and lorries and jeeps, and hundreds of thousands of liberating, occupying troops, for whom the war also was over.

SS-Lieutenant Gerhard Sommer was no longer with his original unit, the 16th SS Panzergrenadier Division, when it surrendered near Klagenfurt. In 1944 he transferred to the 23rd SS Panzergrenadier Division, largely made up of Dutch volunteers. Fighting against the Red Army on the River Oder in April 1945, Sommer's battlegroup was forced into retreat, and managed to make their way into the zone of American advance in time to surrender. Five of the senior Dutch SS officers were arrested immediately, but nobody paid any attention to Gerhard Sommer. He made his way back to the ruins of Hamburg, and tried to find his father and see if anything still existed of his machine manufacturing company.

Lieutenant Georg Rauch, who'd been Anton Galler's adjutant in Italy, went back to the Ore mountains, near the Czech border. The war had passed by his hometown, so he returned to building up his father's cake-making and baking business. Ludwig Goring returned to Ittersbach, between Stuttgart and the Rhine, haunted by his memories of Sant'Anna di Stazzema. Karl Gropler found his home village of Wollin, outside Potsdam, full of refugees who had fled the Russian zone of occupation. He went back to farming sugar beet, potatoes and kale. With three families called Gropler in the village, anybody who went looking for him had to be precise about his identity: but nobody ever came. Karl Gesele travelled from SS service in eastern Germany and met up with Anton Galler to go to Friedrichshafen on Lake Constance, after the 16th SS had surrendered in Bavaria and Austria. Galler then returned to Sankt Polten, west of Vienna, and made plans to emigrate to Canada.

Friedrich Bosshammer, head of the Jewish Section with the Gestapo in Verona, just made it out of Italy alive after partisans tried to assassinate him. He arrived back in Wuppertal, south of Düsseldorf, in summer 1945 and tried to get work as a lawyer. But first, he contacted the HIAG, the fledgling SS Comrades Association, changed his name and received new identity papers and a new war service record. He then disappeared for twenty-three years. Friedrich Siegfried Engel, who had commanded the SD detachment in Genoa, and had overseen the Turchino Tunnel massacres, went back to the suburb of Lockstedt, outside Hamburg, and tried to set up a business importing furniture. Carl-Theodar Schutz, a Gestapo officer who had been at the Ardeatine Caves, went to work for the Gehlen Organisation. Established by the Americans in 1946 in their zone of occupation in Germany, and operating closely with the fledgling CIA, the organisation employed former SS and Wehrmacht officers to operate as intelligence operatives against the Soviet Bloc. It was the precursor to the BND, the German domestic intelligence agency that would be established in the 1950s.

Kurt Winden, one of Herbert Kappler's deputies who had executed prisoners in Rome, went to work for the in-house legal department of a German bank. Joachim Peiper was wanted by the Americans for the massacre of US Army soldiers outside Malmedy in Belgium in winter 1944. The Counterintelligence Corps found him in a PoW camp, and transferred him to an interrogation centre. He was put on trial for the Malmedy massacre. And Karl Wolff? He was imprisoned at Schöneberg, outside Berlin, and appeared as a prosecution witness at the Nuremberg Trials.

Apart from Wolff, what these men had done in Italy between 1943 and 1945 was to make almost negligible difference to how they would fare and function in the new Germany. If Italy in 1944 had been a permissive environment in which the SS could commit war crimes, then in post-war Germany it was to become possible to avoid paying any legal consequences for them. The 16th SS was disbanded in May 1945, its officers and some of its men questioned, and their details entered into one of a number of vast paper databases of an estimated 1.9 million German servicemen and civilian members of the Nazi Party.

The Allied Control Council and Denazification

In 1944 the European Advisory Commission was looking ahead to a point when Germany had surrendered, been occupied and needed governing. They decided that purely military rule of a defeated Germany would be the only workable option for at least three years. Neither the Western Allies nor the Russians knew what the political and military economics of power would be in Germany as the Hitler government surrendered, and the devastated country suddenly shuddered to a stop, like a broken and exhausted racing car that finally runs out of fuel. Would there be organised armed resistance to the Allies? Would the SS or underground Nazi resistance groups like Werewolf 88 fight a guerrilla war against the occupiers? Would there be any money, or food, or medicine or water? Put bluntly, would or could the country function in any way at all?

So the Allied Control Council was established. It was made up of the three main powers of the Western Allies, the United States, Great Britain, France, as well as the Soviet Union. Together they became known as the Four Powers, which became a synonym for the Council as well. It had been one of the many initiatives that had sprung out of the Yalta, and then Potsdam, conferences, and it was set up as the war ended. The Control Council was based in Berlin, and its job was to govern Germany as its sole executive authority – essentially it was a military government that replaced almost every function of the German regime. Its jurisdiction included Allied-controlled Austria as well. The Council split Germany into four zones of occupation, each run by a different one of the four governing nationalities. Each zone was in turn governed by the commander-in-chief of the respective Allied armies deployed there, whose status and power was similar to that of a Roman pro consul, except with soldiers and aircraft and tanks under his command, ready to do his bidding.

These four different commanders then, in turn, made up the executive command of the Control Council. These officers were, respectively, Field Marshal Montgomery, General Dwight D. Eisenhower, Field Marshal Georgy Zhukov and General de Lattre de Tassigny. The French had their headquarters in Karlsruhe, in Baden-Württemberg, near the border of France and Germany; the Russians were headquartered in East Berlin, the Americans in West Berlin and Frankfurt, and the British in Bad Oeynhausen, in North-Rhine Westphalia, 50 miles from Hanover. The Council was signed into being on 30 August 1945, and the entire population of Germany, civilian, military, men, women, children, those inside prison and those outside, were told in no uncertain terms that an entire new set of laws was on its way. For the hungry, desperate, bombed-out, confused and angry German people, it was as though one autocratic regime was going to be replaced with another. Rules, legislation and orders indeed followed, as the country's new governors took over control of the entire infrastructure of a country. British engineers worked to repair the water supply in Hamburg, Russian military policemen tried to clamp down on the black market in East Berlin, the Americans repaired roads, and the French tried to reconstruct hospitals. It was a massive project, almost akin to creating and running a small empire where each of its four different rulers had wildly conflicting ideas about how to execute the task, and very different opinions and ideas about the citizens and just-demobilised soldiers under their control.

For the SS officers, NCOs and men of the 16th SS Panzergrenadier Division who came back to the country from Italy and Hungary, three particular Allied regulations were to make the most substantial difference to their lives; whether they could return to a semi-normal existence as newly demobilised soldiers in the towns from where they had come, or whether they faced arrest, or worse, from the occupying soldiers of the four different nationalities. The first were the regulations concerning war criminals. While the Nuremberg Trials would deliver prison sentences – or the death penalty – to the most senior Nazi Party officials and officers of the SS and Wehrmacht, for the nearly 2 million rank-and-file of the German armed forces, whether they were arrested and tried and imprisoned, or not, depended on the military justice infrastructure of the zone of occupation to which they returned.

For Gerhard Sommer, returning to Hamburg, this would mean he would be under the jurisdiction of the British. Karl Gesele was in Bavaria under the Americans, Ludwig Goring in western Baden-Württemberg under the French, and Karl Gropler in the farming village of Wollin, near Potsdam, on the dividing line of the American and Russian zones. The German Wehrmacht and SS, and their subsidiary civil–military auxiliaries, were all disbanded, the wearing of any sort of uniform was forbidden, and the men and women couldn't convene together in any form of old comrades associations. Meanwhile, any physical remnants of the Third Reich's militarised representation – statues with Nazi eagles, notice boards outside barracks bearing the twin lightning flashes of the SS, anything bearing the words Kriegsmarine, for instance, or Wehrmacht, was banned by the Four Powers, whose men dismantled offending objects, destroyed them, shot at them or just blew them up. But when it came to comrades associations, the SS had already broken this rule, as its returning members discovered.

The second vital set of regulations for the returning SS men concerned potential justice for crimes committed in countries outside Germany. To begin with, this would be predominantly the priority of that country's government, in as much as Denmark or Italy or France could put on trial or request the extradition of German servicemen who had or allegedly had committed crimes there. The Allied Council would extradite Germans to face trial abroad if they were captured in Germany. So the men of the returned SS units knew immediately that they had to avoid arrest.

The third set of Allied regulations concerned the policy of Denazification. The aim of this was straightforward: to remove from any form of power or influence any member of the former National Socialist Party, or the banned organisations such as the SD, the Waffen or Algemeine SS, the Gestapo or any associated intelligence services. The Allies knew this was a massive undertaking – nearly 500,000 of these people were in detention centres across the country already, waiting, in often miserable conditions, for background checks to be carried out on them so they could return to freedom and something of a new life.

These checks, and passing them, were the first step to freedom. Once they had been carried out by military policemen or soldiers, it was straightforward: the man, or sometimes woman, in question would then be given a background form. This attested to the fact that they hadn't done anything untoward in the past, committed crimes, belonged to a unit that had massacred and burned villages in reprisals, taken hostages, run detention centres or served in concentration camps – any of the myriad activities that had been possible for members of the above-named banned organisations like the SS and Gestapo. With a clear background check came a background form. This would subsequently serve as a certificate of employment, a certificate of good, clean, past conduct, a sort of certificate of innocence, of freedom from judicial investigation, a certificate of a *new start*.

The British and the Americans knew they were looking forward to a reunited and probably rearmed Germany, knew that they would be involved in setting it up and probably administering it, and knew that, suddenly, the Soviet Union and the Red Army were the new enemy. They knew, because the Germans told them; and because they could see it every single one of the dozens of times a day an Allied soldier would interact with a German civilian or demobilised soldier. The Germans hated the 'denazification' process, as it was known. So the British and the Americans were very flexible and passive when implementing its rulings. The US and British soldiers knew, too, that up to 40 million people had belonged to the Nazi Party: how on earth were they all to be screened, in a devastated country, just after a world war, in occupation zones where relatively few Allied soldiers spoke German? Of course, it was effectively impossible. The Control Commission knew this before it was even established.

The background check a German completed was called a Fragebogen, or questionnaire. The results of this then decided which of five categories of judicial status he or she would be then allocated. After a shaky start, the Allies quickly changed the questionnaire to a Meldebogen, or background form. For reasons explained below, the former members of the SS, SD and Gestapo found these extremely easy to circumvent. Once one of these two forms had been filled in, the person would appear before a Spruchkammer, or arbitration board, which could be made up of one or more officials like a judge or priest or doctor, who would assign them their categorisation. Once this was done, the individual was considered 'denazified' and got a certificate to prove it. This led to two vital steps forward: employability and freedom from prosecution.

Category Five was the lowest, for people who had been proved not to have belonged to any banned organisation and so were free to head for a new start. Category Four was for relatively minor offenders, such as junior civil servants, public transport officials, municipal engineers – those people who had not been in any branch of the armed forces, but had performed public administrative duties. They were fined, and sometimes had travel restricted, but that was it. Category Three was for soldiers or airmen who'd been in action with the army or navy or air force, but at a low rank – they were just put on probation. Category Two was for black marketers, who could be sentenced to ten years in prison. Category One was for former SS, SD and Gestapo officers, Nazi Party officials or major criminals: theirs was the death sentence, or at the very least up to ten years or more in prison.

What made the most crucial difference to the restrictions in each of these categories was not just what the individual German had obviously done during the war, but which nationality was in charge of the zone where they lived. The British and Americans were lenient,

the French strict, and the Russians verged between being the compliant and tolerant fellow sufferers of a harsh bureaucratic regime to
almost psychotic. Members of the Nazi Party who had been born after
1919 were exempted from any form of strict categorisation, on the
basis that they had not had any form of choice in the matter, and that
the National Socialist regime had made them what they were – effectively co-opting them physically and psychologically. This made it even
easier for every one of the men from the 16th SS, who could legitimately say they had been obliged to join the Nazi Party or SS, or been
brainwashed. So they did. Another way that the SS men could escape
categorisation into the highest levels of One or Two was to ask their
friends, or comrades or officers from their unit or training school to
provide statements of testimony for them at their background checks.
Those people who provided these statements on behalf of one another
started to call the subsequent statements 'Persilscheine', or 'whitened by
Persil', as they were so frequently and consummately falsified.

The British didn't pay too much attention – with an economy at
home exhausted and semi-moribund after the war, the last thing they
needed was to have to support a defeated Germany. Additionally, both
British and Americans knew that, with the Soviet Union the new
enemy in the burgeoning Cold War, Germans were highly likely to
become their new allies sooner rather than later, in a new democratic
Europe with a western treaty organisation co-ordinating a European
defence union that would almost certainly involve the new Germany.
So some British and American soldiers actively supported the move
towards a much more lenient administrative regime for Germany and
the Germans.

Gerhard Sommer was in the British zone, Georg Rauch in the
Russian zone, Ludwig Goring in the French zone, Karl Gesele
and Karl Gropler in the American zone. All of them took the same
approach to resolving their problem of categorisation. If a person had
had a background check, and a resultant denazification certificate that
allocated them to categories Five or Four, then that certificate would
form the basis of their legal, judicial and employment status in the new
Germany for the foreseeable future, until any new government could
begin issuing passports.

So the deal for the SS men was simple: by hook or by crook, get your hands on a Fragebogen with some Persilscheinegen testimony from old comrades, if necessary buy it from whoever necessary, and then you will be free from investigation for years to come. So this is what these men did. Ex-SS men, Nazi Party officials and corrupt ex-Wehrmacht men had, not surprisingly, a very lucrative trade in black market denazification certificates. They could be bought and sold like all the other 'black' commodities: British ration bully beef and navy rum, Players and Lucky Strike cigarettes, American penicillin, French red table wine, American mattress covers that could be used to make clothes, American .45 Colt automatics, sunglasses, or any conceivable form of contraception, medical supplies, alcohol, drugs or food. In the British zone of occupation, after October 1945 it ceased to be classified as a crime to have been in the Waffen-SS, while in the American zone, to be arrested as an ex-SS man required a person to have held a minimum rank of Sturmbannführer, or major.

The men who had been at Sant'Anna di Stazzema were on their way to clearing their first main hurdle to freedom. They would soon be Entnazifiziert, or legitimately denazified. And no group of men was more active in providing fake testimony, or providing a fake Spruchkammer, than the former SS men who were forming the embryo of a comrades association. It would become named the HIAG, or Hilfsgemeinschaft auf Gegenseitigkeit der Angehörigen der ehemaligen Waffen-SS, or Mutual Aid Association of Former Waffen-SS Members. It aimed to help the men of the Gestapo, SD, Allgemeine and Waffen-SS to escape Germany if necessary, but much more preferably, to stay in their new country and infiltrate and take their place in its judiciary, its legal system, its business structure, commerce, media, intelligence services and law enforcement.

This was greatly helped by the fact that the British needed to reconstitute a legal system. A full 90 per cent of judges had been members of the Nazi Party, so the British decided that it would be acceptable if 50 per cent of the judiciary of the German Legal Civil Service could be staffed by what they called 'nominal Nazis'. These judges and legal magistrates would be the people responsible to check the categories on any suspected person's denazification certificate. The British went one step further: they announced in early winter 1945 that unless a person was applying for an official position, they didn't have to fill in a Fragebogen. This led to large numbers of former SS men moving to take up residence in the British sector of occupation – Karl Gesele and Georg Rauch were just two men who decided to go and join Gerhard Sommer in his more lenient, British-controlled zone.

In January 1947, the denazification process was handed over in its entirety to the Germans. For the Allies, it had not been a success, for the Germans, a detested bureaucratic obstacle, made all the more unpopular because it was so easy to circumvent, if laboriously so. All it took, after all, was for a former SS officer or NCO or trooper to pay one or more colleagues or local officials to write glowing testimony about their sterling performance guarding railway stations or looking after orphans on the Russian Front, which was then taken to a judge who had a more than 50 per cent chance of having been in the Nazi Party, who would then assign the person the most lenient category possible. If the SS man wanted to avail himself of a Spruchkammer through the HIAG, then that was even easier. So all of the twelve men from the SS who had been in Italy, apart from Karl Wolff and Joaquim Peiper, were in the clear. Friedrich Bosshammer had disappeared.

The Nuremberg Trials

Apart from the divisional commander Max Simon, none of the thousands of men from the Reichsführer-SS division were detained immediately. The Allies instituted the Nuremberg Trials, which they hailed as the ultimate triumph of justice and reason towards a defeated enemy; the Germans and Italians simply sneered at 'Victor's Justice'. It was to put twenty-one leading Nazis in the dock in its first year, sentencing eleven to death. But many Nazi officials, SS officers and Gestapo men escaped justice. The Americans, British, Russians and French conducted trials both in Germany, as well as in France, Russia and Italy. Many Germans fled abroad to countries where they could hide, or where the governments sympathised with Nazi Germany – Argentina, Paraguay, Spain, Namibia, Syria or Egypt. They changed their names and identities, or they just made sure to be able to blend in to judicial obscurity in the new Germany.

The Allies were most determined and focused on hard justice, legal clarity, and putting the Third Reich's most senior officials and generals on trial. Stalin and Roosevelt wanted to punish the German political and officer corps. The legal ruling that constituted the authority of these trials was called the London Charter, signed by Great Britain, France, the Soviet Union and the United States in London in August 1945. The resultant court was named the International Military Tribunal, and its brief was to try defendants for crimes that fell into the three categories, under which they were charged. These were Crimes against Peace, which involved the planning, initiating, and waging a war of aggression; next was War Crimes, or violations of the laws and customs of war as embodied in the Hague and Geneva Conventions, to which the military forces of most western nations were signatories, and then there were Crimes against Humanity, or the extermination of racial, ethnic, and religious groups and other similar atrocities against civilians. Around 200 Germans in total would be tried at Nuremberg.

On 8 October 1945, Wehrmacht General Anton Dostler was the first German senior officer to be tried for war crimes by a US military tribunal, sitting at the Royal Palace of Caserta, outside Naples. He was accused of ordering the killing of fifteen captured US commandos, who had landed on the coast of Liguria in Italy in March 1944. The soldiers were from the OSS, and the failed mission that had seen them captured was code-named Operation Ginny II. The commandos were all Italian–Americans, whose mission was to try and blow up railway tunnels along the Ligurian coast, so as to disrupt German supply routes. Landed in the wrong place, the OSS men, who were all wearing military uniform, were discovered by an Italian fisherman who called the Italian and German military to investigate. All fifteen Americans were executed by firing squad on the orders of General Dostler, citing Hitler's Commando Order of 1942, in which all commandos and special forces captured on missions were to be shot without trial.

Field Marshal Kesselring had approved the execution order, and Dostler stated that, although he disagreed with them, he was simply following orders. He claimed the Americans were not wearing uniforms, meaning they could legitimately be classified as spies or saboteurs, and thus equally legitimately be executed. The US prosecutors proved that the soldiers were in fact wearing full US military attire. The trial prosecution at Caserta found Dostler guilty, declaring that following and executing orders that he knew to be illegal did not constitute a defence. Anton Dostler was sentenced to death and shot by a firing squad on 1 December 1945 at Aversa, north of Caserta. He was the first German to be tried, found guilty and sentenced to death for war crimes, and his execution was photographed and filmed; the black and white images and footage of him being shot to death by a twelve-man firing squad was disseminated in the American media. The case set a vital legal precedent for the Nuremberg trials.

From the moment that Dostler was found guilty, German generals, officials, and Nazi leaders could not use the clause known as 'Superior Orders' as a defence. This was then codified in Principle IV of the Nuremberg Principles, and similar were included in sections of the Universal Declaration of Human Rights. At Nuremberg, both individuals as well as organisations were charged as criminal. Individuals such as Rudolf Hess, Joachim von Ribbentrop and Field Marshal Keitel were sentenced to death, while organisations such as the Gestapo, SS and SD were declared as 'criminal with criminal intent'. The Dostler Precedent, or Principle IV, at Nuremberg was to mean that regardless of whether Karl Wolff or Max Simon or Albert Kesselring had given orders that supposedly legitimised the killings at Sant'Anna di Stazzema, or Marzabotto, or Fivizzano, the individual officers and NCOs who had followed these orders could be found guilty of war crimes because they had obeyed an order they clearly knew to be illegal.

War Crimes Investigations in Italy

By November 1944, military investigators from the British and American War Crimes Unit, the American and British military police, and legal experts from the US Judge Advocate General's Corps had started to collect enough evidence from Italian survivors to prepare war crimes cases for six of the different mass killings that had taken place in Tuscany in summer 1944. These were, respectively, the incidents at Sant'Anna di Stazzema, Bardine and San Terenzo Monte, Vinca, Bergiola and Massa, the Carthusian monastery at Farneta, and the massacre on the Monte Sole plateau. The British Commission had formed a separate, small, under-resourced unit to deal with SS crimes. The 16th SS Panzergrenadier Division had massacred more civilians than any other German unit in the whole Italian campaign, with a minimum estimated death toll of around 2,500 people. Testimony from survivors of the killings at Sant'Anna di Stazzema and other massacres was thus vital. Among others, the Americans and British wanted to find, arrest, and either execute or imprison a group of SS officers and men who between them had participated in the six different mass killings in Tuscany listed above. Italian Fascist soldiers who helped the Waffen-SS were also targeted in the search, as were at least fifty Italian soldiers who were thought to have taken part in the Sant'Anna massacre.

The investigators were documenting evidence against the 16th SS commanding officer, Major General Max Simon, against Lieutenant Colonel Karl Gesele, Major Walter Reder and Major Anton Galler, Lieutenants Gerhard Sommer and Helmut Lang, and at least twenty SS NCOs and men. But among the SS indictees, the Allied investigators were instructed only to concentrate on Major General Simon: the other officers and men, they were told, would be the responsibility of the Italians. The Allied investigators were still working in newly occupied areas of Italy under the jurisdiction of the Allied War Crimes Commission and its two Investigation Groups at Caserta. In turn these were answerable to the American War Crimes Unit of the US Department of the Inspector General, their Judge Advocate General's Corps, and the Judge Advocate General's Department at the British War Office. London and Washington, however, were clear: they wanted only the very senior SS officers who had given the orders, run the operation and overseen the organisation of the reprisal killings themselves. The officers lower in the chain of command, the NCOs, the men? These would be the responsibility of the Italians.

In Germany, many of those being sought for war crimes in Italy such as Gerhard Sommer and Karl Gesele had falsified their denazification certificates. Living in the British zone of occupation, those below the rank of SS major were not subject to arrest. The British and Americans were not going to put them on trial in Germany or Italy. It was thus comparatively simple for most mid-ranking SS or Gestapo officers, as well as the officers, NCOs and men who gave and took orders at locations like Sant'Anna di Stazzema, to slip through the net after the war.

At a more senior level, complex intelligence deals done by the Americans, internecine arguments between the British Foreign Office and War Office, and conflicting views among the Allies as to Italy's suitability to stage war crimes trials meant that more senior officers also escaped justice. As Himmler's Chief of Staff, as well as head of the SS and Security Police in Italy, SS-Obergruppenführer Karl Wolff was not just potentially heavily implicated in war crimes in Italy, but in the Holocaust, too. Wolff finally escaped trial at Nuremberg, fulfilling his alleged promise to the Americans to appear as a prosecution witness. London believed that the SS general and the Americans may have made a deal concerning immunity for war crimes committed in Italy. This was based upon the reports made after the dissolution of the Operation Sunrise meetings by the British Lieutenant General Terence Airey, Harold Alexander's deputy chief of staff and senior intelligence official. The British weren't certain, however, whether he'd actually done a deal with Allen Dulles or not; the American war crimes investigators were also unsure what their fellow countrymen from the OSS had done; the Italians then received rumour, hearsay and half-truths. The net result was that at a vital moment in war crimes investigations against SS personnel who'd served in Italy, the deal that was, or wasn't, done with Wolff only served to sow enormous confusion and suspicion among three national partners whose efforts should instead have been complementing each other. Wolff himself was released from Allied custody quickly, in 1947, whereupon the new German authorities government arrested him again as part of the denazification programme.

The majority of German service personnel from the 16th SS Division who had carried out atrocities in Italy then found themselves in an extraordinarily lenient judicial environment. The British War Crimes Commission in Italy focused on bringing charges against six Germans: Field Marshal Kesselring and Major Generals Mälzer, Von Mackensen, Tensfeld, Burger, Craseman and Max Simon. The SS men below this rank were to be the responsibility of the Italian national war crimes tribunal system.

As the supreme German commander in Italy, Field Marshal Albert Kesselring was charged with his involvement in the reprisal executions of 335 Italians at the Ardeatine Caves in Rome, and for inciting the killings of civilians in reprisal operation with his 'anti-bandit' rulings of May, June and July of 1944. Also indicted for the massacres in Rome were Luftwaffe General Kurt Mälzer, the military commander in Rome, who was subordinate in command to General Eberhard von Mackensen. Major General Eduard Craseman had commanded the 26th Panzer Division at the time of their massacre of 160 Italian civilians at the Padule di Fucecchio marshes in Tuscany in August 1944. SS Police Generals Burger and Tensfeld were wanted for their role in anti-partisan operations and the deportations of Italian Jews. Legally, it was a unique situation: the British were trying foreign nationals in a foreign country for crimes committed against foreigners.

By the middle of 1945, the British had begun summarising their analysis of German war crimes committed in Italy against the civilian population. 'Report of British War Crimes Section of Allied Force Headquarters on German Reprisals for Partisan Activities in Italy' was the title of the document.[1] It summarises clearly what the British did – and equally importantly did not – know by midsummer 1945 on German operations:

> The British War Crimes Section of the Allied Force Headquarters has investigated fully a number of cases of German reprisals for partisan activity in Italy, committed between April and November, 1944.
>
> A study of all these cases reveals that there is a striking similarity in the facts. The incident invariably opens with the killing or wounding of a German soldier or soldiers by partisans; reprisal activity is then initiated either by the troops immediately on the spot or in more serious cases, by the arrival of definite units and formations specially detailed for the purpose. There is no taking of hostages in the normal sense of the word, but a number of people are selected haphazardly from the local population and are killed by shooting or hanging, whilst whole villages or certain farms or houses are destroyed by fire. In a

number of cases an announcement is then made to the population that the action taken was a reprisal for the death of a German soldier and will be repeated should further attacks on Germans take place.

A typical example is the Civitella atrocity, one of those cases which has been completely investigated. Partisan Bands had been operating in the area, attacking lone German lorries and motor cycles. On June 18th, 1944, two German soldiers were killed and a third wounded in a fight with Partisans in the village of Civitella. Fearing reprisals, the inhabitants evacuated the village but when the Germans discovered this, punitive action was postponed. On June 29th, 1944, when the local inhabitants were returning and were feeling secure once more, the Germans carried out well organised reprisal, combing the neighbourhood.

Innocent inhabitants were often shot on sight. During that day 212 men, women and children in the immediate district were killed. Some of the dead women were found completely naked. In the course of investigation, a nominal roll of the dead has been compiled, and is complete with the exception of a few names where bodies could not be identified. Ages of the dead ranged from 1 year to 84 years. Approximately 100 houses were destroyed by fire; some of the victims were burned alive in their homes.

On December 16th, 1942, Keitel issued an order relating to the combatting of Partisans. This order was captured in Crete. (And in Rome, Florence and Sicily.) On June 17th and July 1st, 1944, Kesselring issued orders on this subject. Other evidence of the issue of this second order to German formations has been found. A comparison of Documents 'A', 'B', and 'C' makes it clear that Kesselring's orders were in accordance with a policy laid down by the Supreme Command. Documents are held proving that this general policy was dictated to lower commands in the German Army in Italy.

Evidence has been found to show that a large number of the atrocities in Italy was committed by the Hermann Goering Parachute Panzer Division. Notable offenders also were 1 Parachute Division, 16 SS Panzer Grenadier Division and 114 Light Division.

The orders of the German Command were made known to the local population in a series of notices which were exhibited in towns and villages throughout German-occupied Italy and were published in newspapers. (A specimen copy of a typical Notice to the inhabitants of Covolo is annexed hereto and marked 'D'.) In the cases on which reliable information is held, it is considered that a conservative estimate of the number of persons who met their deaths at the hands of the German soldiery, is more than 7,500 men, women and children ranging in years from infancy to extreme old age. In the Ardeatine Caves case in Rome, alone, 335 men were shot. Many other reports have not yet been substantiated, but it is certain that the total of innocent Italian civilians who were killed in such reprisals is very much greater than the number given above.

The report then proceeds to list the locations of twenty-one massacres and other killings of civilians that the British had investigated, on which the report was based. It starts with the Ardeatine Caves in March 1944, and moves to the Stia-Vallucciole Valley massacre in April, Fucecchio Marshes in June 1944, San Polo in July, Verruchio and Sarsina in September and the Villa del Albero in Ravenna in November. The summary of the Civitella massacre in the report above shows the British investigative thoroughness. It does not mention any of the killings carried out by the 16th SS Division, particularly those at Sant'Anna di Stazzema or at Marzabotto. This was because the British were relying not just on their own investigative reports of those incidents, but also those of the Americans. But although they had given *their own* reports to the Americans, this crucial arrangement had not been reciprocal. They had not seen the American report on the investigation they had carried out at Sant'Anna di Stazzema. The massacre in the village was going to be included in the indictment used in the trial of General Max Simon and Walter Reder. There were no other defendants nor any other cases referring to the 16th SS' string of killings in Tuscany. And the American report on Sant'Anna so dutifully and painstakingly investigated by Milton Wexler and his colleagues had arrived in Washington with the Joint Chiefs of Staff.

The British and Americans had been investigating massacres carried out in Tuscany by the SS and the Wehrmacht since summer 1944: as the Allied advance moved north and north-westwards, so they came across the evidence of more reprisal killings. As written previously, this information came from Italian civilians, partisans, captured Germans, and physical evidence discovered by the different advancing units. South African and British units had been among those that had fought as far forward as the bottom of the Monte Sole plateau by October and November 1944. Reports of the atrocities carried out by the 16th SS Division in the villages there would be investigated by personnel from the US Counter Intelligence Corps and the Adjutant General's Department, while the British 8th Army would deploy men from the Royal Military Police's Special Investigations Branch (SIB) or the Intelligence Corps' Field Security Sections. These units and individuals would report back to the Allied War Crimes Commission at Caserta. Their reports would also find their way back to London and Washington. One of the first prisoners the Americans had interviewed was the German deserter, Julian Legoli, who had named individual SS personnel. These details had been sent from Florence to the US War Crimes Commission, which on 10 November 1944 was officially charged with the investigation of war crimes in the area of Monte Sole and San Martino.[2]

British war crimes investigators from the Field Security Sections and the SIB had been told about what had taken place at Monte Sole as early as November 1944. This followed reports from the British and South African units who had been deployed in the area. But the fact that the Germans only withdrew from the plateau in February 1945 was to make physical access to the Monte Sole plateau impossible until spring 1945. Communications between the British and American investigators was reportedly poor, and the British were sometimes unaware that the Americans were also carrying out investigative operations in tandem with their own. Logistical support for both of them was limited, especially for the British, and although they could take testimony from the Italian civilians displaced from Monte Sole to areas further south, by then under Allied control, they couldn't get to the villages themselves – access to the scenes of the crimes was obviously impossible while they were occupied by the Germans and Italian Fascist soldiers. The British War Crimes Commission, and the Judge Advocate General's Department in London, were looking for the more high-ranking officers reportedly responsible for each crime they were looking into. The British investigation fell into three separate and distinct phases. The first was the initial gathering of information, which began in November 1944, and this was followed by two separate periods of work led by different officers and non-commissioned officers. The fact that the departing German troops had mined various areas on the approaches to the Monte Sole plateau further complicated the operations.

The pace of the British investigations can be gauged by the timings of the investigation by the SIB into the massacre at Padule di Fucecchio, west of Florence. On 23 August German army troops from the 26th Panzer Division – a unit of the army, not the SS – executed 174 civilians in an area of marshland outside Fucecchio, 20 miles outside the Tuscan capital.

Three sergeants from 78 Section of the 8th Army's Special Investigation Branch began their investigation on 5 February 1945 into the events that had taken place between 6 July and 23 August 1944. The report into this was sent by Sergeant Charles Edmonson to his superiors on 12 June 1945, when the war had been over by five weeks.[3] The military police NCO, who was both a former member of the British Household Cavalry and a one-time mounted policeman, would be one of the men investigating what happened at Monte Sole. Padule di Fucecchio is roughly equidistant between Florence and the sea, in an area liberated by the Allies in August and September 1944. That more than five months elapsed before the SIB looked at one of the biggest German massacres that had taken place in the area explains something of why the British could not begin substantial investigations into the events at Monte Sole until spring 1945. The Germans had to pull out of the area, for one thing, and investigators were occupied with other events as well.

But timing, the decisions made by commanding officers of Allied units, available manpower and evidence all had a part to play in deciding when a war crimes investigation could begin. As has been written, the first British and American soldiers arrived in and around Sant'Anna di Stazzema days after liberating Pietrasanta, and just weeks after the massacre took place. Monte Sole would take longer, and it would be spring 1945 before Sergeant Edmonson would lead a British team there. Another inquiry would follow in the summer, and yet a third in March 1947.

Meanwhile, the investigations led by the Italian authorities after the war differed hugely from one to the other, depending on the individual who carried it out. Sometimes they were very efficient and effective indeed, sometimes they got nowhere, and little effort was made by the investigating police officers. Major Vito di Majorca's investigation into the killings at Sant'Anna was just as thorough as the British or American ones. Yet Captain Carlo Galli of the carabinieri from Bologna, eventually to be tasked with finding out what had happened in the Monte Sole operation, was the opposite. Nobody from the Allied teams had informed him of what they were doing, so the reports that Galli was to send to the Prefect of Bologna and then the General Attorney of the Supreme Military Court in Rome from June 1946 to May 1947 were insubstantial. There is one possible explanation for this: Galli was to be dispatched to Monte Sole and Marzabotto with instructions not to discover too much, to allow the Allied teams to take the lead and come up with the evidence. The Italians at that point were much keener that the British and Americans investigated major war crimes, as then the SS men responsible a) stood a far higher chance of being found and sentenced, and b) sentenced to death and executed, something that Italy couldn't do, as it had banned the death penalty in 1944.

So when in May 1947 – after two years of investigating – Carlo Galli reportedly still wasn't sure of the name of the exact SS division responsible for the massacre at Monte Sole, this was not entirely surprising. Galli would have worked hard *not* to find out details, especially when one considers that he had physically met the British officer – a Lieutenant Jones – who was carrying out an investigation at the same time on the same events, and obtaining far more useful evidence. Also, the few relevant documents collected by Galli allegedly got lost between Bologna and Rome. These circumstances did not even change after the intervention on 22 February 1947 by the mayor of Marzabotto, who asked Allied Headquarters in Italy that testimony from the town hall be submitted in the trial against Field Marshal Albert Kesselring, which was beginning at that point.

II

THE FIRST WAR CRIMES TRIALS

Principle IV of the Nuremberg Trials, the legal precedent that dealt with the question of 'Superior Orders', had been set in practice by the Americans, when they put Wehrmacht General Anton Dostler in front of a firing squad for ordering the execution of the US soldiers captured during a commando raid in Liguria. The Allies also wanted any war crimes trials they held, including those forthcoming in Italy, to follow other existing laws or conventions or penal codes too, such as the provisions of international law and the Geneva Conventions. The British thus had to prove in Italy that a German commander had been personally responsible for inciting or ordering his men to facilitate breaches of international law.

Lieutenant Colonel P.M. Marjoribanks-Egerton reported in spring 1945 that the master copy of the *British Manual of Military Law* from April 1944 had had an important section annotated. Across the clauses about reprisals and hostage execution, lines had been drawn in red ink, and a new section of paper pasted over it. This was because the British were anticipating forthcoming war crimes trials against the Germans and Japanese. So with a military criminal code already in keeping with the new Nuremberg Principles, the British proceeded.

Hamstrung by the absence of American investigative files, and not knowing what deal had or hadn't been done with Karl Wolff – or others – two further factors then confused their judicial intentions. Firstly, the difficulty in tracking down witnesses in Italy meant that evidence gathering was slow, and the trials could not begin before 1946.

Secondly, London was adamant that it only wanted to bring cases in which it stood a significant chance of success: the chances of obtaining convictions against mid-level or lower-level SS officers was thus non-existent, given the difficulty Italian witnesses had in recognising them or naming them. Neither the British nor the Americans had interviewed any SS NCOs or mid-ranking officers from the 16th SS Division, for the simple reason that they did not know where they were. Lastly, the British did not trust the Italians to carry out war crimes trials correctly. The Italian government accused the British of dragging its heels: Colonel Richard Halse, one of the prosecutors in the trial of Albert Kesselring, went so far as to say that because of its history of twenty-two years of Fascism, followed by what he called its *volte face* surrender to the Allies, it could not be considered as an 'ally' to the British or Americans, merely a co-belligerent.[1] Hopes for continuing and effective justice for war crimes in Italy were then further damned when the British announced in early 1946 that it was not to be British policy to bring war crimes perpetrators to justice in Italy except where the victims were British servicemen. It was small wonder, then, that the British Embassy in Rome, in spring 1946, warned of the possibility of riots and assaults focused against British soldiers and civilians in Italy, a result of significant anti-British feeling among Italians over the failure to prosecute more Germans wanted for war crimes.

The Trials of Albert Kesselring and Max Simon

Kesselring's own trial began in Venice on 10 February 1947. It was immediately adjourned for a week, after the chief defence counsel told the court that he had only been given twelve hours to study the charges against the field marshal. The court then reconvened on 17 February. Dressed in a dark grey tunic and black tie, Kesselring had two British military policemen behind him, and his Wehrmacht and civilian legal briefing and counsel team at his side. As already mentioned, it was an exceptional event – a British military court, putting on a trial of foreigners, in a foreign country, for crimes committed against foreigners. Thus it was presided over by a military officer. Acting Major General Sir Edmund Hakewill-Smith was a fighting soldier who had won the

Military Cross at Ypres on the Western Front in 1918, serving as an officer in the Royal Scots Fusiliers. He then went on to command a division in north-west Europe in 1944 until the end of the war: he was not, however, a lawyer. Pictures of the trial show him sitting under a large British Union Flag, and under him he had four British Army lieutenant colonels. The legal expertise was that of the chief prosecutor, Colonel Richard Halse from the British Army's Legal Corps. He had already prosecuted, and obtained the death penalty in, the two trials in Rome in November 1946 of Luftwaffe General Kurt Mälzer and Wehrmacht General Eberhard von Mackensen. They were the respective military commanders in Rome, subordinate to Kesselring, judged responsible for the reprisal killings of 335 Italian prisoners at the Ardeatine Caves in March 1944. This was also the incident that formed the basis of one of the charges against Kesselring.

Kesselring himself had spent six days at the trials of Mälzer and Von Mackensen, giving testimony in support of them. He had been imprisoned since 1945, firstly in Luxembourg, then for five months in solitary confinement at Nuremberg, and then for a month in Britain at the London Cage in Kensington. Here he was debriefed about his war experiences: in his memoirs he recalls that one of the interrogating officers was Jewish, and that he, Kesselring, warned him that if the Jews continued their policy of revenge against the German nation, they would be sowing what he called the seeds of antisemitism.

There were two principle charges against Kesselring: the first was that he had been involved in the reprisal killings of 335 Italian citizens at the Ardeatine Caves in March 1944. The second was that he 'had encouraged and ordered the forces under his command to kill Italian civilians as reprisals, as a result of which numerous Italian civilians had been killed'.[2]

One of the prosecution's arguments was, curiously, based upon the German Military Code of Justice, which had been in force throughout the Second World War. This said that although an order given by a senior officer to commit a crime abnegated the responsibility of the more junior officer who carried it out, legal action could still be taken against them if they either exceeded their orders or knew they'd been ordered to commit a crime. In fact, this was essentially a mirror of the Principle IV from Nuremberg.

Kesselring's defence didn't invoke the Principle IV from Nuremberg, but explained the chain of communication of orders, arguing that the former field marshal was not responsible for what had happened subsequent to him giving them. There were twenty-one defence witnesses, and only nine for the prosecution, many of whom were absent from the court, but whose testimony was contained in a list of sworn affidavits.

With the first case, concerning the execution of civilian hostages in response to the bombing in Via Rasella, the defence and the prosecution clashed over whether Kesselring only gave orders to his Wehrmacht and SD subordinates – Mälzer, Kappler, Von Mackensen – to execute, as hostages, prisoners who had already been condemned to death in Italian prisons anyway.

The defence said he had, and that this showed that he was executing his orders from Hitler, to kill ten Italians for each German killed in Via Rasella, in the most humane way possible. A second argument from the defence was that once Kesselring had passed on the order to his subordinates in the SD, it was no longer his responsibility as to how these orders were carried out. One senior official at the trial was to say that 'the real defence of the field marshal is that I never executed any order, and that everything was passed along the chain of command, in a message to the SD'.[3]

The court aimed to clarify and attribute responsibility to Kesselring for the killings of civilians carried out by his subordinate officers in direct response to his orders. Kesselring's defence counsel consisted of four German lawyers, headed by Dr Hans Laternser, who, as seen, argued that responsibility for anti-partisan reprisals had been passed to the SS and SD and thus was not in the former field marshal's area of control. When it came to the second set of charges concerning reprisal actions taken against the Italian civilian population, the defence said that the 'anti-bandit' orders given by Kesselring stressed to his men that they should be tough, carry out tough operations, but all within the constraints of the law. The prosecution said simply that the rulings were against the laws of war and had simply encouraged troops under Kesselring's command to commit atrocities.[4]

One of the most important prosecution witness statements were those of Lieutenant Colonel A.P. Scotland, who commanded the

London Cage where Kesselring had been interrogated. Colonel Scotland's testimony stressed that Kesselring's anti-bandit orders, issued in June and July 1944, made it clear they were responsible for guerrilla warfare conducted with the utmost violence even against women and children, giving a green light to all the excesses against civilians carried out by his subordinates. Scotland's evidence went on to argue that Kesselring had had supreme command and control over all anti-partisan operations, even those that Wolff may have authorised himself, as such operations, said Colonel Scotland, could only have been co-ordinated with Kesselring.

The relationship between SS and Wehrmacht was thus collaborative, not subordinate, and thus the Luftwaffe field marshal would have had authority, knowledge of and command and control over anti-partisan operations – and the subsequent killings of civilians – even when Wolff himself may not have been aware of them. In court, when Kesselring proceeded to say that his orders against partisans and civilians were understandable, his guilt, said the prosecution, was established. He blamed Italian partisans for breaking international law, and the Italian Fascists for carrying out massacres. He said that the civilian population in areas controlled by partisans effectively shared the same objectives as them, and therefore those arrested could only be partisans or their leaders. Equating the civilian population with armed resistance fighters – including hundreds of babies and children – saw Kesselring doomed. In his summing up, General Hakewill-Smith said that:

> The charge is a much more serious and grave one, and that is that the field marshal did deliberately and knowingly when he produced the relevant orders, was having them produced in such form that he knew what the results would be, and that he intended by bringing these orders into existence, to bring about these results. The very question that the court wants answered is this, 'Can you shoot, in certain circumstances, a person by way of reprisals?'[5]

Kesselring was found guilty on 6 May, on both charges. He was sentenced to death by firing squad, which was considered more honourable than hanging.

Both the Italians and the British had planned a major trial to take place for the campaign of SS and Wehrmacht reprisals, but this never took place. In Padua between April and June 1947, SS-Brigadeführer Willy Tensfeld, Lieutenant General Eduard Crasemann and SS-Gruppenführer Max Simon of the 16th SS Division were put on trial by the British. Tensfeld was acquitted and Crasemann received a ten-year sentence.

Yet much more controversial was the trial of the SS major general, who arrived in court in Padua in an extraordinary legal position. He had already been sentenced to death by another court four years previously. The Soviet Union had held a war crimes trial in the city of Kharkov between 15 and 18 December 1943. The military tribunal of the Fourth Ukrainian Front had an individual and novel approach: they tried three Germans and a Russian for war crimes – prisoners, physically present in court – committed locally against Russian soldiers, civilians, Jews and Red Army PoWs that the Germans had carried out in the region between October 1941 and August 1943. They also laid accusations and charges against six senior, absent German officers, one of whom was Max Simon, charged with war crimes carried out by his then-division, the SS-Totenkopf. It was the first public war crimes trial in Russia, and each of the defendants present represented a different branch of the German armed forces. The Waffen-SS was represented by one Lieutenant Hans Ritz, a prisoner of war captured in 1943: along with the three other defendants, representing respectively the German Wehrmacht intelligence service, or Abwehr, the German Secret Field Police, or GFP and the locally recruited Kharkov Security Detail. The four men were found guilty of atrocities against the Soviet people and the Russians executed them. As the commanding officer of the SS Totenkopf unit responsible for participation in killings of civilians, soldiers and PoWs, Max Simon was sentenced to death *in absentia*. At Padua, he received the death sentence too, but this was almost instantly commuted to life imprisonment, and then to twenty years in prison. But one of the Waffen-SS's leading war criminals would be pardoned after only seven years. How? And why was he pardoned by the very military and legal establishment that had imprisoned him in the first place: the British? The decision to hand down the death sentence to both Kesselring and Simon caused concern and resentment in the one country where it would have been expected to be welcomed: Great Britain.

The former Luftwaffe field marshal had earned the respect of some of the senior Allied commanders against whom his men had fought in Italy. These included Harold Alexander, who sent a telegram to the new British Prime Minister, Clement Attlee, whose Labour Party had won the General Election in July 1945. Alexander's telegram said that 'as his old opponent on the battlefield, I have no complaints about him. Kesselring and his soldiers fought us hard but clean.' This was a message whose contents could obviously refer to the battles both in Sicily and on the Italian mainland in which the Allies had confronted German troops. Yet as the senior Allied commander in Italy, with access to every single piece of intelligence available, Alexander, of course, could not be unaware of the reprisal actions carried out by the Germans. This was obvious. The massacre at the Ardeatine Caves was just one incident of which Alexander was aware: after all, it had been his message warning German commanders and troops about the consequences of reprisals that had been air-dropped and distributed in such large numbers in late 1944. Was it Kesselring's trial to which he objected, or the imposition of the death penalty?

Lieutenant General Oliver Leese, who had led the 8th Army during Operation Olive as well as the battles to take parts of the Gothic Line, was among those who added their plaudits. Leese used the phrase 'British Victor's Justice' to describe the judicial fate of Kesselring. He described him as 'an excellent soldier who had fought his battles fairly and squarely'.[6] The death penalty had been abolished in Italy in 1944, and many Italians opposed to the former Fascist regime saw it as a legacy of this. The British, however, had expected Italians to welcome the imposition of the death sentence for the German held responsible for the draconian anti-partisan rulings, and the reprisal massacre at the Ardeatine Caves. They were perplexed: weren't these trials meant to be aimed at accommodating and reconciling the Italian public with the Allies, and wasn't muscular post-war justice one of the best ways of doing this?

The Italians thought that the Allies would be harder, faster and more efficient than themselves in providing a tough punishment for German officers such as Kesselring. But on the other side of the legal fence, in London, the thinking was different. If the Italians were not going to impose the death penalty on those who had committed large-scale war crimes against their fellow countrymen, then why should the British? To what extent were they there to punish war criminals on behalf of another country? Italy was not Germany: the country had surrendered in 1943 and a very substantial percentage of its population had welcomed the British, Americans and Commonwealth troops as allies and liberators. The War Office in London issued instructions to Alexander's successor as Commander in Chief of British Forces in the Mediterranean: in late 1946 they told Lieutenant General Sir John Harding that no more death sentences should be imposed, and those that had been should be commuted. So Generals Mälzer and Von Mackensen escaped a firing squad. And so on 4 July 1947, Albert Kesselring's sentence was commuted to life imprisonment.

Much more obtuse and seemingly confusing was that the same lobby was behind the commuting of the death penalty for other senior Axis commanders, even including Max Simon: even to the most militarily sympathetic former soldier who had fought against him, Simon was clearly a mass murderer, even though he professed not to have known what was being done by his subordinate officers in Tuscany or outside Bologna.[7] At his trial in Padua in March 1947, Simon had said that, 'I knew the men who did it [carried out the massacres at Sant'Anna di Stazzema and Marzabotto] were under my command, but I did not know about it until afterwards, and all I can do is to take the responsibility.'[8] So even the most generous-hearted of his supporters – and these were men who had served in combat in Italy and seen the horrific human toll it had taken on the civilian population – could not claim ignorance of the facts of Simon's operational behaviour.

At first, Kesselring was sent to Mestre Prison outside Venice, and he was then moved to Wolfsberg in the province of Carinthia in Austria. In 1947 he was then transferred to Werl Prison in Westphalia. An influential group in Britain lobbied not just for his release from prison, but also for the death sentences handed down to Von Mackensen and Mälzer to be commuted. This group was headed by Lord Maurice

Hankey, who had served in Prime Minister Neville Chamberlain's war office, and during the First World War as secretary of David Lloyd George's war Cabinet. A pacifist, and extremely competent civil servant and then government minister, he underestimated the potency of Fascism between the wars, and he saw how the First World War had left victims in its wake – his younger brother Donald was killed in action on the Somme in 1916. He left the government in 1941, where his last position was as Paymaster General, but remained active and influential on the fringes of lobby politics afterwards. In 1950 his book *Politics, Trials and Errors* was published, in which he put his case against war crimes trials and argued that the British and Americans had no right to put the Germans or the Japanese on trial for crimes they had committed during wartime.[9] Part of his position was based on a firm belief that war crimes trials and the imposition of the death sentence left military commanders like the Germans and the Japanese with less incentive to behave honourably in war, while he also thought that executing war criminals and senior military commanders did nothing for post-war justice, reconciliation or for the millions of victims the two world wars had left behind.

Had the lobbying group opposed to war crimes trials and the death penalty only involved him and like-minded pacifists, it would have had profoundly less influence than it did. What was much more surprising were the other figures who supported his position: the Admiral of the Fleet William Boyle, the historian Basil Liddell Hart, and, of course, Harold Alexander. In Italy the Pope, Pius XII, supported the idea, but this was almost certainly based upon the basic tenets of the Catholic Church rather than diplomatic and political pragmatism. When Churchill regained the position of Prime Minister in 1951, one of his many priorities was the early release of senior German military figures held in custody. The Hankey group, consulting with Churchill, started working on initiatives on how best to see this put into practice – Churchill, a formidable admirer of the military and naval hierarchy, thought it was inappropriate to convict a senior military commander. By the time Kesselring received a life sentence, and Von Mackensen's and Mälzer's sentences had been commuted from the death penalty, there were, of course, still senior German military officers serving prison sentences, mostly in their own country at the judicial hands of the Allies. One of these men, who was to be imprisoned in Italy, was Max Simon, the officer who had commanded the 16th SS Division at Sant'Anna di Stazzema.

It was to come as no surprise that the initiative for early release was to find huge support in Germany, where the release of military prisoners was becoming an enormous political issue. West Germany and NATO were both to be established in 1949, along with the European Defence Community. Konrad Adenauer, the first German Chancellor, saw the principal battle in post-war Europe as that between Christianity and Marxist Communism. An utterly committed European integrationist, he pushed the urgency of German rearmament to the sympathetic Churchill in London and Alcide de Gasperi in Rome – the French objected strongly – saying in a speech in 1949 that one of the prices for Germany's political and economic rapprochement at the heart of the new Europe should be an amnesty law that would see the release from prison and stay of execution of Nazi, and other, German war criminals.[10]

Now that the Cold War was a real and effective political and military dividing line between the Americans, Europeans and the Soviet Union, the rehabilitation of senior German officers and political figures who were in prison was a priority for the Germans. But other parties were thinking about them as well. Churchill was, by summer 1945, so concerned about the threat posed by the Soviet Union that he had, in his dying days as Prime Minister, ordered his senior war planners to prepare an extraordinary contingency plan called Operation Unthinkable.[11]

Churchill was secretly afraid that the Americans could pull out of the territories they had occupied and liberated in countries such as France, Italy and Germany, and divert their forces to the Pacific for the attack on Japan. Secondly, he was deeply concerned that Washington might also withdraw its troops, airmen and sailors from the European continent because of the enormous domestic unpopularity of keeping a massive army in Europe after four long years of war, expensive in both human and material terms. Both actions by the Americans would leave Great Britain vulnerable and exposed. Churchill also didn't trust the Russians not to default on their deals made and promises given at the Yalta Conference. He was in a belligerent, worried and frightened mood, and despite the triumph of victory in Europe, he saw the vast, looming spectre of the Russian threat.

So in May, then June and July 1945 he requested his planners and chiefs of staff to come up with a plan that would see the British Army, Navy and Air Force, accompanied by her allies, make a surprise attack against the centre of the Red Army line around Dresden. One of Operation Unthinkable's aims, as the report said, was to impose upon Russia the will of the United States and the British Empire. The will of these two countries could be defined as a square deal for Poland. It was to be a protracted war after a pre-emptive strike, and yet it would almost certainly see the beginning of the Third World War. The plan was top secret, written by a very small group of senior British officers in the Cabinet War Office who, along with Churchill, numbered about twenty.

The plan was to attack and cripple Russia and its forces before the Red Army could do the same to the Western Allies. And to assist the Allies in this attack, their new war against the Soviet Union, with its massive numerical superiority in men and equipment, one of the requirements of the strategy was the co-opting of up to 100,000 former German servicemen to fight alongside the British, Americans and other forces. The assistance and support of the Americans would be vital. The Russians outnumbered the Western Allies, realistically, three-to-one: yet the superior quality of Allied men, training and equipment offset some of these advantages in manpower and quantity of equipment the Russians held. Forty-seven Allied divisions would go head-to-head with 170 Russian ones. The plan foresaw the possibility that Britain could lose access to Iraqi and Persian Gulf oilfields, and Russia could even ally with Japan. Yugoslavia would be involved, undoubtedly, Austria could be invaded by Russia, and there would be total war in Central Europe, again, within weeks of the conflict having just ended. Yet the operation to cripple the Soviet Union once and for all would lead, saw the report, to total war, which would be long-lasting.

By June, Churchill was ready to review the plan and the options, after the document was signed by some of the men who had prepared it: the British First Sea Lord, Admiral Sir Andrew Cunningham; General Sir Alan Brooke, Chief of the Imperial Staff; and Air Chief Marshal Sir Douglas Evill. Churchill saw it then as a hypothetical contingency.

However, in as much as the potentially devastating plan affected the men of the former German armed forces, it saw ten divisions of them being initially included. These 100,000 German servicemen would be both former Wehrmacht soldiers, and almost certainly those men who had fought in the Waffen-SS. The co-operation of their generals, the men who still held their loyalty, was thus vital for him. Was it conceivable, therefore, that former generals like Max Simon were potentially, and hypothetically, of more use to the Allies outside of prison than in?

In Germany, two leading newspapers and magazines, including the influential *Stern*, ran a series calling for justice for Kesselring and other senior German officers. The British, having been obliged to commute the death sentences they had imposed themselves on defendants like Kesselring, said that the Italians should now take over all war crimes trials for the atrocities committed in their country for those under the rank of general. Kesselring and Mackensen and Mälzer were dealt with, Simon's release from prison, and future pardon, was in hand, and Italy was told it could prosecute minor war criminals. There would be no Italian Nuremberg.

The Americans, meanwhile, had put Wehrmacht General Anton Dostler in front of a firing squad for ordering the execution of US soldiers captured during a commando raid in Liguria; they also tried and shot Heinrich Andergassen and two other Gestapo officers in Pisa in 1946. Max Simon was sentenced to death by the British court in Padua in 1947, which was then commuted to life imprisonment. He was to be pardoned by the British, and released in 1954. Also, by 1947 the British War Crimes Group from Caserta and their personnel were so stretched for resources they even had their vehicles taken away, limiting their ability to carry out investigations. The Group then moved en bloc from Italy to Austria. By mid-February 1948, it was effectively over: no Germans would in future be tried by British military courts for war crimes committed against Italian victims, said a message sent on 19 February from London to the head of the War Crimes Group, South East Europe.

The Italians had wanted to stage their own version of the Nuremberg Trials, what they called '*una piccola Norimberga*', a little Nuremberg. But a number of factors prevented this. Almost all the defendants they wanted for trial were living in Germany or had disappeared, and Germany would not extradite them. The Yugoslav government had imprisoned hundreds of Italians for war crimes committed in Croatia and Slovenia: Italy feared they would be executed, or at best never repatriated, if they put Germans on trial in Italy. The German and Italian governments were concentrating on a policy of mutual rapprochement, economic links and military co-operation in the run-up to the creation of NATO: the Russians were now the enemy.

So, although the Italians took over trials from 1948 onwards, they sentenced only thirteen Germans, including the former Gestapo chief in Rome, Herbert Kappler. The one exception to this rule was the trial of a crucial SS company commander from the 16th Division, Major Walter Reder, who was tried by an Italian court in 1951 for the massacre at Marzabotto. But that was it. The British had concentrated on providing justice by bringing cases against generals only, believing that the Italians themselves would put a substantial number of Germans on trial. The Italians, for their part, thought the British would do this. Both sides had expected the Americans to help more, and the Italians were to feel very strongly let down that the Allied response seemed to have benefited Germany and not them.

The Kesselring Trial Brings Italy and Germany Closer Together

Alcide de Gasperi was the Italian Prime Minister and the founder of the Christian Democracy Party: he had been a committed anti-fascist, serving a prison sentence in 1927, and becoming the last prime minister of the Kingdom of Italy and the first of the new Republic. He was returning from the United States when the verdict against Kesselring was announced, and had just finished forming the latest in a number of Italian coalition governments that were designed, with American, German, British and French encouragement, to sideline the communists and socialists. A strong favourite of the United States, Germany, Britain and the Vatican, he was pro-European, anti-communist, and determined to forge the basis not just of a future

European Union but of a common defence policy that would lead to the establishment of NATO. To this end, he saw the crucial importance of a stable and democratic Germany that could rearm itself in security. Some of his Italian political critics were to say of him that his priorities included German political and economic security much more than Italy's. He allied himself closely with his fellow Christian Democrat in Bonn, Konrad Adenauer, who would become Germany's first post-war chancellor in 1949.

A man who fervently opposed the Nuremberg trials, Adenauer was to say at a Christian Democratic speech in Hanover in 1949 that the 'Waffen-SS were soldiers like every others'. Former SS General Paul Hausser, who had commanded the Liebstandarte Adolf Hitler regiment in Italy during the mass killings on Lake Maggiore and at Boves, used the words as the title of his own book, which sought to redeem the post-war reputation of the Waffen-SS. So between De Gasperi and Adenauer, the two men were very anxious to limit the scope of war crimes trials and investigations in Italy. That Kesselring, Kappler, Von Mackensen, Mälzer, Simon and SS Generals Burger and Tensfeld had been tried was enough for them.

He and the Allies were agreed, however, that one major trial should still be carried out in Italy that covered all of the crimes committed by the 16th SS Panzer Division: as Walter Reder was in custody, and his command and control responsibility was not in doubt, De Gasperi, Churchill, the Germans and the Americans agreed he should be tried. And the other officers and men of the 16th SS? For now, Reder was sufficient. The killers of Sant'Anna di Stazzema were now one more step away from any form of effective justice.

12

Amnesty in the New Italy

In Tuscany, the Mancini, Pieri and Pardini families were still living in Pietrasanta, at the foot of the mountain below Sant'Anna. They were accommodated with other displaced people, sleeping six to a room in semi-destroyed houses. Many of the people around them were survivors of other SS atrocities in Tuscany. When news broke in April 1945 that Mussolini had been captured and killed by Italian partisans, there were two immediate and large-scale reactions in the towns on the Tuscan littoral. Firstly, wild celebration that the Fascist regime was now gone for good. Secondly, instant revenge by local partisans against any Fascist sympathisers or soldiers they could find. The Italian Fascist soldiers who participated in the killings at Sant'Anna had tried to flee northwards with the Germans, but many had remained stuck, in hiding, in Tuscany. As the Second World War ended, the Italian partisans ignited a blowtorch of revenge along the Tuscan coast. The fathers of Enio Mancini and Adele Pardini decided, in early summer 1946, to stay in Pietrasanta. They wanted to help an Italian judicial tribunal that was conducting an independent investigation into some of the massacres in Tuscany: this was being held under the authority of the government in Rome and not the British or American military administrations. But instead, they ran head-on into the first of many obstacles to justice for the massacre carried out in their village.

Palmiro Togliatti was a firmly committed communist, and from 1927 until he died, he was the leader of the Italian Communist Party. He didn't just have close ties with Moscow, he had become a citizen of the Soviet Union in 1930, and admired in his speeches, his actions and his writings what Stalin had achieved: he thought that a similar model of political communism could work in Italy. For four years in the 1930s, he was Italy's representative to the Comintern, the international organisation of national communist parties, and in 1951 Stalin offered him the position of Secretary-General of the Cominform, which had succeeded the Comintern. On paper, there could be no politician in Italy – or wider Europe for that matter – who seemed less likely to please the increasingly conservative centre-right politicians and former military leaders in Italy, Great Britain and Germany. At a time when Churchill had been considering an unprovoked assault on the armed forces of the Soviet Union, and when Italians, Yugoslavs and Russians were embroiled with the British and Americans in the divided, strategic Adriatic port of Trieste, Togliatti should have been international anathema to Western leaders. But Alcide de Gasperi in Italy had chosen him as his deputy prime minister, and with him in government it seemed as though the Italian communists – many of them former partisans – were inside the political fence, looking out, rather than the other way round.

Togliatti had been Minister of Justice in De Gasperi's coalition government for the first year after the war, so when, in 1946, Italy held a referendum that banished forever the Kingdom of Italy, institutionalising its new republican status, a general amnesty was announced negotiated by Italy's former Comintern leader himself. It became known as the 'Togliatti Amnesty'. The deal was simple: both former Fascists and former partisans would either receive a pardon, or reduced sentences for crimes committed during the war. The partisans had often killed Fascist prisoners or civilians, while the Fascists' crimes carried out while they were Germany's allies, and under the authority of the Salo Republic, were legion.

The amnesty went through the country's Parliamentary Assembly in June 1946. Sixty-four Fascist *Camici Neri*, or Blackshirt troopers, who had taken part in the killings around Vinca and Fivizzano in summer 1944 had received life sentences or long terms of imprisonment. Under the new law they were pardoned. Inside Italy's overcrowded prison system, there were about 12,000 Fascists and partisans imprisoned

– more of the former, not surprisingly, after the death of Mussolini and the end of the war. Such was the atmosphere of collective amnesia among the Fascists in the country, both in and out of the prison system, that jokes sprung up about it. Suddenly everybody had been a Christian Democrat or Communist partisan, nobody had *ever* supported Mussolini or the Germans.

One popular joke went: three men in Rome decide to take part in a memory competition in summer 1946; the prize is 20,000 lire, shoes for all your family, and a guaranteed supply of Lucky Strike cigarettes, penicillin and US Army canteen food for a month. (That, in 1946, the latter three items should be among the prizes showed exactly what the priorities were for most Italians in their starving country.) So there is a long line of competitors queuing round the block near the Circus Maximus, and eventually the three men get to the front. The competition is to see who has the best memory, and what they can remember.

'I can recite every name in the Rome phone book from memory,' says the first man, and then proceeds to do so.

'Hmmm, not bad,' say the judges, who tell everybody very loudly that they are, of course, three former partisan leaders.

'I can remember the name of every piazza, street and *vico* [alleyway] in the greater Rome metropolitan area,' says the second man, reciting a mammoth list of names.

'That one's going to be hard to beat,' say the judges.

Then the third man steps forward, and says simply, 'I can remember being a Fascist.'

He's the clear winner, and has approximately thirty seconds to enjoy his prizes before the crowd stone him to death with cobbles.

Italians might have made jokes about it, but in reality, the amnesty was more of a compromise. The Communist Party accepted that some Fascists were going to be let out of prison, and the Christian Democrats agreed that left-wing partisans could be pardoned. The Togliatti Amnesty covered the period leading up to and including 31 July 1945: any crime committed subsequently was punished as normal. Death sentences were reduced to life imprisonment, life to thirty years, while sentences of over five years were reduced by two-thirds. Senior Fascist officials – many of whom had been killed anyway at the end of the war – remained untouched by the amnesty, which rather optimistically wanted to rekindle a spirit of reconciliation in the new Italy.

Of course, it had the opposite effect. The amnesty excluded crimes committed for material gains – such a black market murders – and crimes committed with what was known as excessive cruelty. There were protests about the latter clause, as rape and horrific sexual violence, normally but not always carried out against women, were not included in this clause and could be pardoned. The intricacies of Italian law, however, specified that although sexual violence was pardonable, practices such as pulling teeth or fingernails were not. Under this ruling, one of the Italian Fascist soldiers who had assisted the Gestapo in the Via Tasso prison in Rome, where Colonel Montezemolo had his fingernails removed, could still be imprisoned.

One sweeping clause immediately extinguished any hopes for independent and effective Italian justice for the Italian Fascist soldiers who had participated in the killings at Sant'Anna. It stated that any Italian Fascist soldiers or police officers who were suspected of involvement in any atrocities – such as that at Sant'Anna – that had been led and coerced by the Germans would be subject to an immediate amnesty.

One of these incidents concerned the involvement of Italian Fascist soldiers in the killings committed around Fivizzano and Vinca in August 1944. Colonel Giulio Lodovici was the leader of the Fascist troops who had assisted the Germans in the operations there. He was arrested in 1948, and brought to trial, but was released because of a lack of evidence. Sixty-four different Italians were brought to trial following the massacre and sentenced to life imprisonment or lengthy prison sentences, but under the terms of the Togliatti Amnesty, they were all released and pardoned a short time after. A masked Italian had killed Adele Pardini's mother, one of many women murdered at Sant'Anna di Stazzema. Under the amnesty he had, effectively, just walked free. And now that the Togliatti Amnesty was in place, former partisans in Pietrasanta and the neighbouring villages were that much more reluctant to take revenge on former Fascist soldiers. The Italians who had collaborated with the SS at Sant'Anna had returned home, and lived free, sometimes in the same towns and villages as the families of their victims.

Italian Vice-Commissioner of Police Vito Majorca, a senior police officer from the Tuscan seaside town of Viareggio, had begun an investigation into the killings at Sant'Anna – one in May 1945, and now the second in August 1946. He had carried out interviews with as many as ten of the survivors in Sant'Anna about the presence of Italian soldiers and collaborators there on 12 August 1944. These Italians, he said,[1] were essentially porters or guides, as well as 'participants' in the different actions in which they had accompanied the Germans. Yet the verification of this was considerably difficult. They were used as porters, like Aleramo Garibaldi, who admitted openly what they had done: carried munitions and weapons for the Germans, because if they didn't they would have been shot. Especially in the case of Aleramo, where his wife and children had already been killed. (See Chapter 7.)

Then there were the interpreters that the German military used. The survivor Avio Pieri had said, for instance, that while they were taking him towards Valdicastello after being forced out of his house, he heard one of the soldiers, with a mask over his face, speaking Italian. He remembered him saying to an old woman who was tired of walking that she should sit down, and he said it in a perfect Tuscan dialect. One woman, Nicola Badalucchi, had a brother who had been deported to work in Germany. She found herself in Valdicastello with her family, and discovered that the SS who had taken the column from Valdicastello to Lucca were all Italian SS police. Not just this, but she had met and recognised two of the men in Pietrasanta afterwards, called Francesco Gatti and Egisto Cipriani.

The man who killed Adele Pardini's mother was certainly Italian, she said, with a typical accent in the dialect of Versilia, around Pietrasanta. Survivor Angelo Berretti said that her sisters, who at the time of the killings on the morning of the 12th were walking towards the mill, had arrived at the top of a mountain and heard another group of men. They were telling each other to try harder, to get to the summit. All in fluent Italian.

Marietta Mancini said that her husband Daniele had recognised another soldier who was Italian, among the Germans, who opened fire on him because he'd been recognised. Arnaldo Bartolucci said that he saw a column of men coming from Monte Ornato, and he heard the first one of these men saying to the others in perfect Italian that they should move, *avanti*, *avanti*, they said. Lastly, Ettore Salvatori said too that among the men who took him in a line to be shot, there were several men speaking Italian, three of them, who said that the night before they had been threatened with death by the SS and taken to the German headquarters to work the following day.

On 19 July 1946, the Charge d'Affaires at the American Embassy in Rome composed a telegram. He marked it 'Urgent' and 'Secret' and addressed it to Washington DC, for James F. Byrnes, the American Secretary of State for Foreign Affairs.[2] It was the interpretation of how the new amnesty law would affect relations between the United States and Italy, and particularly, how it would benefit the former:

> We are not of the opinion that general amnesty decree of new Italian Republic (Presidential decree No. 4, June 22) is contrary to interest of US in assuring that Fascists and Fascist institutions are eliminated from Italian political and economic life. Briefly decree which grants amnesty for common crimes within certain limits also grants amnesty for political crimes. Amnesty affecting the first class has been compared with general amnesty granted by President Johnson after Civil War to ex-Confederates since it applies to Italian citizens guilty of collaboration with Germany or rebel Mussolini government etc., after Italian surrender September 8, 1943. The second class covers political crimes committed earlier but excluding crimes committed by persons in important posts of command and for crimes involving serious physical violence or profit. In decree there is also provision for pardon and commutation (as distinct from amnesties of penalties for political offenses excluded from the operation of the general amnesty). Briefly there are: death penalty commuted to life imprisonment, life imprisonment commuted to 30 years, all other sentences of imprisonment over 5 years reduced one-third.

None of the above categories of crimes, or pardoning thereof, affected America's position in Europe. What did was one word – Communism:

Covering letter to draft decree when submitted to President Council
of Ministers referred briefly to established Italian practice of granting
amnesty for common offenses on historic dates such as founding of
republic and said with regard to amnesty for political crimes that 'A
political and social peace is necessary' for Italy and that new republic
must meet this need; that amnesty should not, however, apply to more
serious offenses or in cases where political crimes were committed
by persons in high public, political or military office; that for these
cases, the persons involved must suffer their full punishment; and in
conclusion that at this critical moment of Italian national life, present
amnesty will contribute to creation in country of new atmosphere of
unity and harmony necessary for economic and political rehabilitation of Italy. It is reported that decree was largely drafted by Togliatti,
Communist leader and then Minister of Justice. In any event, draft
decree emanated from Justice while Togliatti was Minister. In letter
dated July 8 to AFHQ on decree, chief commissioner reported that
in his opinion shared by chief legal officer and political advisers there
is nothing in decree which transgresses Moscow declaration on Italy
or long armistice terms.[3]

The irony was that the decree, drafted by the Communist leader
Togliatti himself, could potentially have marginalised the very communists he was seeking to protect. The American government were thus
fully supporting the pardoning of Italian Fascists. The masked killers
from Sant'Anna would go free, and the United States could now be
added to the list of countries, Great Britain and Germany included,
which appeared set on blocking forms of effective justice for those SS
men and Italian Fascists who had committed crimes in Tuscany and in
Emilia-Romagna. Max Simon was now about to be pardoned by the
British. That left only one man still to face justice: Walter Reder. And
although he was to be tried in an Italian court, the long arm of British
intervention was going to reach all the way from London to Bologna.
Reder was almost the only member of the 16th SS Division who was
to appear – and talk – in public, at any time between 1944 and 2007.
His trial was vital.

13

The Trial of Walter Reder

Former SS-Major Walter Reder was handed over to the Italian authorities on 3 May 1948. He had been in prison in Austria, where he was taken after his arrest at his mother's house in Salzburg by the US Military Police on 9 May 1945. The time that it took to bring him to trial was caused by two main factors; the lengthy and problematic investigations carried out, that had resulted in 4,000 pages of documentation that had been gathered. The Italians had also wanted to wait for the completion of the other trials conducted by the British, particularly of Kesselring and Simon. The trial of Reder was thus held in front of an Italian military tribunal in Bologna in September 1951: it formed a sequel not just to the trials of Kesselring and Max Simon, but to efforts made by the Allies to see that effective justice was carried out in Italy for the SS crimes committed in Tuscany and elsewhere in 1943–45. It was a vital sequel to the other two trials in as much as it was carried out by the Italians: here, at last, were Italian prosecutors taking responsibility for investigating and trying war crimes that had taken place in their country. The testimony and evidence in the trial was based to a large extent on material gathered by American and British war crimes investigators, to which the Italians added their own material. Reder was charged with offences alleged to have been committed by him when he was in command of the 16th Reconnaissance unit of the 16th SS Panzergrenadier Division, which in turn formed part of the German units in Italy under the command of Field Marshal Kesselring.

With crowds of hundreds of Italians protesting outside the court house, the one-armed ex-SS officer arrived in court in a two-piece grey pinstripe suit and black tie. In subsequent days he would replace this with an Austrian military-style tunic, with Austrian national emblems on the lapels. The court heard a lengthy description of Reder's character from his defence team: born in Freiwald in 1915, he was a subject of the Austro-Hungarian Empire. He had distinguished himself as a leader of front-line troops, had served in France and then in Russia. He had been wounded at the Battle of Kharkov in March 1943, subsequent to which his left arm had been amputated. He was awarded the Knight's Cross of the Iron Cross for his service in Russia, and in May 1944 was transferred to Italy, fighting in Tuscany. The division to which he belonged was mentioned by Field Marshal Alexander in his report on the operations between 3 September 1943 and 1 July 1944.[1]

In particular, speaking of the fighting at Cecina on 29 June to 1 July 1944, the British commander-in-chief observed, 'The 16th Panzer Division had been brought in here to strengthen the German defence and fought with skill and fanaticism.'

Later, referring to the struggle for Rosignano during the first week in July, Alexander recorded, 'The town was defended by the 16th Panzer Grenadiers against the 34th United States Division with the same stubbornness as they had shown at Cecina.'

Reder's unit, however, was withdrawn from the front line where they were facing these Americans and moved north. A large detachment of Italian partisans known as the Red Star Brigade were positioned on the top of a strategically located plateau south of Bologna, from where they could control road and rail access running north and south to this city. The German front line was to the south, their headquarters in Bologna to the north, and the partisans threatened the access between the two. The action taken by Major Reder's unit against these partisans was the subject of the court proceedings.

The court sat in front of three Italian judges: Reder's defence counsel was made up of both an Italian and an Austrian lawyer. He pleaded not guilty. The first testimony to be presented by the prosecution were the affidavits of three German SS PoWs from, respectively, the 2nd and 5th Companies of Reder's reconnaissance regiment.

On 29 September 1944, they said, the whole Reconnaissance Regiment of the 16th SS Division, the Aufklarungsabteilung, was involved in a reprisal action against Italian civilians because of partisan activities. The action took place, they stated, in the San Martino and La Quercia area, south of Bologna. In this massacre about 800 women and children were killed, they had been told afterwards by their commanding officers.

The principal witness was an SS trooper from the 2nd Company called Willi Kneissl. Subsequent to his testimony, there came that of Julien Legoli. He was described to the court as a young Alsatian university student, who had been conscripted into the SS in May 1943, and transferred to Italy and the 16th SS Division just before the beginning of the operation on Monte Sole. Some days after the operation began – Legoli said it was three – he deserted, and then, after what must have amounted to nearly a month on the run, he surrendered to the Allies on 1 November 1944. His testimony was based upon what he had personally seen while in action with Reder's regiment:

The sergeant positioned the platoon (20 men), around the village and the shooting, using light weapons, lasted for about 10 minutes. The order was given to ceasefire and our soldiers entered the buildings finding them abandoned and without weapons … As we approached one house we heard a scared woman screaming. Our senior corporal, Knappe, approached a window of this house and without looking inside he threw in a hand grenade. Four of us then entered building and we found a dead woman about 50–60 years old. Without any doubt she was killed by the grenade. The entire village was then burnt … Then we were given permission to rest … Our short rest was interrupted by 30 to 40 women and children approaching under escort by three SS soldiers.

They asked the platoon leader, Boehler, what they were supposed to do with them. Our leader said 'they have to be shot'. The women and children were lined up against the wall of the house where the old woman was killed. They tried to run away but they were caught. Boehler ordered the corporal, Pieltner, to execute them with a machine gun. I heard Pieltner whisper an objection to the order. Boehler took out his revolver and threatened Pieltner, who then shot the women and children. This happened around 11–12 am. The corpses were left where they fell.[2]

Meanwhile, SS-Hauptmann Wilfried Segebrecht was the Commander of the 1st Company of the reconnaissance regiment, which was in action on the morning of 29 September.[3] The same version of these events had already been given in the military tribunal trials of Major General Max Simon. The Reder trial, meanwhile, heard about the killing of the commander of the Red Star Brigade, the recuperation of badges and documents, and the confirmation by Italian prisoners that the individual killed was indeed Commander Lupo, Musolesi's nom de guerre. The killings on and around the Monte Sole plateau took place at eighteen different principal locations.

Fourteen people from the Migliori family were killed in the hamlet of Vallego di Sopra ('upper' Vallego), some of whom were refugees who had already fled Bologna. The unit responsible was the Support Regiment of the 16th SS Division. Calisto Migliori told the court:

On the 29th of September, I and my family were still in bed. Suddenly we were woken up by voices in the courtyard and someone beating on the house door. It was my brother and two friends who had come to tell us that the Nazis and Fascists were coming from Creda (down in the valley) and it was possible to hear hand grenades and machine guns being used there. We had woken up in the dark, no electric light and it was still night. We talked about what to do. The common opinion among us was that the adult males needed to hide while the women, the children and the elderly could stay at home. I stayed in the courtyard for a little while and saw them coming in silence. My mother and father, and my wife insisted: 'Run and hide yourself. They won't harm us.'

So I went alone. As I was walking away, my 10-year-old son, Armando, screamed to me: 'Daddy, take me with you! But he was bare footed and in his night clothes and in the dark his mum couldn't find clothes and shoes. So I went alone. The Nazis were already close. They saw me but they didn't say anything. I was quite convinced there was nothing to fear. I thought that if they let me go, then my parents, my wife and children would have been safe. I was almost in the woods when I heard the first shots and the bullets whistled close to me. I hid among the bushes. In the woods I didn't hear shots but I was very confused and the fear for my beloved meant that I didn't think clearly. I wanted to go back home but at the same time terror held me. I remained in the woods all day long and throughout the night. Early the next morning I decided. There was this bright moon, I approached the house. I trembled. In the courtyard I saw something lying on the ground: I knelt and touched the cold body of my father. Near the stable I found my mother, also killed. I lost my mind and I ran away to the woods. Some friends then told me: 'They killed them all.' For twenty-seven days I wandered the woods in the rain and cold. I ate grass and raw chestnuts.[4]

Reder was not slow to present his own writing, too. This is an extract from an essay and memorandum called 'The Partisan War', written by him in 1949:

The methods of combat of these communist partisans were without scruple, full of tricks and regardless of the safety and lives of the civilians living in the area. Every house, even those inhabited by non-combatant civilians, was used as a fortress. Houses where women and children seemed to be living peacefully were also places from where German troops were shot in the back with machine guns. Some women and girls were participating as active armed combatants along the same lines as the Russian female battalions. The fact that during the fighting houses used by the partisans as fortresses and resistance nests were destroyed, and that even the civilians suffered losses and damages, is clear. But it is not the fault of the German troops and their Commanders.[5]

The court was told about one of the eighteen different principal massacres that made up the Monte Sole anti-partisan operation, that took place over the week of Friday, 29 September to 5 October. In and around the two hamlets of San Giovanni di Sotto and San Giovanni di Sopra, fifty-one people were killed, of whom twenty-nine were women and thirteen of them children or teenagers. The two villages lay next to each other on a slope – *di sotto* being the one below, *di sopra* the one above it. The 5th Company of Walter Reder's reconnaissance regiment carried out these killings, which was led by SS-Lieutenant Max Saalfrank.[6] One of the families in San Giovanni di Sotto was called the Fioris:

> In San Giovanni di Sotto at 7.00 in the morning, Mario Fiori saw houses burning in the area. He and his brother-in-law, Gaetano Sandri, ran into the woods and hid in a ditch covered in greenery while the soldiers shot in their direction. All the men of San Giovanni di Sopra ran away while the women and children remained at home.
>
> 'We left them at home,' Gaetano Sandri declared, 'we were convinced that they had nothing to fear'. Gerardo Fiori, brother of Mario, living in San Giovanni di Sopra, saw 'a group of about 30 German soldiers coming towards my home'. He ran into the woods as well and hid in a ditch (…). Soon afterwards the same soldiers reached San Giovanni di Sotto. Malvina Stefanelli saw them arriving while she was in the courtyard: 'When they were close to me I realized that one of them was signalling to me to go away. I went away and went to the closest woods.' Her daughter, after seeing the houses all around burning had already run away with other people and was hiding in a shelter between the two San Giovannis.[7]

The evidence against Walter Reder was damning: his argument that the 728 people killed were all partisans did not sway the prosecution nor the Italian military judges at Bologna. The defence's argument and witness testimony that the 730–760 civilians killed in the seven-day operation were just that, civilians, many of them women and children, did. There was an argument that Reder, because of the overwhelming evidence against him, could only be found guilty, and it was because of this that the Allies had originally handed him over to the Italian judicial system rather than try him themselves. The trial was held in Bologna, which was a traditional political centre of the Italian Communist party, not because of this, but because it was the nearest large town or city to the location – Monte Sole – where the events took place, and thus the local seat of justice. The decision to hand Reder over to the Italians was a compromise designed to make the people of the nation where his crimes were committed feel included in the judicial process. Italy, as has been written, could not execute him, and after the commutation of death sentences in the trials of Kesselring, Mälzer and Von Mackensen, he could not be given the death penalty.

The Italian desire for justice carried out by themselves was to be partially sated by the trial of Walter Reder: the British did not want demonstrations, riots or violence against any of their dozens of military and diplomatic facilities in Italy, and the Italians wanted justice, and a perpetrator. Sant'Anna di Stazzema might have been one of the most notorious and high-profile massacres, but Marzabotto and Monte Sole was the biggest, both in terms of the number of victims and the enormous geographical area over which it was spread. The public attorney in Bologna at the trial was a man called Piero Stellacci; this legal role is known in Italian as a *pubblico ministero*, or public minister, but it means the local government legal arbiter. Having attended the entire trial of Walter Reder, his opinion was as follows:

> Soldiers distinguish themselves from killers because they have a sense of the limits and boundaries of their own actions, because they're honourable. The truth is this: Reder, like others like him, belonged to a military class of people without scruples and without morals. The fact that the Nazis lost the war is simply an occasion for us to be able to judge Reder, and be able to punish him. He'll be condemned not because he's one of the conquered, but because he's a delinquent, because he fought the war with the methods and spirit of a delinquent, an idiot, in the certain belief that he'd never have to account for his actions.[8]

On the opposite side of the coin, one foreign commentator who followed the trial closely was the English historian Frederick John Partington Veale, or F.J.P. Veale. An iconoclast, follower of Oswald Mosley and sometimes revisionist interpreter of historical events, Veale wrote a biography of Lenin, and of Frederick the Great, as well as a history of warfare. He was convinced that war crimes trials were the epitome of the phrase 'Victor's Justice'. Like Lord Hankey, he was firmly opposed to them, and it was no coincidence that Hankey, who as has been written was the influential leader of the group that protested at the death sentence handed down to Kesselring and the three German generals, wrote the forward to one of Veale's books. He was convinced that the trial of Walter Reder was specifically staged for the Italians, and that the operations at Marzabotto had been subject to historical reinterpretation. He also appears to have read conflicting Italian and American and British reports of the trial. Veale's theory is that, despite repeated investigations, neither the British nor the Americans could find enough evidence to link Reder to the Marzabotto killings, so they handed him over to the Italians, who allegedly could. If this were merely the opinions of a respected, though highly biased and politically far-right historian, it would be one matter of contention. But Veale, by extension Lord Hankey, Field Marshal Harold Alexander and other members of the group, were very close to the ear of Winston Churchill. And in Italy, reportedly to Pope Pius XII. Veale commented:

> Accounts of the war crimes trials which followed the Second World War are rendered tedious by the fact that precisely the same issue arose in so many of them. Exact statistics are not available but probably in at least three-quarters of these prosecutions the complaint against the accused was that he had dealt harshly with civilian irregulars and terrorists who had been attacking his troops in the rear. In all these cases there was generally only one issue to be decided: were the victims of the accused inoffensive civilians so unfortunate as to have found themselves in the midst of hostilities or were they really combatants in civilian dress? War crimes tribunals invariably accepted the former contention.
>
> The Italian war crimes tribunal which tried the Italian charges against Major Reder adopted the novel course of accepting both contentions. The gallant but muddle-headed officers who composed this tribunal held as a fact that the inhabitants of a few tiny villages in the mountains south of Marzabotto in which a gang of communist terrorists was surrounded and annihilated by troops some of whom were under the command of Major Reder, were ruthlessly slaughtered

as a reprisal for the atrocities previously committed by this gang of terrorists. At the same time the tribunal held that the inhabitants of these mountain villages had well-earned the Gold Medal for Valour collectively awarded them posthumously 'for heroically resisting the Fascist attack.'

As we have seen, the British military authorities had already brought to trial and convicted Major Reder's commander-in-chief, Field Marshal Kesselring. They had also afterwards disposed of his immediate superior, the divisional commander, General Max Simon, at a war crimes trial at Padua in January 1948 at which he had been sentenced to death and then sent to join Field Marshal Kesselring in Werl Prison. With regard to Major Reder therefore two obvious courses were open to the British military authorities.

If they came to the same conclusion as the American authorities that he had no case to answer, their plain duty was to release him at once. If however they were satisfied that a prima facie case against him had been made out, they could put him on trial before a British military tribunal as they had done with his superior officers, Field Marshal Kesselring and General Max Simon. Neither of these courses were adopted. On the 13th May 1948 Major Reder was handed over by the British military authorities to the Italians so that the latter might try their own charges against him.[9]

On 31 October 1951, Walter Reder was sentenced to life imprisonment, the sole defendant to be imprisoned for the killings and reprisal operations at Marzabotto. He was taken from the Bologna courthouse to the military prison at Gaeta, on the Mediterranean coast between Naples and Rome.

However, SS Major General Max Simon, wanted for war crimes in the Soviet Union, Italy and Germany, would soon be a free man. He was pardoned in 1954 and released from prison.

A photo of survivor Lilliana Mancini in the museum at Sant'Anna di Stazzema. (Museo Storico di ant'Anna di Stazzema)

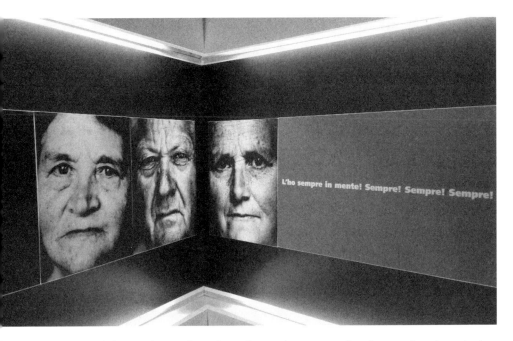

'I have it in my mind always, always, always,' says the caption next to the photos of survivors in the museum at Sant'Anna di Stazzema. (Museo Storico di Sant'Anna di Stazzema)

The Pieri sisters, killed in the massacre on 12 August 1944. (Museo Storico di Sant'Anna di Stazzema)

Adele Pardini is at the bottom right in this photo of her sister's First Holy Communion in Sant'Anna di Stazzema. (Museo Storico di Sant'Anna di Stazzema)

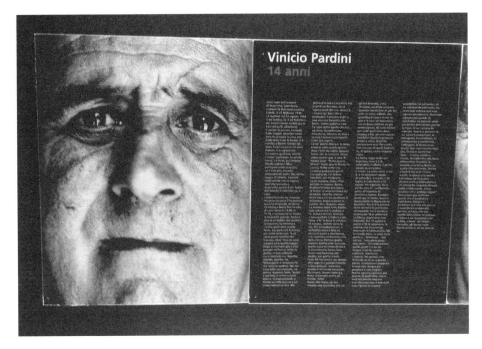

Vinicio Pardini was 14 at the time of the massacre. (Museo Storico di Sant'Anna di Stazzema)

Adele Pardini outside her home in Pietrasanta, October 2019. (Author's Collection)

Tuscan partisans at the liberation of Florence in August 1944. (Istituto Storico della Resistenza Toscana)

Enrico Pieri at the memorial in Sant'Anna di Stazzema. (Author's Collection)

The view from Sant'Anna di Stazzema to the Tyrrhenian Sea, October 2019. (Author's Collection)

The name of each of the hundreds of people killed is inscribed on this memorial stone at Sant'Anna di Stazzema. (Author's Collection)

Enrico Pieri, a survivor of the massacre, talks to Italian schoolchildren in the church at Sant'Anna, October 2019. (Author's Collection)

nio Mancini at his house in Valdicastello, October 2019. (Author's Collection)

A street sign in Pietrasanta remembers 'the fallen of the Gothic Line'. (Author's Collection)

Italian partisans pose with a captured German MG–42 machine gun. (ISREC Imperia)

American troops from the 92nd Infantry Division with a German prisoner, Lucca, Tuscany
September 1944. (ISREC Lucca)

14

SS Men in the New Germany

By the mid-1950s, the Cold War had been in progress for nearly a decade. The Americans, British and Italians were by now facing off Marshal Tito's Yugoslav armed forces, as well as the Russians, across an explosive dividing line running through the city of Trieste, an old, historic and strategically vital port on the Adriatic. For the Allies, Italy's political and military co-operation in holding this line, and Germany's commitment to rearmament, economic growth and becoming part of the new democratic Europe was considered far more important than bringing ex-SS men to justice. The German SS men who were still wanted in Italy – and relatively few were – had by now been amply assisted in disappearing into a new civilian life in Germany by another factor. During the mid-1950s, it was estimated that 77 per cent of the German judges working in war crimes trials, in Germany itself, were themselves former members of the Nazi Party. Germany's priorities were now economic recovery, not denazification, and forging closer allegiances with France and Italy. The number of war crimes trials plummeted.

Konrad Adenauer was the new, first German Chancellor. On the one hand, he was a committed European integrationist, who saw that the future of Germany lay in reunification, strengthening relations with its former enemies, such as France, Great Britain, the United States and other European countries. Italy was included in this. But he had to play a careful hand: he had a domestic electorate who had just come out of one of the most brutal wars Europe had ever seen, and balancing his commitments to them, and the political pragmatism required to take his country forward into a new Europe, was a major challenge. One pressing matter was how he was going to deal with the question of former German soldiers still in custody, and those wanted for war crimes? He was opposed to the process of denazification, and so he proposed introducing an amnesty law that would cover those war criminals and alleged war criminals – i.e. those who had been tried, and those who hadn't – from the SS, SD, Gestapo, Wehrmacht or the Nazi Party.

In an induction speech that he gave on 20 September 1949, he said that he would request, from the Allied High Commissioners, what he called a 'corresponding amnesty' for any sentences given to people in the above five categories.[1] How was he going to keep the entire ex-military and civilian infrastructure of the Third Reich, its supporters and families, on his side? This was millions of people. Adenauer was a canny and consummate political realist, and he was very keenly aware of the threat of resurgent nationalism if his political decisions were, or were seen to, exclude those who less than four years before had been fighting for their country, or supporting a dictatorship. He saw the denazification process as one of his main obstacles. It seemed to still promote and encourage the concept of enmity, of difference, an antagonistic approach that divided not just Germany but the whole of the European continent into victors and losers, the right and the wrong, those for the future or those against it. The spectre of nationalism loomed heavy in the shadows, waiting to pounce again if he got things wrong. He said that denazification would encourage what he called 'extreme nationalism as all those who did or had supported the National Socialist Party would be excluded from normal German life forever'.[2] So the amnesty provisions that came into law directly benefited those who Adenauer wanted to keep onside, including 3,000 former members of the SS, SA, Gestapo and SS who had taken part in deportation operations.[3]

How did this affect the dozen men from the SS and the Gestapo who had returned home from Italy five years before? For Gerhard Sommer, who in 1950 was 29 years old, it meant he was free. Four things had led up to this point: firstly, he had not been indicted in Italy, and neither was any court or inquiry in Italy looking for him. Secondly, he lived in the British zone of occupation, and was not liable to arrest because of his former SS rank Thirdly, his denazification certificate was forged with the help of HIAG, the SS old comrades association. Fourthly, he had committed no crime in the new Germany, and his past was not under scrutiny as he did not hold a government position, rather he worked with his brother-in-law for his father, and was expecting his second child.

Georg Rauch, who had been the adjutant of Anton Galler, had also forged his denazification certificate. Karl Gropler, farming in Wollinn outside Potsdam, had not needed to, and Anton Galler had by now emigrated to Canada. Karl Gesele, meanwhile, was in negotiation both with HIAG and the residents' association of the Spanish seaside town of Denia, outside Valencia.

One factor that would have a major bearing on the safety and security of the former SS men was the increasingly warm relationship between Italy and Germany, which meant that the judicial future of men who had served in the SS and SD and Gestapo in that country was not just an extremely low priority, it was now an embarrassing obstacle to both sides' political economic partnership.

One of the major priorities for the new Chancellor was German rearmament. On 25 June 1950, the Korean War had broken out, and the United States and Great Britain agreed that West Germany had to be rearmed. Why? Partly because they were sitting on the border with the Soviet Union, and they had to be prepared to counter any form of threat from them. In East Germany, their leader, Walter Ulbrich, was saying that both West and East Germany would soon be reunited under communist rule. This pushed Adenauer's administration as far as it was possible towards Britain, France and the United States, so the Germans then agreed to allow their new army to function as part of what was called the multinational European Defence Community, as this was the only way the highly nervous French would agree to German rearmament.

It was not surprising, however, that in a political environment where former members of the SS and Gestapo were being offered an amnesty, and where large parts of the former judiciary, civil service and armed forces of the Third Reich now found themselves at peace, and looking for employment, that former Nazi Party officials would find positions within the new government. But when it emerged that Adenauer's State Secretary and Cabinet chief of staff was a man called Hans Globke, it caused considerable controversy. Not only had he been involved in drafting antisemitic race laws under the Third Reich, he had also served as the chief legal advisor to the Judenreferat, the Office for Jewish Affairs in the Ministry of the Interior that had been headed by Adolf Eichmann. But Adenauer decided to do something that would send a universally understood message to all of the former members of Germany's armed forces who had even the slightest fear that they could be arrested. As part of his integration strategy, Adenauer kept Globke as part of his administration.[4] To men like Gerhard Sommer, Ludwig Goring and Karl Gesele, the message was clear: you have nothing to fear in the new Germany.

By now, in 1950, West German rearmament was becoming a German, and European, priority. The Italians, Germans and French were starting to co-operate on economic, industrial and energy issues such as nuclear power and steel production. Discussions were under way between six European countries to formalise and sign the terms of the European Coal and Steel Community. These were, respectively, France, Germany, the Netherlands, Belgium, Italy and Luxembourg. Sharing and mutually harnessing energy resources and regulating industrial production between the six countries, via a common market, would reduce the material potential of any of these countries to go to war with each other. Rearmament by Germany was also seen as vital, given its geographical proximity to the Soviet Union and its political and economic place in Europe. But Adenauer saw that those former German soldiers who were still in prison comprised a fearsomely large obstacle to this. So he continued pushing the Allies to free them, and especially to release from custody in Spandau Prison in Berlin the so-called 'Spandau Seven'.

These former high-ranking Third Reich officials included Admiral Karl Dönitz, who had been commander of the German Navy, and very briefly indeed, the successor to Adolf Hitler as the head of the German government. Rudolf Hess was the Deputy Führer of the Nazi Party in 1933–41, Albert Speer had been Minister of Armaments and War Production, while Walther Funk had been Reich Minister of Foreign Affairs. Along with Erich Raeder, Konstantin von Neurath and Baldur von Schirach – the latter had been head of the Hitler Youth – these men had either been sentenced to long terms of imprisonment by the Nuremberg Trials, or given life.

The higher echelons of the former Wehrmacht then pushed the envelope forward very dramatically. Four senior ex-generals were among those invited in 1950 by Adenauer to a secret meeting at Himmerod Cistercian monastery in the Rhineland. The subject on the agenda: German rearmament.

The former senior officers and their colleagues had put together a document, the so-called Himmerod Memorandum, which outlined their vision of the new German army. They wanted the Allies to accept this. They also wanted the Allies to make a statement that the Wehrmacht had fought a clean and honourable war. This, they said, was the price of a new military beginning. The Allies were prepared to do this, and so in January 1951 the first Supreme Allied Commander in Europe – the head of the new North Atlantic Treaty Organisation – issued a statement. The great majority of the Wehrmacht had acted honourably, said General Dwight D. Eisenhower.

Adenauer also managed to negotiate with the Americans that, of the roughly 102 German prisoners facing a death sentence in Landsberg Prison, ninety-five had their sentences commuted. Then in 1951, denazification ended under laws passed by the West German parliament, the Bundestag. The British and the Americans had seen it as an obstacle to the creation of the new Germany they wanted; Germans saw its abolition as the key to a new freedom. Especially the former members of the Waffen-SS and Gestapo.

The Tilsit Einsatzkommando Trial in 1958 suddenly changed this. An SS officer and nine other members of an Einsatzkommando group were charged with the killings of 5,106 Lithuanian Jews: all ten men were convicted, with the judges recommending that from that point on, Nazis or SS men who had held positions of command and control responsibility be charged as a matter of priority. Following this, German Chancellor Konrad Adenauer set up what was called the Zentrale Stelle der Landesjustizverwaltungen zur Aufklärung nationalsozialistischer Verbrechen, or Central Office of the State Justice Administrations for the Investigation of National Socialist Crimes, known for short, mercifully, as the Zentralle Stelle. Investigations in Germany suddenly increased. Seeing the way the judicial wind was blowing, officials in the German government whose sympathies still lay with the Nazi Party sought to minimise the fallout against former members of the SS.

How did this affect men such as Gerhard Sommer, living in Germany? Or Karl Gesele, on the run in Spain? Italy had, meanwhile, waived any compensation claims against Germany under the terms of the 1947 Paris Peace Treaties. The effects of this were felt immediately. So when a group of seventeen survivors from Sant'Anna tried to apply for compensation to rebuild their village, they were told by the regional authorities in La Spezia that there wasn't any money available at all. By 1959, Enio Mancini was doing his national service in Bolzano in the Sud Tirol. He returned to Tuscany in 1961, and to Pietrasanta in 1964. He wanted to help rebuild some of the destroyed houses in Sant'Anna di Stazzema, but he had no idea where to start. Justice might have been denied to him and Adele and Enrico, all now in their 20s and 30s, but they wanted their property back.

What was the Italian government going to do about it? What, indeed, were the German government going to do about it? The answer was effectively nothing. In 1961, Germany paid Italy 40 million deutschmarks under the Bilateral Compensation Agreement; for the Italians, European integration and suppression of communist subversion were now two priorities, and the country agreed that none of its citizens would pursue personal compensation claims against any German or against the German state. The agreement contained one other vital clause that would affect the former members of the 16th SS Division now living in freedom in Germany. It specified that no German citizens could ever be extradited to Italy on war crimes charges relating to the Second World War.

The plot then thickened. Both the Italian and German governments were now trying to put the horrific incidents of the war behind them; they realised that it was in both of their mutual interests – though not, of course, in the interest of the victims – if any war crimes prosecutions or related extraditions were immediately halted. Staff at the German foreign ministry in Bonn, their embassy in Rome, and the Italian Chief Prosecutor in Rome had begun an exchange of letters in 1959. They were working out a strategy for dealing with culpability for Germany's crimes committed in Italy. The killings at Sant'Anna, and the massacre at the Ardeatine Caves in Rome in 1944 were still the two most high profile. This strategy involved the Italians at every turn. Herbert Kappler, the Gestapo chief in Rome, had been imprisoned for this massacre in 1948 in Rome, but none of his SS or Gestapo subordinates who carried out the actual shootings had been touched. Correspondence between the Italians and Germans explains why.

Kurt von Tannstein was a foreign ministry official working at the German embassy in Rome in the 1950s: he had joined the Nazi Party in 1933, and worked under Hitler's Foreign Minister Joachim von Ribbentrop. Other German foreign ministry officials, all former Nazis, were in charge of the Kappler case in Bonn. Von Tannstein said at the time that the 'priority was putting the affair to rest, as desired by both the Italian and German sides'.[5]

One Italian diplomat from the ruling Christian Democrat Party said that on the day that the first German criminal was extradited, there would be a wave of protests in countries that were demanding the extradition of Italian criminals. Fearful of damaging good relations with Konrad Adenauer's government – itself a Christian Democratic Union – and reminding Italians of the extent to which communist partisan groups had fought against the Nazis, the Italians decide to bury the evidence. Twelve SS and Gestapo officers were still wanted for the Ardeatine Caves massacre; Italian civilian prosecutors were due to reopen proceedings the following year. Just before they did, the chief public prosecutor in Rome, Massimo Tringali, visited the German Ambassador Manfred Klaiber at his embassy.[6] The German kept notes of the meeting.[7]

Tringali said the Italians had no interest in bringing any German wartime executions in Italy to the public's attention, and so German officials should confirm to his office that none of those accused were still alive, or that they couldn't be found anywhere, or, even if they could, they couldn't be extradited from Germany to Italy. Ambassador Klaiber had been a member of the Nazi Party since 1934, as had his colleague at the foreign ministry in Bonn who was handling the case.

So not surprisingly, the answer that came back from Bonn to Rome was that, indeed, the wanted SS men could not be found. Of course, at least some of these former SS men were alive and at liberty in Germany. A former SS captain who oversaw the execution teams in the Ardeatine Caves was called Carl-Theodar Schutz: he was on the Italians' wanted list. At the time, he was reportedly working for the German intelligence service, the BND. Another SS officer, Kurt Winden, had helped select the victims of the Ardeatine massacre. In 1959, he was working as the head of the in-house legal department at Deutsche Bank in Frankfurt.[8] The Germans were getting away with murder. By the early 1950s, none of the SS killers from the 16th SS Division, bar two – Max Simon and Walter Reder – had been touched.

In 1956 the Italian Foreign Ministry and the Ministry of Defence, under their respective ministers Gaetano Martino and Paolo Taviani, wondered if it was worth continuing any further inquiries or attempts to have arrested, track down or apprehend any former German servicemen or Nazi Party officials who had committed crimes in Italy in 1943–45. How they did it, and why, and what happened, was to remain secret for nearly forty years. In 2003 a large Italian government report would finally tell the story, once the hidden truth had begun to emerge.[9]

So the Italian government in 1960 decided not to file almost any more extradition requests to Germany. They gathered thousands of wartime documents, including some of those of the Allied and Italian war crimes investigators. These included the investigations done by Milton Wexler at Sant'Anna di Stazzema, the British inquiries in and around Pietrasanta, the carefully worded report about dentistry and human remains from Sant'Anna, some sheaves of pages concerning other atrocities in Tuscany and elsewhere in Italy, the two Italian investigations from Sant'Anna, as well as war crimes inquiries from the Balkans and the Aegean and Ionian Sea.

Included was material that had been investigated, collated, reported and interviewed, going back as far as the Italian invasion of Ethiopia. It was quietly locked away in a cupboard in a ministry of defence building at Palazzo Cesi-Gaddi in central Rome. The cupboard was padlocked and then turned to face the wall. Why had this happened? What was there to hide?

15

The Cupboard of Shame

The cupboard stood facing the wall for nearly forty years. Some of the files sat on the shelf next to it. Italian governments changed, as did the country itself. The road from the Second World War to the 1990s had been long and varied, and the country's priorities vis-à-vis its neighbours in NATO and the European Community changed. The April 1948 elections had secured another victory for the Christian Democrats, led by Alcide De Gasperi, who eventually agreed to lead his country towards NATO membership. Italy's Foreign Minister, Count Carlo Sforza, was a major supporter of Western European integration, and saw Italy's inclusion in NATO as part of this: he signed the North Atlantic Treaty in Washington in April 1949. Membership of the Council of Europe followed a month later.

Alcide De Gasperi served as Prime Minister for seven years, and after his death the country's political instability worsened. Between January 1954 and July 1972 there were fifteen different governments, albeit each with a Christian Democrat prime minister. From 1972 onwards, Italian politics was dominated by one of De Gasperi's protégés, Giulio Andreotti, who led a Christian Democrat government seven times.

From the late 1960s until the early 1980s the country was marked by what became known as the Anni di Piombo, or Years of Lead, which referred to the period of vast economic crisis after the 1973 oil prices crash, accompanied by the rise of both extreme left-wing and extreme right-wing terrorism, involving groups such as the Red Brigades. The Years of Lead culminated in the assassination of the Christian Democrat leader Aldo Moro in 1978, and the terrorist bombing of Bologna railway station in 1980, where eighty-five people died. It was the worst security incident in Italy of its type since the Second World War, and the Italian secret service put the blame on a neo-fascist organisation called the NAR, or Armed Revolutionary Nuclei, several members of which were imprisoned afterwards. The war crimes files in the cupboard, meanwhile, remained untouched.

It was only in the 1980s that the country had its first non-Christian Democrat governments, signalling that the terror of communist rule that been a constant since 1945 was diminishing. The British, Americans and the Germans had been quick to support every Christian Democrat government with huge amounts of development funding in order to be able to maintain some political hold over them. Gradually, the economy picked up, largely driven by manufacturing sales abroad, mostly of cars, food and luxury goods: tourism boomed. Italy became the world's fifth largest industrial nation. But then, as a result of the spending policies of the socialist Prime Minister Bettino Craxi, Italian debt rocketed, passing 100 per cent of gross domestic product. And still nobody disturbed the files sitting in the Ministry of Defence building.

Italy and Italians started rebelling in the early 1990s, questioning government, the building blocks of society, and particularly their nation's relationship with three other foreign powers that seemed perpetually to be telling Italy what to do, politically, financially and militarily. These were the United States, Britain and Germany. Italians appreciated the common defence security represented by NATO membership, but hated having to have American nuclear missiles based in the country. Still smarting bitterly at the Second World War – and the absence of justice for war criminals – being told how to behave in terms of monetary policy by Bonn and Berlin was galling in the extreme. The British lectured the Italians about political economic development – in short, the country wanted to define itself, for itself, to itself. It was helped by the fact that between 20 and 40 million foreign tourists visited Italy each year in the years from the 1980s onwards. But in the early 1990s, Italians tired of corruption, political dysfunction and a stumbling economy. Extensive governmental corruption uncovered by the Mani Puliti or 'Clean Hands' investigation meant that people were demanding radical reforms. The Christian Democrats split into different factions, the Communist Party reformed itself as a centre-left democratic party, and then came the advent of self-serving politics, 'the politics of the self', as Silvio Berlusconi's political era was christened. And still the untouched war crimes files slumbered on.

Nothing further was done to investigate what happened at Sant'Anna di Stazzema. Enrico Pieri, Adele Pardini and Enio Mancini grew up, moved abroad, returned to Italy, and waited. They changed from being young adults to grown-ups. Nothing happened. In 1991, Enio Mancini opened a museum in Sant'Anna, dedicated to preserving the memory of the massacre. Parties of Italian and German diplomats and politicians came to visit, each promising that the case would be reopened with the German government. But nothing moved. Until 1994.

In that year, an Italian military prosecutor in charge of the investigation into the participants in the Ardeatine Caves massacre in Rome found stunning new evidence in the locked cupboard in the government ministry in Rome. Military prosecutor Antonino Intelisano was in charge of the investigation for the prosecution against former SS officer Erich Priebke, involved in the Ardeatine Caves massacre. He was looking at evidence in the files held in the Palazzo Cesi-Gaddi, in Via della Acquasparta. He saw the wooden cupboard, turned against the wall, and wondered why it was locked. So he asked the cleaning and maintenance staff. Nobody knew anything. It's been like that for ever, said one. So Intelisano decided to open it.

The war crimes described in the files stretched from the Aegean to the Balkans to Tuscany and to the south of Italy, with 13,000 pages of testimony and depositions in total. The witness statements came from Italian civilians, German PoWs and Allied soldiers, collected as the Allies advanced up Italy in 1944 and came across different towns and villages where the Germans and Italians had committed atrocities. The Italian media immediately nicknamed the cupboard the *armadio della vergogna*, or 'the cupboard of shame'. It also contained extensive witness statements collected by British military investigators and lawyers from Sant'Anna di Stazzema.

These were the files that had been locked away and forgotten for forty years. Apart from these, it also contained the details of other different massacres. They included Marzabotto, the Ardeatine Caves, the killings at San Polo in Tuscany, the massacres of Italian officers on the islands of Leros, Kos, and Karpathos, and a variety of incidents in Yugoslavia. Prosecutors from the Italian military attorney's department and deputies from the parliament immediately convened, and met to decide what to do. Firstly, it appeared an imperative that they should open latter-day investigations into the war crimes committed in their country in the Second World War. But where to start? Secondly, it was an imperative to find out why the contents of the cupboard had been covered up and hidden for so long.

The government set up two boards of inquiry. The first convened in 1999 and was called the Council of the Military Judiciary, made up of a trio of army judges and prosecutors. The second inquiry in 2001 was led by a commission of several different members of parliament. Both decided on the same approach: investigate why the files were there, and then reopen investigations into their contents. Both boards of inquiry came to exactly the same conclusions: the primary reason why the Rome military prosecutor had decided to hide the files was to avoid any potential diplomatic or humanitarian embarrassments with the German Christian Democrat Party in the 1960s, when Italy's priorities were embracing the democratic community of the European Union, the security of NATO, and accessing enormous post-war development funding from the World Bank, the United Nations and the International Monetary Fund. Maintaining good relations with Germany was considered vital, as it was the richest country in Europe and sat on the front line with the Soviet Union.

The second reason, the commissions discovered, that the files had been hidden was because a lot of them contained information about crimes committed by Italians in ex-Yugoslavia, which had been at war in 1991–95, and again, over Kosovo, in 1999. It was feared that Italians could still be put on trial for crimes committed in Yugoslavia, or Albania, or indeed in Eritrea or Ethiopia. There was a third reason, reported the respective commissions, the last of whom was to deliver its report in 2003. This reason was to conceal war crimes whose investigation could reveal that the SS, SD or Gestapo perpetrators had also worked as agents for the governments or armies or intelligence services of Italy, Great Britain or the United States.

Investigative commissions headed up by the chief military prosecutor in Rome and the President of the Italian Parliament's Chamber of Deputies announced in 2001 that investigations would formally resume into those war crimes whose details were in the Palazzo Cesi-Gaddi files. Some limited investigative activity had already begun in the mid-1990s, but it would require governmental authorisation for Italian military prosecutors to open investigations into individuals such as the SS men, who had been in Tuscany in 1944, who were citizens of and resident in a foreign country – Germany – that was also part of the EU and NATO.

Thirty Italian deputies and senators were involved in the writing and collating of the 2003 report, which was eventually presented to the president of the Senate of the Republic, Marcello Pera, in 2006. It ran to 430 pages, and was a chronology of events from 1943 to the end of the 1990s.[1]

By 1944, it said, the Italian Ministry of Foreign Affairs had compiled a list of German war criminals, and France, at this point, was concerned about war crimes carried out by the Italian Fascist military in Corsica. By 1945 a ministerial commission was set up by the Italians, an all-party group headed by liberal politician Aldobrando Medici Tornaquinci, who was a ministerial under-secretary of state. It included an army officer, university rector, academic, former partisan, and a foreign ministry official, among others. At a meeting in May 1945 with the United Nations War Crimes Commission, the Yugoslavian representative said that he was just back from his own country, and that he and his government had proof of war crimes committed by up to 600 Italians. This was one of the foremost worries of the Rome authorities. Another was that the case of the Ardeatine massacre should be tried in Rome, by Italians – the commission had, by this stage, travelled to Allied headquarters at Caserta, where, they said, they were struck by the accuracy of the Allied investigations.

In the July 1945 British report into war crimes and reprisals, the Italians saw one British conclusion: 'the shooting of old men and of women and children and the atrocious cruelty with which it was done are completely indefensible.'[2]

Another comment they noted in the report was written by a British officer:

If these high-ranking officers of the German Army are to be brought speedily to a fair trial, it can be done only by British Courts and the matter is one in which we should interest ourselves since we played a major part in fostering the very partisan warfare which led to the reprisals.[3]

By April 1946, the report said, there was still an ongoing plan to have a big Italian trial in Rome or Milan, especially as by that year the American and British investigators had passed on to the Italians their documentation of inquiries carried out at fifteen places, including Sant'Anna di Stazzema, the monastery at Farneta, and Bardine San Terenzo.

The changing politics of Europe and the Cold War were illustrated by reactions to Kesselring's death sentence – Harold Alexander said he and his men had fought 'hard but fair', and one of Winston Churchill's secretaries was quoted in the British report as saying that when he heard about it, 'Churchill had telephoned to say he was distressed about the Kesselring sentence, and might raise it in the House of Lords.'[4]

By February 1948 the Judge Advocate General's Department in London had told the British War Crimes Group for South Eastern Europe that from then on no more Germans would be tried for crimes committed against Italians – the Americans and British at this point were deciding about handing Walter Reder over to the Italians, so they could put him on trial. By this time too the file on Sant'Anna di Stazzema was still sitting with the Italian military prosecutors' office.

By this point, the report stresses, German rearmament, European integration and the threat posed by the Soviet Union were the order of the day – co-operation between France, Germany and Italy on developing nuclear power were considered more important than the thorny question of extraditing German war criminals. So by autumn 1956 to spring 1957, Minister of Defence Paolo Taviani and Foreign Minister

Gaetano Martino were already planning to conceal the war crimes files, not wanting to compromise the image of Germany's new armed forces as it rebuilt itself.[5] The chief military prosecutor in Rome, Enrico Santacroce, was the one who began to physically implement this plan. And so the files were chosen, placed in the cupboard and locked away.

The most high-priority files in the 'cupboard of shame' were those relating to the massacres at Sant'Anna di Stazzema and at the Ardeatine Caves. In the intervening years of 1960–95 the latter had both achieved iconic status among Italians as a symbol of the failures of international justice to hold strong to the promises of 'Never Again' made at Nuremberg. But for the Italian investigators, their problems were just beginning. They knew that their best chance of obtaining convictions was to concentrate on SS massacres for which nobody had previously been indicted, tried or served time in prison. This counted out the Monte Sole killings, as the indictments of both Walter Reder and Max Simon had focused on the incidents in and around Marzabotto. That left Sant'Anna di Stazzema. The next decision that faced Antonino Intelisano, the chief military prosecutor in Rome, and Laura Boldrini, President of the Chamber of Deputies, was who to appoint to lead the investigation? They needed somebody qualified and determined, who knew Tuscany and its history, and who had a track record of dealing with complex military investigations.

The Chief Military Prosecutor in La Spezia was a highly capable, understated and extremely smart man called Marco De Paolis. Since the discovery of the files in the Palazzo Cesi-Gaddi, De Paolis had been looking at the killings in Tuscany carried out by the 16th SS, and had written a book about the reprisal operation at Sant'Anna di Stazzema.[6] He would lead an investigation to try and put together cases against the killers from Sant'Anna di Stazzema that would hold up and stick in court. And once these cases had come to court, see if they could be used to persuade the Germans to bring their own investigations.

Having begun working on the Sant'Anna case file in the mid-1990s, De Paolis was well aware that any successful investigation would stand or fall on three primary considerations. Firstly, the indictees had obviously to be alive at the time of investigation and trial, and in reasonable health, given that they would be, by definition, in their 80s and 90s.

Secondly, there had to be prima facie evidence that they had not only been at Sant'Anna, but that multiple witnesses could place them there. So instead of looking for individuals who had been part of a unit or sub-unit that had been at Sant'Anna on 12 August 1944, and then working backwards to prove their guilt, why not, he thought, do it in reverse? Find the individuals from the SS who had been there, against whom two or more witnesses could testify, and prove they were part of a wider criminal enterprise? The legal concept of the 'joint criminal enterprise' was then forming the basis of several high-profile international war crimes cases being prepared against politicians, generals and paramilitaries from several countries in the former Yugoslavia. What if, thought De Paolis, we applied the same approach to Tuscany in 1944?

Make Sant'Anna di Stazzema one enormous crime scene, place the guilty SS men there, with witnesses who know whom they are looking for? It had worked at the International Criminal Tribunal for the former Yugoslavia in The Hague. It could work in La Spezia. If he could find the killers who were still alive. Thirdly, if they could be proved to have had some form of command and control responsibility, it would make a successful prosecution much easier.

So De Paolis started his investigation from two novel lines of approach: he knew from experience that if he tried to implement an individual series of investigations against certain men who he knew to have been at Sant'Anna di Stazzema, and prove that they had been culpable of murder, he would be lost. The defendants would simply offer a defence that they had been misidentified, that they had been following superior orders, that they had been elsewhere. No. He needed to make the village and its surroundings one collective crime scene in which the various sub-units of the 16th SS Division had all been intricately involved. And to co-ordinate an investigation between Germany and Italy he needed help from the former. So he approached somebody he knew who had previous experience of such investigations.

Kurt Schrimm was a 55-year-old German prosecutor from Stuttgart, who had, since September 2000, been in charge of the Centrale Stelle, or the Central Office of the State Justice Administrations for the Investigation of National Socialist Crimes. Located in an old prison building in Ludwigsburg, 5 miles north of Stuttgart in

Baden-Württemberg, the yellow stone of the construction nestles into the walls of the town itself, and during the Third Reich's administration it was used to house political prisoners. Now, it is Germany's centralised organisation that co-ordinates the hunt for any remaining Nazi war criminals, run both at the level of the German Federal Government, but also answerable to its sixteen regional administrations and their respective justice ministers.

Schrimm, a silver-haired, determined and capable man, was from Baden-Württemberg itself: he had worked as a Stuttgart public prosecutor since 1982. Murder, disappearances and organised crime were his remit, as well as crimes committed by or against Germans living abroad. It was this competency that was to make him the choice to run a huge war crimes investigative unit. Since many of the killings carried out by the SS, Gestapo, Einsatzkommandos and Wehrmacht had taken place off German soil, investigating them sixty years later required a consummate ability to work as a combination of police officer, lawyer and international diplomat.

As we have seen in earlier chapters, before the foundation of West Germany in 1949, war crimes investigations in Germany, and in the territories conquered or administered by the Third Reich, were the responsibility of the Allied forces – British, American, Russian – who had liberated them and then administered them. These obviously included Germany and Italy. The Ulm Einsatzkommando trial in 1958 of Gestapo, SD and SS officers who had murdered 5,106 Lithuanian Jews, changed that. Konrad Adenauer decided that the Zentralle Stelle should be set up. At first, the office only investigated killings that occurred outside Germany, and against civilians.

Then German law changed in a way that would have a fundamental effect on the operational manner in which the country investigated war crimes. It could now look into crimes committed both inside and outside Germany without any statute of time limitations. Once an investigation had been initiated and suspects identified, and a case prepared, the Central Office then passed – and passes – its files and ongoing investigation over to both federal and regional prosecutors for further action.

Schrimm knew exactly how this worked from personal experience of hunting a former SS officer, living in Germany, who was wanted for crimes committed in Italy. The Central Office investigated all categories of crimes carried out by the Waffen SS and SD, the Gestapo and Wehrmacht, involving crimes that formed part of the Holocaust, in and out of concentration camps, and those – like Sant'Anna di Stazzema – that involved civilians targeted in reprisal operations. It also targeted the state officials who had run the Third Reich's criminal operations. By 2002, when Marco De Paolis was planning his investigation in Italy and Germany, the office had been involved in tracking down and prosecuting 7,000 German war criminals. They had also co-operated with the investigative and law enforcement agencies of Great Britain, France, the United States, Brazil, Italy, Russia and such countries as Canada.

Schrimm was to make the perfect counterpart to Marco De Paolis. His involvement in the case of SS officer Friedrich Engel had shown this. The so-called 'Butcher of Genoa' had executed 246 Italian hostages in 1944 in reprisal for the bombing of a Genoa cinema that had resulted in the deaths of five German sailors. The executions had been carried out above the Turchino tunnel, which overlooks the coast outside the Ligurian city. Schrimm had worked with prosecutors in Hamburg and in Italy, and in 2002, Engel had been brought before a German court and sentenced to seven years in prison after being convicted of fifty-nine counts of murder. The court had then freed him because of his age – he was 91 – and the German court of appeals was then to reverse this judgement, saying that although Engel had ordered the executions, the case of 'criminal murder' had not been proved. No new trial was to be permitted.

This was partly because he had been investigated by German authorities in 1969 but no charges were laid and the case ended in 1970. As Schrimm and De Paolis were in contact about Sant'Anna di Stazzema, the Italians were in the process of requesting that Germany rearrest Engel. An investigative programme from the German state television broadcaster, ARD, had tracked down Engel to his house in the Lockstedt suburb of Hamburg. Yes, he said, he had been partially responsible for killing fifty-nine prisoners, but he had only been following the orders of Adolf Hitler. ARD found him pushing a wheelbarrow in his garden, in the same suburb where he had lived peacefully since the end of the

Second World War. After the war he lived openly in Hamburg. He told them that he had set up a company importing and exporting furniture and travelled to the United States, Europe and Japan, but never went to Italy. He told the Italian newspaper *Corriere della Sera*:

> I am responsible, but only in part for the execution of fifty-nine Italian prisoners of war. For me to have resisted would have been impossible. Imagine, if you can, how you would have resisted the personal wishes of the Führer. Yes, I was involved. I did not oppose it. And I regret it immensely. They died as heroes, as martyrs. They didn't cry; they didn't shout, they didn't ask for pity.[7]

However, he told the newspaper during the interview at his home, he 'rejected' a Turin military court's 1999 conviction of him for another three massacres:

> False, totally false. I do not have a terrible record in Italy. I love its music, its art, its melodic language. I love that city [Genoa] and its people. I would have liked to have known it better, learned its history. I'm sorry, I am truly sorry for the pain I have caused.

Schrimm and De Paolis then started to plan the investigation into the massacre at Sant'Anna di Stazzema. It transpired that the files discovered in the Rome archive had also been dismissed in 1960 by order of the military public prosecutor: in 1996 the Inquiry Commission of the Council of Military Magistrates opened into this decision discovered this to be true, and it was confirmed by the Parliamentary Commission of Inquiry. So from 2001, De Paolis and Schrimm worked on interviewing living witnesses, mostly in Tuscany, and developing a case from the wartime documents. Initial investigations in Germany carried out by a firm of lawyers in Hamburg, and the Zentralle Stelle in Ludwigsburg, revealed that there were at least three former SS officers, fifteen NCOs and one private soldier still alive and living in freedom in Germany who had participated in the killings at Sant'Anna di Stazzema. The lieutenants and sergeants had what is termed 'significant command and control responsibility' at Sant'Anna.

But German prosecutors then hit a brick wall: they were blocked access to any of their suspects' wartime SS records, or current personal details, such as where they lived. The investigators persisted, and discovered the men's whereabouts and wartime records. What the prosecutors and lawyers in Italy and Germany most wanted was at least one former SS man who would be prepared to do the unthinkable: stand up in court and testify against his old colleagues. To their surprise, a former SS man broke ranks and decided to testify. Ludwig Goring had been a Rottenführer, or corporal, in the 16th SS at Sant'Anna di Stazzema on the day of the massacre in August 1944. The Italian and German investigations were now under way, and when Goring was approached by prosecutors and investigators, he surprised them by his decision to give testimony in any forthcoming trials. He confessed to killing twenty women at Sant'Anna. He was the first German in any war crimes investigation to have co-operated fully with Italian magistrates.

When the Italian and German prosecutors finally came for ex-SS Sergeant Alfred Concina, he was living in a retirement home in the town of Rechenberg-Bienenmühle. A small and old Saxon settlement, Rechenberg is filled with half-timbered houses, and the view from the cobbled square in the centre is of the hills, of ski resorts. It sits outside Chemnitz, in east-central Germany, 2 miles away from the mountainous border with the Czech Republic. It was 15 December 2003, and for fifty-eight years the old NCO had not spoken about the incidents that had taken place at Sant'Anna di Stazzema. When the time came, fourteen people were there to see him, arriving in the day room at the retirement home. There was a German prosecutor from Chemnitz, a German lawyer acting as a defence counsel, and Marco De Paolis, the Italian prosecutor from La Spezia. In addition, there were two German police officers from the Regional Crime Office in Baden-Württemberg, two additional Italian policemen, and a senior German superintendent and a commissioner from the Homicide department in Chemnitz. Then two more lawyers, Concina's son-in-law Gerd Schieck, his daughter Brigitte, and an Italian court interpreter.[8] The latter was instructed to carry out an open and frank interview, 'conforming to the truth'. Concina was advised to answer in an equally open and frank manner, and not to confer with the defence lawyer.

The first question to Concina from the Italian prosecutor was simple:

> You are suspected of having taken part on the 12th August 1944 in
> Italy, in the location of Sant'Anna di Stazzema, in an action of the SS
> in a capacity of SS Sergeant and head of a platoon or a squad thereof,
> of the 7th Company [of the 16th SS Division].

His lawyer replied that Concina would not make any statement about
what had happened on 12 August 1944.

'But what was the name of the commander of your company?' asked
De Paolis.

'He was called Sommer,' said the former NCO.

'What did this man called Sommer do, where was he located?'

'I'm sorry, but after sixty years, I don't know.'

'What was the name of Sommer's subordinate?'

'He was called Burmeier and he's dead.'

'How did you receive the orders for the action?'

'I don't know anybody who gave an order. We left and that was
it, enough.'

'Sommer was the commander of the company from the 11th and
then from the 13th onwards?'

'Yes, Sommer was in that period the company commander. For the
12th, I will avail myself of the facility to not reply.'

'How many men were in your squad?'

'In a squad there were ten men, and a platoon was made up of
three squads.'

'Do you know a certain Bartelewski and Gelsenkirchen?'

'The names don't mean anything to me.'

'When did you join the SS?'

'I first arrived in that pile, that heap, in 1944, but to be honest it
wasn't there that I wanted to go. First I was in the air force in ground
crew, and then was transferred to the SS.'

'Do you still have any documents pertaining to this period in question?'

'No, nothing.'

'Do you remember the name of your unit?'

'It was the 16th SS Panzergrenadier Division, the Reichsführer-SS.'

The interview is then marked that, on the advice of the defence lawyer, no requests for proof of evidence were requested by the defence. Concina agreed with the written record of what he had said. He had nothing further to add.

The interview then closed, and the twelve lawyers, prosecutors and police officers left, leaving Concina alone with his relatives. It was just one of a large variety of interviews that De Paolis, and the German prosecutors, were about to carry out with former SS men.

16

THE TRIALS

Marco De Paolis had assembled a team of bilingual legal researchers, and together they worked with their counterparts from the Ludwigsburg War Crimes Commission and the Stuttgart prosecutor's office. They had made a list of ten primary suspects whom they wanted to interview, and then a secondary list of potential suspects. The difficulty was that they were not sure, until they met them, whether these old ex-SS men were even still alive. Until they arrived to see them in person, it was always unsure. For instance, when one of the legal researchers had found the telephone number for Albert Piepenschneider, who had been at Marzabotto with the 16th SS, the resultant phone call did not help to clarify things. No, he's not here, in fact this is not his number, said a woman whom, it transpired, was his wife. The former SS man himself then picked up the phone, and confirmed that it was indeed him, and yes, he had served in the 16th SS Division, but no, he had never been near Marzabotto. De Paolis and the German research team were under no illusions as to what they were up against. In his own words, the investigation 'annoyed them' (the SS men) and he was aware that he was up against harder than average men, men who'd never said sorry, men who had never co-operated.

They used two primary methods to find their suspects. The first was their SS and war records, which were held in two different locations. One was in the State Military Archives in Freiburg, another in the government's separate personnel archives in Berlin. The difficulty was that these gave last-known addresses of the former SS men at the last time their personnel files had been updated. In some cases this had not been done since the mid-1940s, when they arrived back in Germany, were demobilised and then applied for their denazification certificates. Many of the men had obviously moved home since then, and given the age of the suspects – they were all in their 80s and 90s – a number of them were in retirement homes. The list of the ten main suspects to whom they wanted to talk had been taken from witness statements gathered in the course of the British and American investigations carried out between 1944 and 1947, and the Italian carabinieri investigations that had followed them.

SS-Sergeant Werner Bruss, who had joined the SS 'not out of any ideological motives but to get away from a father who was an alcoholic', had been in the 5th Company of the 2nd Battalion of the 35th Regiment, and in 2003 lived in Reinbeck, a suburb of Hamburg. Alfred Concina, who had served under Gerhard Sommer in the 7th Company, was from Oelsnitz in Saxony, and at the time of his first interview by Marco De Paolis was in the Johanna Rau retirement home in Rechenberg-Bienenmühle. Ludwig Goring, who served as a sergeant in the 6th Company, under the command of SS-Hauptsturmführer Anton Galler, lived outside Karlsbad in 2002.

Karl Gropler, the agricultural worker from Wollin, near Potsdam, who had joined the Hitler Youth in 1937 and the SS in 1942, still lived there. Georg Rauch, meanwhile, was the son of the miner from the Ore mountains in Saxony who had joined the Hitler Youth when he was only 12 and was an apprentice baker. He had ended up serving as Anton Galler's adjutant. In 2003, his Bundesarchiv service record listed him as having moved to the town of Rummingen in Baden-Württemberg. Like every citizen in Germany, Rauch had a social security number, and the prosecutor's team in Ludwigsburg could see that he applied for and collected his state pension in Rummingen. The pension approval form also contained his most recent address. Cross-referenced with the German telephone records for 2002, Rauch was pinned down to the town near the French border. German telephone records had not been fully put online by 2001, and so the team from the Central Office in Bavaria were hoping that none of their suspects had moved house since the books were last updated the preceding December. The age of their suspects was an unexpected factor that would help the investigators: older people moved house less, were more dependent on state facilities, and tended to visit hospitals, care homes and clinics more often. They left footprints. As Kurt Schrimm the prosecutor said, these were people for whom they had only started looking from 1995 onwards. The men from the 16th SS had not been investigated before, and after fifty years of freedom assumed they were safe.

Horst Richter was another one of the primary suspects. Wounded three times before he even got to Italy in 1944, he had become a platoon commander in the 5th Company. In 2001 his address, and phone number, were listed at number 14 Weberstrasse, in Krefeld, a satellite town of Düsseldorf. Heinrich Schendel, another ex-sergeant, came from Ortenberg outside Essen, and still lived there. Alfred Schöneberg came from Koblenz, but in 2001 lived outside Düsseldorf. The lead suspect, the man most wanted by the prosecutors in Italy and Germany, was Gerhard Sommer. In 2001 he had not yet moved into a retirement home and still lived in the Hamburg suburb of Lockstedt. So, with the suspects' residential details established, the prosecution team went looking for them.

When the fourteen people came to see Alfred Concina on 15 December 2003, this was by no means an abnormally large number of police officers, lawyers, prosecutors and defence counsel to attend the interview of one suspect: it should be borne in mind that this was the largest collective war crimes hunt ever carried out for former members of the Waffen-SS since the 1950s, and the German governments at both federal and regional level were incredibly cautious and nervous. They knew they had to get it right. Under interview a second time, Alfred Concina remembered that he had been at Sant'Anna and said that it had been a real carnage, a mess, but he said he'd never killed anybody. He then made an inadvertent error. Sommer's orders were orders, he said in the interview. He had only been doing as he was told. Incriminating his former commanding officer, he showed firstly, that he had no idea that his former lieutenant was still alive, and secondly that he was not in touch with him. Sommer was then still living in the Lockstedt suburb of Hamburg. When prosecutors from Ludwigsburg came to interview him, he at first refused to talk to them, and then said that the action at Sant'Anna di Stazzema had been an operation strictly against partisans. Ludwig Goring in Karlsbad admitted that he had been at Sant'Anna, and that he had killed twenty-five women with a machine gun. The memories still haunted him, he said. The Italian and German prosecutors then offered him immunity if he would come and testify in Italy, but at the very last moment before he was due to travel, he changed his mind.

The trial eventually opened on Tuesday, 20 April 2004, in the Tuscan port of La Spezia.[1] The ancient port city sits north of Carrara and Massa and Pietrasanta, but it is part of the same coastal region, and it too had seen its share of killings carried out by the Germans in 1944. The trial was what the survivors, the region of Versilia, and Italy itself had been waiting for since 1944. Every television channel, newspaper and radio station from the country was there, most of them hoping to catch a glimpse of a live German defendant, but that proved impossible. Marco De Paolis balanced the feat of leading the prosecution, questioning survivors, talking to the hundreds of family relatives who had come to see the trial, while simultaneously discussing the situation with the numerous Italian politicians from every party who used the trial to prove their – mostly heartfelt – judicial and humanitarian credentials by giving statements outside the court. There was a strong feeling of Italian unity in the face of some veiled hostility to the Germans. When the German ambassador from Rome decided to visit the court hearings on one day, to demonstrate repentance, and reconciliation, the police security detail from the La Spezia Polizia di Stato warned against, fearing that he could be barracked, insulted and possibly attacked by relatives of the victims.

There were ten defendants: Sommer, Rauch, Concina, Gropler, Richter, Schöneberg, Bruss, Schendel, Sonntag and Goring. All of the former SS men had adamantly refused to come to Italy, and were represented *in absentia* by Italian lawyers. Only one German man attended; a former member of the 16th SS called Adolf Beckert, who had been offered immunity. He was accompanied by his wife. Just after the military tribunal, consisting of three Italian judges, had opened, Beckert broke down in tears and then he immediately started asking for a pardon from one of the nieces of a survivor who was in the gathered audience. Claudia Buratti very politely said thank you to him for coming to Italy, but added that she could not pardon him.

Then, in the opening statement by the prosecution, the court heard from the testimony that had, among others, been given in August and September 1944 to the British, the Italians and the Americans. They then heard interviews given between then and 2003 (and sometimes after) to German and Italian prosecutors. The prosecution read out the background details of each of the accused, their SS career, the summary of the interviews they had given in Germany, and the question of their presence in, and culpability for, the massacre at Sant'Anna di Stazzema. The presentation ran to dozens of pages – lawyers would interrupt, the judges would ask questions, witnesses would try to protest at what was being said – but in those opening days of the trial, the court in La Spezia heard a summary of what these ten men were alleged to have done in the hills above Pietrasanta on an August morning sixty years before. The court listened, Tuscany listened, the survivors and relatives listened, and Italy listened as Marco De Paolis and the prosecution counsel made their opening.[2]

Werner Bruss had been involved in an Einsatzkommando in the Ukraine and Russia. He was promoted to sergeant and transferred to the 5th Company of the 2nd Battalion, with whom he saw service in Hungary. He reiterated in letters sent to the German investigators that he had joined the SS not out of ideology but to get away from his father, who was an alcoholic. He said that he had never been interviewed before about what had happened at Sant'Anna di Stazzema, and that on the day in question he had only heard about the events after twelve midday. He wrote this in a letter that was sent to this future La Spezia tribunal on 10 June 2002, including the fact that on 12 August he was with a group of four to seven men who were told to go and take up a position on a flank on a hill, to prevent the arrival of any partisans. After three hours of this, without having heard any shots, or strange noises, but having only seen a pregnant woman walking with a baby, they were told to return to the old factory where they had spent the preceding night. Only on arriving there, when they asked their colleagues if they should return the civilians to their houses, did he hear from them what had happened. However, the testimony given cannot remotely be taken

as reliable as, even though he claims to have been out on a flank protect-
ing the side of the operation, his claim not to have heard any shots or
strange noises seems impossible, given that everybody else interviewed,
however far away they were, heard repeated amounts of gunfire.[3]

The presence of smoke coming from Sant'Anna alone would have
told him that something had occurred. It is impossible that as an SS
sergeant on this kind of operation he could not have known what was
happening. Anyway, by his own admission, he was on this 'cleaning'
operation to prevent the flight and movement of any partisans. Given
Kesselring's repeated orders, and Bruss' experience on the Eastern
Front, he had to have known what was happening.

Alfred Concina had been interviewed on two occasions, in July and
December 2003. After initially refusing to talk about the events, he had
then confirmed that his commanding officer had been Gerhard Sommer,
that the operation had been a real *grande porcata*, a mess, and that he had
killed civilians and partisans. He remembered that sixty to eighty of
his colleagues had arrived outside the church at about eight o'clock in
the morning. He remembered that an order had been given to kill the
women and children and old people in front of the church, and then to
burn them, using furniture. He recalls a cupboard being used. He said
that orders had been given, but he couldn't recall by whom.

Ludwig Goring was at Sant'Anna di Stazzema: documents taken
from the Bundesarchiv showed him very clearly to have been present
on that day.[4,5] He also admits it in his own interview in March 2003,
in which he said that on the day in question he was carrying an MG
42 machine gun. After a couple of hours, he and his squad of men,
about twenty of them, were told to go down to a group of houses. In
front of one of them was a gathering of perhaps twenty to twenty-
five women, sitting on the ground. There was also his company
commander present, a lieutenant, and another officer whose rank
insignia on his shoulders suggested that he was a lieutenant colonel
in the SS. He was nervous and impatient, and he told him (Goring)
to position the machine gun and to open fire on the women. He had
the only machine gun and the other men had their rifles and sub-
machine guns. He opened fire, and used up an entire cartridge belt.
There was no need to administer any coups de grace. The order was

given to burn all the bodies, and they poured petrol on them. At that moment, however, a child who must have been about 10 years old, on fire, ran away like a blazing human torch.

The officer told two or three men to go after him, without catching him. Goring said that he was completely aware of having shot the women, and knew that civilians were not to be touched, but that he had received orders, and as far as he was concerned, orders were orders. He was also afraid that if he didn't obey orders, he himself would be given a summary position in front of a firing squad. He was aware of having killed twenty to twenty-five people, and was aware of his criminal responsibility.

Karl Gropler was interviewed in person by both Italians and Germans on 13 June 2003. He remembered the bloody mass killings at Kharkov in 1943, when he was a member of an SS unit there. He was shown a picture of Sant'Anna di Stazzema and recalled that an operation had been carried out there. Interviewed for a second time on 22 December 2003, he recalled that there had been certain operations against partisans, but could not remember any specific details.

Georg Rauch, however, as one of the 2nd Battalion's adjutants, had been involved in the planning of the operation, but had not actually participated in it. Rauch himself, however, had what he considered to be a clear alibi. He said in an interview on 11 December 2002 that at the time of the operation it would have been impossible for him to have been at Sant'Anna di Stazzema, because at the time concerned he was recovering in hospital after being wounded in an air strike by the Royal Air Force.

To this effect, in 1946 he had asked another colleague from the SS, whom he had met in Bavaria, to write a testimony on his denazification certificate that he never committed any crimes against humanity. This statement was entered on 2 November 1946, and said that Rauch had been in hospital in Pavia from the beginning of June to the end of August 1944. This information, however, was contradicted by documents found in the German Federal Archive, which on a career record update from October 1944 showed no record of his ever having been wounded. As one of the unit's adjutants, during an operation in which every officer of the battalion was involved, it was inconceivable that he could not have been present during the planning or execution stage, or both.

The first mention of Horst Richter's name had come up when the American investigative commission had interviewed the SS deserter Willi Haase, and under interview all he would admit by 2002 was that he had been in the village of Sant'Anna that day.

Heinrich Schendel said that he couldn't have been at Sant'Anna di Stazzema on 12 August 1944, as he had only arrived with the unit on the 17th, and the day after, the 18th, he had been wounded and transferred to hospital. But this information given in an interview by him on 1 October 2002 to Italian and German investigators was incorrect. In October 1978, applying for his pension, he said on the form that he had in fact arrived with his SS unit on 1 August.

Alfred Schöneberg was 'placed' in Sant'Anna di Stazzema and Pietrasanta on the day of the massacre both by one of his commanding officers, and by Bruno Terigi, the Italian interpreter who had worked for the Wehrmacht before the arrival of the 16th SS.

When Heinrich Sonntag was interviewed on 3 March 2003, he first said that he had never heard of Sant'Anna di Stazzema, and had certainly never been there.

And Gerhard Sommer? His name had first come up in the investigations carried out by Major Milton Wexler in the immediate aftermath of the massacre, where the Americans, in trying to put together a list of some of the SS officers who could have been present, heard his name mentioned by several German prisoners of war. He was also interviewed in July and December 2002 by Italian and German personnel, but said that although he had been in command of a unit in 1944 in Tuscany, the first time that he had heard of the name of Sant'Anna di Stazzema had been in 2002 when a television documentary team from ARD had made a film about it and interviewed him.

He was incredibly reticent under questioning and said he could not remember the name of any of his commanding officers, nor the position he had held in whichever unit it was that he had been in. He said that there had been actions against partisans, but he had never participated in a single one and could not remember any of them. The prosecution said that it was simply inconceivable that an officer such as Sommer could have been unaware of the major actions his unit was taking part in that summer in Tuscany.

Proceedings were under way. The SS had arrived by four different routes, they had substantial weaponry, which included flame-throwers. It was a straightforward fight against partisans, said the opening piece of testimony, drawn from an interview with Gerhard Sommer. Seven different witness statements – read verbatim from 1944 and 1945 – then testified that this was far more than an operation against partisans, it was designed to kill the inhabitants of the village.

'Not so,' argued Alfred Concina in his sworn statement from the retirement home near the Czech border. 'We only wanted to isolate the men, take them away for labour duties, and capture the partisans.'

'Then why machine-gun nearly 120 women, old men and children in front of the church and set them on fire?' asked the prosecution of his defence counsel.

'He wouldn't know,' he said, 'he [Concina] was in the church at the time. He couldn't see what was going on. He's told you that.'

'But it was Lieutenant Sommer who gave the orders to open fire on the women and children outside the church?'

'Lieutenant Sommer gave the orders,' said the defence, reading. 'We just did as we were told, more than anything we didn't want to get attacked by partisans.'

During the trial, the lead prosecutor Marco De Paolis argued that the ten defendants, a lieutenant and nine enlisted men, *chose* – and he emphasised this word – to participate in the killings and were not just following orders.

'Not true,' said Luigi Trucco, the defence lawyer from La Spezia for two of the men – Gropler and Rauch – who argued that the hearing was based on flimsy evidence and that 'justice should not be a vendetta'.

'The verdict is irrelevant,' said survivor Enio Mancini, present in the court, and who as we have seen had been 5 at the time of the killings. 'But we are asking for two things – justice, as far as it is still possible, but also truth. The trial is helping us with that.'[6]

The defence also argued that the exact nature of the participation of the defendants could not be clear, as the chain of command was not clear, that the Hague Convention allowed the use of such measures against guerrillas, and that it could not be proven that any intentional or particular acts of cruelty were involved.

'Shooting a 3-week-old baby and her mother and her sister with a machine gun does not, in your learned opinion, constitute intentional cruelty,' asked one of the prosecuting council?

De Paolis said that the defence's argument that it was all a 'battle against the guerrillas, which may have degenerated somewhat, but which was legitimate nevertheless', was inadmissible. It was Gerhard Sommer who had given the orders, he said, as well as his superior, Anton Galler.

For a year, the ten men from the 16th SS were on trial at the military tribunal in La Spezia. Nine survivors, including Enio Mancini, Enrico Pieri and Adele Pardini, were constantly present in the court room. Hundreds of relatives of the victims would arrive by coach, and court proceedings were broadcast in an old cinema nearby. The town became the focus for international justice, although, as De Paolis said after one particularly long day in court, in the early summer heat, it looked as though justice was going to be denied.

Ludwig Goring's testimony was to prove crucial. Having incriminated himself by confessing to killing twenty-five women with an MG 42 machine gun, he then gave firm and reliable testimony about four of the other defendants. And after a trial lasting nearly a year, the judges withdrew to consider their verdict. On 22 June 2005, Francesco Ufilugelli, Enrico Lussu, and Enrico Zanone announced their sentencing decision:

> In the name of the Italian people, the Military Tribunal of La Spezia pronounces in public audience the sentence against the defendants: condemned to life imprisonment, and ordered to pay costs to relatives of 100,000 euros each.[7]

Dozens of the relatives of survivors wept. The prosecution congratulated each other, but as one member of the prosecution council was to say to the media gathered outside, it was now the turn of Germany to show that it was a civilised, developed and democratic country – it should extradite the defendants or put them on trial in Germany.

Following the trials, the Italian Ministry of Justice and Ministry of Foreign Affairs in Rome issued arrest warrants for all the defendants, filed extradition requests and demanded compensation. The German government refused to act on any of this, despite repeated requests from Rome and Brussels. Despite not being in court, Sommer, Schöneberg, Sonntag and four others lodged an appeal, while the other three accused accepted their sentence. On 21 November 2006, the Court of First Appeal in Rome rejected the defendants' appeal. Those of Sonntag and Schonenberg were non-applicable since both of them had died in 2006; in 2007 an appeals court ruling in Rome confirmed the life sentences against Gerhard Sommer, Gropler and Rauch.

A year after the first trial in La Spezia had finished, another one started, on 13 April 2006. This time seventeen German soldiers from the 16th SS Division, again, *in absentia*, were going on trial for the killings at Marzabotto. One of the defendants, called Albert Piepenschneider, who was 78, was interviewed by the media in front of his house in Germany, but did not understand the questions very well, and laughed. An old red-faced man, on the phone afterwards he admitted to having been in the 16th SS but not at Marzabotto. Another man, Albert Meier, aged 79 from Essen, said he was in bed when called by a journalist and interviewed. Yet a third, a Bavarian farmer called Franz Stockinger, laughed nervously at the accusations, while his wife tried to cover up on the phone that he was present. Another man talked anonymously, not about Marzabotto, but about Sant'Anna di Stazzema. He said it was simple, the action was against partisans, to get the civilians to flee. It was like a hunt; the people were rounded up and then taken together in front of the church, and in front of this building, under a crucifix, they were gathered together and then shot.

One prosecutor from Ludwigsburg then commented that journalists could ask any questions they liked, seemingly without any form of procedure, but this was partially to do with the established practice of many Italian and German journalists, who had appeared to be able to find the suspects in Germany before the prosecution could. 'We just looked in the phone book,' said one television journalist from Hamburg.

In the second trial at La Spezia, all the seventeen defendants were absent, and almost all of the information on them came from the files from the Armadio di Vergogna. The charge was called 'a joint violent endeavour against civilians', and all the accused were, on 13 January 2007, sentenced to life imprisonment. The prosecution had endeavoured to demonstrate that an operation of this scale and of such 'homicidal uniformity' could not have been planned without the active consent of the soldiers of the four companies of the Reconnaissance Regiment of the 16th SS Division.

Antonio Politi was the consultant to the military prosecutor at the trial, and he provided more details by using the same maps that had been drawn by Walter Reder himself prior to the operation. Reder, he said, always claimed to have ordered his men to respond to fire 'without any regard to civil population' and to set fire to those houses where shooting against his soldiers was coming from. Some German soldiers contradicted this version of the facts, claiming that Reder's orders were in fact to 'exterminate the civil population'. The testimonies from survivors supported this second version of the facts, because there had emerged a pattern of very uniform behaviour by all the SS units and platoons engaged in these operations in Tuscany, even when they had not engaged with partisan forces, as at Sant'Anna. 'On the contrary,' said Politi, 'the major part of the massacres took place in locations where there were no partisans.'

This modus operandi perfectly matched the German counter-insurgency doctrine that was in practice at that time. Politi said that, based on the evidence, everything was prepared in advance and what happened was the result of precise orders given before the beginning of the operation. The opposite thesis – that the massacres were reprisals that were ordered after or in anticipation of armed resistance – conflicted with overheard or monitored radio connections between the troops and between their platoons and headquarters. In reality this was how German SS forces operated during counter-insurgency operations.

'The whole population,' said Politi, was considered 'automatically to be actively supporting the partisans' and subject to the consequences of that. This doctrine had been elaborated and trialled on the Eastern Front and they were inspired by the contempt 'inculcated' in the troops towards partisans, and the population in those areas where partisans operated. Such a mentality spread to the Italian front, and especially after the fall of Rome when the Germans army started to withdraw to the north and felt it necessary to protect their lines of communication. In this context the Germans considered women and children as essential helpers of partisans' groups. The massacres had the strategic goal of practising a 'scorched earth policy' in areas where partisan groups were located.[8] Politi's theories were proved by what the former members of the 16th SS said themselves.

Private Theobald Kurz was interviewed about the La Spezia trial, and talked about meetings held after the war by veterans of the 16th SS Panzergrenadier Division, who published a book, referred to previously. It was an attempt to absolve themselves for any responsibility for what happened at Monte Sole. Corporal Wilhelm Kusterer served in the 16th SS' reconnaissance unit responsible for the operation, and in his explanation seems not to be able to make a distinction between 'civilian' and 'partisan':[9]

We had to defend ourselves. By 'we' I mean my unit. It was like this: 12-year-old children were armed and they shot at German soldiers. Thus they were partisans. We defended ourselves and of course during the combat we killed partisans too. In Marzabotto it was just military actions in the context of a war. We were ordered to carry out an operation against the civilian population. By this I mean against the partisans. Their brigade was called Stella Rossa. I can confirm that it was an anti-partisan action against the Stella Rossa group.

17

VOICES OF THE SS

The German lawyer in Hamburg who represents some of the survivors of the Sant'Anna di Stazzema massacre is called Gabriele Heinecke. A human rights attorney, she also works with and on behalf of Enrico Pieri, and the organisation of survivors of Sant'Anna that he heads. She and they have taken on the might not just of the German legal system, but of the country's tortuous relationship with its past. She also represents victims of German war crimes committed in Greece. She has written a book about the massacre at Sant'Anna and in 2016 was made an honorary citizen of the small Tuscan village.[1] One of the focuses of her work on the Sant'Anna massacre was and is the case of ex-SS Lieutenant Gerhard Sommer. Along with the nine other defendants, he was sentenced to life imprisonment at the trials in La Spezia. But subsequently he lived in freedom in Germany and was not extradited back to Italy to serve his sentence.

German prosecutors in Baden-Württemberg – of which Stuttgart is the capital – had begun their own investigations in 2002 against seventeen former SS soldiers, but these were halted in 2012 by Stuttgart prosecutor Bernhard Haussler because of an alleged lack of evidence. Eight of the unnamed SS suspects were reportedly still alive at this point, but Haussler could not find sufficient evidence to find them guilty of murder or accessory to murder – the only two charges on which Germany's Statute of Limitations had not, in the case of the suspects, run out.

'Belonging to a Waffen-SS unit that was deployed to Sant'Anna di Stazzema cannot replace the need for individual guilt,' said Haussler in a statement. 'Rather, for every defendant it must be proven that he took part in the massacre, and in which form.'[2]

The statement from Stuttgart, on behalf of its chief prosecutor Claudia Krath, said that the prosecutorial teams had tried to do everything possible but could not find enough proof, as they had not been able to ascertain with any degree of certainty the number of victims, as the village (Sant'Anna di Stazzema) was full of refugees who'd come from elsewhere, and for each single action that took place during the massacre there had to be a single accusation against that (particular) person and this hadn't been possible. It had also not been possible to verify that it had been an act of reprisal and that it had been co-ordinated, said Krath's office, as the original plan could have been to single out the partisans and then deport the men for work in Germany, and that things went wrong only after these first decisions had been taken. The prosecutor underlined, again, that merely belonging to a unit of the SS that had been deployed to Sant'Anna did not imply participation in the massacre. Krath also said that her and her team 'had done everything possible, and felt the weight of their responsibility'.[3]

Heinecke accused these prosecutors of delaying proceedings, and said that the state prosecutor in Stuttgart had for ten years resisted the rulings of the La Spezia court:[4]

> In 2007, I asked again to look at the documents, and only after my threat to request a forced procedure before the court did Prosecutor Haussler let me know I could go to Stuttgart … I spent a day's work in a draughty corridor of the Public Prosecutor's Office in Stuttgart. They told me there were no free rooms, provided me with a table and a ramshackle chair between the coffee machine and the stationary cupboard. The material was in a chaotic state … not in chronological order, impossible to find your way. This method of hindering my work was constantly practiced until the Stuttgart investigation was shelved on 26 September 2012.[5]

Yet German penal law prohibited the extradition of a suspect like Gerhard Sommer, who, even though sentenced in Italy, could not be transferred back there without his own consent.

'He can't talk his way out of the massacres, saying he wasn't directly involved,' Heinecke said of Sommer. 'He was the one who autonomously gave the order, or passed it down the chain of command.'[6]

Professor Carlo Gentile from the University of Cologne, meanwhile, is a leading expert in the study of German war crimes committed in Italy in the Second World, and author of several books and academic papers on the topic.[7] He has also appeared as an expert witness in war crimes trials. He said that prior to 2013, there were also flaws in previous investigations carried out by German prosecutors. However, after the decision by the Stuttgart prosecutor's office in 2012, Heinecke went back to a Federal German court to overturn the decision of these officials from Baden-Württemberg and was successful. There were now new grounds to bring Gerhard Sommer to trial.

For his part, Gerhard Sommer had remained resolutely unrepentant, since long before the La Spezia trial. In 2004, he had told a German television crew (see p. 239) that he had 'an absolutely clear conscience'. In 2007, an Italian government report said in its findings that the wartime documents about Sant'Anna, found in the so-called cupboard of shame, were definitely concealed by the chief public prosecutor in Rome in the early 1960s to avoid damaging relations with Germany. This was then followed by another damning report, this time from the Rosenburg Project in Bonn, an investigative initiative run by a former justice minister, that examined the history of the German Ministry of Justice itself. Seventy-seven per cent of senior Justice Ministry officials in 1957 were former members of the Nazi party, the project found; while from 1949 to 1974, 55 per cent of the entire upper echelons of the ministry were former Nazis.

'During the early post-war years, the Federal Minister of Justice was riddled with lawyers who – in their capacity as officials in the Reich Ministry of Justice and other agencies – had served as willing accomplices of the Nazi regime,' said Heiko Maas, Federal Minister of Justice and Consumer Protection, in the forward to the report, researched and written by an independent academic commission from January 2012 onwards.[8]

The legal concept of collective and individual guilt for a single action, had, curiously, been given new hope in the trials that took place in the aftermath of 9/11. One of the al-Qaeda cell based in Hamburg,

Mounir el Motassadeq, had been sentenced by a German court to fifteen years in prison. He was convicted of 246 counts of being an accessory to murder, one for every passenger aboard the four flights that were hijacked on 11 September. The court ruling had major implications for prosecuting Nazis. If Motassadeq was guilty of aiding and abetting murder, then so too, by legal extension, were people like those SS men who had in any way facilitated mass murder in Italy. Lawyers at the Central Office in Ludwigsburg had got to work, and this was believed to be the background to the Stuttgart prosecutor's operations. The Central Office said there was enough evidence against the wanted men from Sant'Anna for them to be tried and convicted in Germany of 346 counts of murder committed with unusual cruelty.

It was against this background of activity that Enio Mancini travelled to Hamburg in 2008, to try and confront any of the ex-SS men who were still alive.[9] He was encouraged to do so by a new and determined chief prosecutor in Hamburg called Lutz von Selle. But he says he were blocked access to a nursing home where ex-Lieutenant Gerhard Sommer was then living. However, unbeknown to him, Stuttgart had opened its own investigation into seventeen unnamed former SS soldiers – eight of whom were still alive – but kept the details of it completely covert. Gabriele Heinecke and Marco De Paolis claim not to have known the details of it. And it was in 2012 that the German prosecutors in Stuttgart decided to suddenly close it, out of the blue.

The mayor of Sant'Anna di Stazzema then was Michele Silicani, a survivor of the massacre. He was 10 in 1944. He said the decision by the German prosecutors was scandalous, and that he would bring as much pressure as possible on Italy's Minister of Justice to lobby Germany to reopen the case. The Germans' primary reason for shelving the case was, they said, that the testimony of Italian victims and survivors, collected by the Allies, was unreliable. However, justice and human rights officials in Germany and Italy now strongly believed that the evidence against the living and dead SS men was overwhelming; and successful prosecutions in the case would set a legal precedent for Germany, under which it would be obliged to investigate and bring charges against every single former SS, SD, Gestapo and Wehrmacht man or woman in Germany, alleged to have committed war crimes, who was still alive.

So it seemed that by the end of 2012, hopes were fading for any form of prosecutions that might result in imprisonment for the SS men who had been at Sant'Anna di Stazzema. The Italian foreign minister, Giulio Sant'Agata, told the German foreign minister Guido Westerwelle that Italy would still continue to push Germany either to extradite, or put on trial in Germany, war criminals sentenced *in absentia* in Italy. But by 2013, the Germans' only response was to agree to fund a joint German–Italian project, a study of German war crimes committed in Italy in the Second World War. This was published as *The Atlas of Nazi and Fascist Massacres in Italy*, and when the investigation finished, it revealed that the number of Italian civilians killed by Germans and Italian Fascists was around 22,000, double previous estimates.[10]

However, while the project was ongoing, Gabriele Heinecke had, as mentioned on the previous page, managed to get a federal prosecutor to go over the heads of the Stuttgart office. The Sant'Anna case, not surprisingly, had stark parallels with other war crimes proceedings that had taken place in Germany in the preceding fifteen years.

When former SS-Hauptsturmführer Friedrich Engel, who then lived in Hamburg, was sentenced to life imprisonment *in absentia*, in 1999, by a court in Turin on 246 counts of murder, the Hamburg District Court had subsequently sentenced 'the Butcher of Genoa' to only seven years in prison. He was found guilty and convicted on the charges of executing fifty-nine Italian hostages at the Turchino Pass in May 1944. But the German Federal Court of Justice overturned the judgement of the Hamburg Regional Court on 17 June 2004, ruling out a retrial. The Federal Court had ruled that shooting hostages had been a legitimate reprisal for the attack on the Odeon Cinema in Genoa – in which five German sailors were killed – and thus the shootings could not be classified as murder. It could be classified only as a voluntary manslaughter, as there had not been cruel and unusual circumstances to the killings. Because this is subject to a statute of limitations in Germany, the shootings could not be the subject of a murder charge. The fact that Engel was then 89 also meant that the proceedings could not be carried out. This case had similar ramifications for Sant'Anna di Stazzema.

When, in 2002, the German investigation from Stuttgart into the killings at Sant'Anna had originally begun, prosecutors and investigators were keenly aware that the provisions of the statute of limitations could pose a formidable obstacle. The proceedings were terminated at the end of 2012 with an announcement from the Stuttgart prosecutor's office that they were closing the investigation. As already written, Gabriele Heinecke then managed to override this decision – but there was another obstacle. On 5 August 2014, the Higher Regional Court in Karlsruhe overturned the decision to use the Stuttgart public prosecutor in the ongoing case against Gerhard Sommer.

Eventually Gabriele Heinecke closed the investigation, after a surprise regional court ruling that Sommer clearly suffered from dementia, and would thus be unfit to stand trial. He would have been likely to have been charged with up to 342 cases of premeditated murder with 'special and unusual cruelty'. How had this happened? How had Gerhard Sommer got away with murder?

The road from Sant'Anna di Stazzema to the closure of the investigative case against him was marked by very few moments when he emerged from obscurity into the public eye. By 2012, he was the world's highest-ranking, most-wanted living SS war criminal; that he had also been convicted of mass murder and sentenced to life imprisonment *in absentia* made his case even more exceptional. A father of three children, and the co-manager of a machine export company, he never uttered a word of contrition or apology for his actions in Italy in 1944. When one of the investigative programmes of ARD, the German public service broadcasting group, had interviewed him in 2004, he was adamant: he had a clear conscience.

On 11 April of that year, a television crew from the *Contrasts* programme met Sommer in front of the house where he was living in a suburb of Hamburg. 'We'd like to ask you about something that happened a long time ago, in the time of the 16th SS Panzergrenadier Division,' they asked. 'You were in this division?'

'That was correct,' answered Sommer, also confirming that he had been a company leader in the 2nd Battalion of the unit. Asking how the television crew knew about this, he was told that it was on the basis of documents extracted from the archives of the Wehrmacht and the SS.

'For me,' said Sommer, standing in the driveway of his house, shovelling away the snow, 'this time is done. I have no reproaches, I have an absolutely clear conscience, and I don't want to know anything about this now.'[11]

When Gabriele Heinecke was asked by the Martyrs Association of Sant'Anna di Stazzema to file a counterclaim against Sommer, following the Stuttgart ruling in 2012, the prosecutor's office in that German city refused her access to the files of evidence that they had assembled against the accused. To show them to her, said the prosecutor, would be prejudicial to him.

Since the beginning of 2005, and after the death of his wife, Sommer had been living in the CURA Old People's Home in a suburb outside Hamburg. The retirement home in Volksdorf is about 6 miles northeast of the city centre of Hamburg. The affluent suburb is set in the middle of some woods, and the home is called Haus Lerchenberg. Sommer then lived in a two-room apartment on the first floor; his wife, to whom he had been married for nearly sixty years, died in 2002. He had three daughters, the eldest of whom was then 62, while the third one looked after her father.

On 12 August 2005, the sixty-first anniversary of the Sant'Anna Massacre, protesters from an anti-fascist organisation distributed leaflets at Volksdorf train station, and attached their statement to the garden fence in front of the retirement home: on it were the names of 434 of the victims of the killings. The message read:

> On August 12th 1944, 300 members of the 16th SS Panzergrenadier Division (arrived) in the Italian mountain village of Sant'Anna di Stazzema and killed 560 people, including 120 children. Among the killers was also the one in the CURA senior housing complex in Hamburg Volksdorf, Gerhard Sommer. He was convicted as a war criminal in Italy.

Then in April 2007, a German newspaper journalist from Hamburg decided to visit the CURA home, to interview the manager and other residents, and see if she could talk to Gerhard Sommer as well. Friederike Gräff worked as the arts editor for TAZ-Nord, the Hamburg and northern German affiliate of *Tageszeitung*, or 'Daily Newspaper'. Run by its employees and owned by a co-operative, the paper was left-leaning and had been founded in Berlin in 1978.[12] Her article stands out, partly because she was one of the few journalists to see Sommer alive in the last decade of his life, and also because the article – excerpted, translated and footnoted below – was one of few that described the living conditions and surroundings of a man who was at the time one of the world's most-wanted living Nazi war criminals. It also revealed the extent to which Sommer was not the only one whose wartime past still evoked memories. His subsequent whereabouts were not a secret to local residents, or residents of the retirement home. By early 2013 Sommer's residence in Volksdorf was even to be listed on Wikipedia.

In the aftermath of the broadcast of the ARD documentary in 2004, and when another German newspaper reported that Gerhard Sommer was living in the CURA old people's home in Volksdorf, he had gone to see the manager, a German man called Achim Tobola. Gräff interviewed him:

The day a newspaper wrote that he was living as a war criminal unmolested in a nursing home in Hamburg-Volksdorf, Gerhard Sommer went to see the house manager. 'So I don't fall off my chair,' says Achim Tobola. They went to the breakfast room together, Sommer was nervous and gave him the article. 'I'll read it first,' said Tobola. Then he called the lawyer for CURA, the company that runs the retirement home, and asked what to do in such a case. What do you do if a resident, as a former SS man, is sentenced to life imprisonment for the murder of 560 people in Italy – and continues to live with you under one roof?

What do you do when demonstrators gather in front of the house and residents write letters requesting [that] Sommer moves out while the others have coffee with him? It is as if an experimental set-up had been set up in Haus Lerchenberg: how do the old people react when the Third Reich meets them again, and everyone can drop by and see the result?

Gräff then wrote that the manager said there were three clear groups in the home: those who ignored Sommer's past and socialised with him, those who were silently neutral, and a third group who refused to talk to him at all. This latter group, discovered the journalist, included an old woman called Elli Kortenhaus, who had been a teacher during the war and wanted Sommer moved out of the home. 'Why?' wondered Gräff.

Kortenhaus was 83 years old in 2007, said the *TAZ* journalist in her article. An energetic and combative woman who, to the care home's directors, seemed much younger. There always seemed to be something she was holding back, they would say, something she'd seen that she couldn't quite talk about. She wrote a letter to the management asking that Sommer be moved out. The management invited her to talk to the board of CURA, the association that runs a string of nursing homes across northern Germany. So Elli, Achim Tobola, Gerhard Sommer and his daughter had a meeting. Sommer said little, but his daughter assured both Elli and Tobola that her father had never been to Italy in his life.

'Rubbish,' said Kortenhaus, 'there's a film made about German war criminals in Italy, and I have seen it.' It was called *Angel of Death: On the Trail of German War Criminals in Italy*, and in it she had recognised Sommer.

It was the same documentary film made by ARD and broadcast in 2004. One scene shows Sommer, a white-haired man in a woollen hat who is shovelling snow in front of his driveway in Hamburg. I have no reproaches to make, he says, asking the journalists to leave his driveway.

Kortenhaus said to Gräff that she had got to know the SS and knew exactly what 'kind of criminals they were'. She had had a job as a teacher in the war, with the family of a man who was in charge of what she euphemistically called 'a labour camp'. With his wife, she did her best to help the camp inmates, introducing sewing and carpentry classes. She never forgot the SS.

Nor did another resident of the home, called Gundula Bernhard, aged 79, whose husband was a Jew. His mother died in Auschwitz, and his father in turn starved to death with two other brothers in a ghetto in Budapest. Her husband, she says, was in a devastatingly morbid mood all of his life. All of this, she said, coloured her attitude towards Sommer. Bernhard told Gräff that one other old woman that she knew, who had also attended a showing of the ARD film, had also been reminded of her past by the documentary:

In 1986, when she was 60 years old, she went to a pastor because there was one thing that did not leave her in peace: that at the age of 17 she had sworn an oath on the Nazis at the Reich Labour Service. 'They say everyone did it, but it doesn't matter,' she says. The pastor told her that she shouldn't stop at this guilt. That she could do something now. Now, after seeing the film about the SS men in Italy, she says she would like to 'speak to the one who feels guilty'. She would like to tell him what the pastor told her.

The man she was referring to in the documentary was Ludwig Goring, the only one of the defendants to have been charged in Germany.

Gräff was about to leave the home after talking to Kortenhaus, until she saw the very man that she – and thousands of others, Italian survivors included – wanted to see. Gräff wrote:

On leaving the Lerchenberg house, when Elli Kortenhaus wants to accompany [Gräff] to the exit, she suddenly stops at the gallery: 'He's sitting there,' she says, pointing to a suntanned man in a shirt who is talking to an old lady sitting at a table.

He hadn't replied to the letter asking him to speak. Instead, his daughter called and said that her father was now 86 years old and unable to do so. They would have had bad experiences with newspapers. 'He has a lot of friendships,' she says. 'But there are also people – which I can understand – who have different experiences during this time, Jewish fellow citizens who have different experiences.'

The daughter sounds friendly on the phone, [but] actually she doesn't want to say more, but then she says that her father's past is not an issue in Haus Lerchenberg. People lived their lives, they didn't talk to each other much. One quickly asks how she lives with all this. 'It affects our generation,' she says. 'It cannot be helped. You have to deal with that for a long time. 'And then, at the end: I can only tell you: my father is innocent, so I can live with it.'

There Graff's newspaper report ended.[13]

By the time of the end of the Stuttgart prosecutor's investigation, as Gabriele Heinecke attempted to launch a new set of court proceedings, the crucial question for the Hamburg prosecutor was whether it was possible to meet and discuss things with the 93-year-old former SS officer.[14] On 26 October 2013, the Forensic Medical Service in Hamburg determined that Sommer was unable to negotiate due to intellectual restrictions. But, they said, another review of Sommer's health was expected in 2014. Accordingly, said Heinecke, Sommer could be expected to participate in a court process, he was mentally resilient, his thinking was not impaired. Of course, she said, a trial was a huge burden for a 93-year-old, but if certain precautions were taken, it would be possible to minimise the risk of damage to his health.

'Current reports,' she said euphemistically, 'assume that negotiation skills are slightly restricted.'[15]

There were also many, she said, who considered the German judicial investigation to be a disgrace.[16] When the Italian military prosecutor Marco De Paolis made non-stop requests for assistance from the witnesses and suspects to the German investigative authorities, the Central Office of the State Judicial Authorities for the Investigation of National Socialist Crimes then awarded the 2002 trial investigation to the Stuttgart public prosecutor. The reason, reportedly, was because most of the fourteen accused, and also the oldest of them, came from Baden-Württemberg. And then after ten years, Chief Prosecutor Bernhard Haussler stopped the investigation on 26 September 2012 due to a lack of evidence and definitive proof. During the decade of investigation, it was not possible to provide individual proof of guilt for the murders at Sant'Anna di Stazzema. In the meantime, it took Heinecke a year to gain access to the Stuttgart files. She had never, she said, experienced anything like that before.

By June 2013, and as the Hamburg lawyer for Enrico Pieri, she had applied to the Higher Regional Court in Karlsruhe for enforcement of the indictment, wanting a trial to begin in Germany after the collapse of the Stuttgart process. By 2013 only four of the accused were still alive. Against three of them, ruled the Karlsruhe prosecutor, the application for a trial was inadmissible. One had disappeared, one was in hospital and the third had already given self-incriminating and conflicting evidence so was disbarred from giving testimony or appearing in court. The fourth was Gerhard Sommer. But by this time the 93-year-old former SS officer had been consulting, and been consulted by, psychologists and experts in geriatric health. As a result of these consultations, in the fourth week of May 2015 it was ruled that he had advanced dementia. On 29 May, Hamburg prosecutors said that he would not have been able to address the court, and so would simply have been a 'passive object of public prosecution'.[17] The prosecutors said that if the former SS man had been deemed fit to stand trial, he would 'with high probability have been charged with 342 cases of murder, committed cruelly and on base motives'.[18]

'The military court in La Spezia found that he was responsible as the commander of the company in Sant'Anna di Stazzema. There was no reason to assume that the old men, the women and children who were slaughtered in the church square of Sant'Anna had something to do with partisans,' said Heinecke. Nor was she to be encouraged or placated by the fact that Mancini and his fellow survivor, Enrico Pieri, the president of the Martyrs Association, received the German Federal Order of Merit last spring:

> The thought that the two should be brought to finally draw a line, with the Cross of Merit, and to no longer insist on prosecution because of this award ... what do you say? What do you say too to former SS men like Albert Meier who was at Marzabotto, and said after his trial that: 'they got what they deserved'? Or SS man Franz Stockinger who was also at Marzabotto, and laughed about it?[19]

In 2014, Karl Gropler, one of the men from the 16th SS sentenced at La Spezia, still lived in Wollin, an old and peaceful little town outside Berlin. He was then 93. He couldn't be extradited to Italy, and his village defended him. Simone Gropler said:

> My brother-in-law is innocent. He's old, tired and ill and only wants to be left in peace. Remember that at the time these incidents were supposed to have happened, he was wounded and still convalescing. The Italian court sentence is a political one. Here he's not anonymous, we've all lived here for generations, and I can tell you, he wasn't there in Italy that day.

In the village bar, Krause's Café, the waitress would say only one thing.[20]

'He's one of us, he always attends the old comrades meetings, he's always well-behaved. We'd like to wait for a German sentence before judging him.'

'The inhabitants of Wollin should go to Sant'Anna di Stazzema,' said Gabriele Heinecke. 'There they'd understand how the horror goes on day by day, there they'd see how German justice goes so slowly that these people will be dead before the justice system finishes its work.'

She was to be proved right

But perhaps Heinecke's most telling words were among those she delivered on 19 March 2016 in Sant'Anna di Stazzema, when she received an honorary citizenship of the village:

Sixty years after the end of the Second World War, German soldiers were sentenced abroad for Nazi war crimes. German society wondered – why were they sentenced in Italy and not in Germany? There is no interest in this subject; entire generations of students have learned nothing in history lessons on German crimes. Silencing crimes was the defining element of post-war history in Germany. I am happy to have interrupted this silence a little with you.[21]

18

German Apologies
and Reconciliation

The reactions to the German judicial decision in Stuttgart and Hamburg came thick and fast. The government in Bonn, aware that it was facing a possible public relations disaster, sought first to minimise the damage. The facts were very simple: for ten years, the country's law enforcement, legal and judicial system had investigated, and tried to bring to court, ten old men wanted for one of the worst war crimes committed against civilians, outside of the Holocaust, in the Second World War. In the interim, all of them had been found and interviewed by Italian prosecutors, and some by Italian and German journalists. What had happened? How would the government deal with it? There were a number of factors involved, and at a state, regional and individual level, the Germans tried to regain some of the lost ground.

Differences between Italian and German laws, and the possible availability of permissible evidence, meant that it may have been difficult to expect both German and Italian courts to achieve the same results. German Minister for Foreign Affairs, Guido Westerwelle, decided to confront the question back in 2012:

I understand there is disappointment, but I am also certain Italians understand that we must respect the independence of the judiciary. That said, we have an obligation to pay active tribute to the memory of the crimes that were committed in Sant'Anna, Marzabotto and other places.[1]

The key phrases in Westerwelle's speech were 'independence of the judiciary', and 'the expectations of the families of the Italian victims'. What he was stressing was that the German judiciary had throughout the whole ten-year process remained independent of the government's influence, and that the key interest and focus of the German legal system had been to see that justice was done, was seen to be done, and to present a result to the German – and Italian people – that was in keeping with the law. The Italian historian and war crimes expert Carlo Gentile said that he could not believe that there had not been some effort made by the Germans to 'slow things down', suggesting that if the search for the surviving SS men could be drawn out long enough, the chances were that they would have died in the interim. Professor Gentile is a Doctor of Philosophy and a professor of modern history at the University of Cologne, and has appeared as an expert witness and consultant at several war crimes trials in Italy, Germany and Canada. He has written four books and academic research papers on the story of German war crimes in Italy in the Second World War.[2]

One possible theory is that the Germans may have shied away from putting the SS men from Sant'Anna or Marzabotto on trial in their home country, because to do so would then oblige them to open legal proceedings against every single other SS, SD, Gestapo and Wehrmacht individual who had committed war crimes. If they had put, say, Gerhard Sommer and Karl Gropler on trial for crimes committed in Italy, then could have been liable potentially to investigate the case of any still-living German serviceman who had allegedly committed war crimes while serving in Russia. If Moscow decided to open a series of war crimes trials against German soldiers who had served there in in 1941–45 – possibly committing crimes – then the legal onus on Germany to put these men on trial at home would have been enormous. It is also a possibility that the Germans felt that there was not enough available or reliable evidence to link defendants to crimes with which they might be accused

As it was, says Gentile, it is hard to believe there was no deliberate effort made by the Germans to slow down the legal procedure. It is a strong argument – it can be argued that if an effort were made to make the judicial process the absolute slowest possible, then ultimately the defendants would, simply put, be all dead or incapable. The German statute of limitations on manslaughter meant that it was possible for a defendant to escape prosecution for this if thirty years had elapsed in between the time of his or her crime and their trial. This meant that effectively anybody arrested after 1973 for war crimes carried out in 1943–45 could invoke the statute. Many did. Only in 1979 did the Bundestag vote to lift the statute of limitations on murder, whether perpetrated in the past or in the future, whether committed by Nazis or others.

Another – slightly less likely – possibility is that the Germans would have been hesitant to prosecute the SS men who had been at Sant'Anna because, by doing so, they would then have potentially opened themselves up to multiple compensation claims. The Italian tribunal at La Spezia had awarded damages of 100,000 euros against each defendant. If a German court had ordered any of the former SS men who were found guilty to pay similar compensation, they could have been on the receiving end of other, potentially costly, claims from the families and relatives of the hundreds of victims of Sant'Anna.

The expectations of the families of the victims, meanwhile, was behind much of the Italian governmental reaction. Italy, said its Foreign Minister, Giulio Terzi di Sant'Agata, would demand that Germany 'goes after' Nazis found guilty of war crimes by Italian courts. The word is translated from the Italian word *cacciare*, meaning 'to hunt'. He said that his government would continue to insist that Germany applied Italian rulings, i.e. respected the rulings of Italian courts. Although as a rule the German government does not extradite its own nationals, extraditions are possible within the EU and to international criminal courts, such as the International Criminal Court in The Hague. The Germans had taken another route: they spent over a decade investigating the alleged perpetrators of some of the killings at Sant'Anna di Stazzema, and then closed the investigation before anybody was brought to trial.

Its extradition policy is absolute – any war crimes trials could only see custodial sentences if the German defendants were tried in their own country. At the time, di Sant'Agata was speaking at the launch of a report written by Italian and German historians that focused on the estimated 600–700,000 Italian soldiers who, after being taken prisoner following the 1943 Armistice, were deported to German work camps as, effectively, slave labour. The report proposed that a memorial should be built on the site of a Berlin labour camp where many of the Italians died; it also suggested something that would come to fruition – the setting up of an archive of Nazi war crimes committed in Italy.

While both foreign ministers were bemoaning the decision of the Stuttgart prosecutors in 2012, they were also full of praise for the idyll of the European Union, the united Europe that that year had just won the Nobel Peace Prize. But surely, in praise of a united Europe, shouldn't the justice of one country be the requirements of other member states? Germany's relationship with its own past and present, with reconciliation and its recent history, is complex. Italians do not have this issue – 'We never confused Nazism with the German people,' said Romano Franchi, the mayor of Marzabotto, in reaction to the news about the Stuttgart prosecutors.

In Pietrasanta, Enio Mancini simply said that while Germany was always quick to tell Italians to do their homework on the economy, 'Our German friends should do theirs on their history.' Adele Pardini's sister, Cesaria, sighed that, 'There was no logic to this, it is not fair.' Mancini said that he would shortly be returning to the German government the medal that they had given him, saying that the Stuttgart acquittal was scandalous. Even a newspaper owned by the disgraced former Prime Minister Silvio Berlusconi had a comment to make, as *Il Giornale* described the German judge's decision as a 'slap in the face from Stuttgart'.[3]

In summer 2015, Enrico Pieri and Enio Mancini each received a telephone call, completely out of the blue. It was from the same mobile phone number in Germany. When Enio Mancini answered his, a foreign voice ascertained that it was him, and then said simply:

'My uncle saved your life in 1944.'[4]

The German man on the phone was called Andreas Schendel, a writer and self-defence instructor in Aachen. His uncle, Heinrich Schendel, had been the teenage SS soldier who had saved the lives of Enio and his childhood friends on the day of the massacre at Sant'Anna. Now his nephew wanted to visit the village, meet survivors, and apologise to them if he could. His uncle had been a difficult, aggressive and secretive man. When he died in 2014, his family found his diaries: in them was his personal description of what happened on 12 August 1944 in Tuscany. So his nephew, Andreas, visited Sant'Anna, and met with survivors.[5] Adele Pardini and one of her sisters came to meet him, and although their reserved, yet generous, tolerance could not match his effusive, compulsively reconciliatory nature, they said afterwards that they had been pleased that he had come. It was one of the first times they had ever met a German who had come to Sant'Anna because they wanted to, not because – like ambassadors and politicians – they had to. It was a huge step forward. Reconciliation was reached at a personal level, if not at a governmental one.

In summer 2019, the German President Frank-Walter Steinmeier then visited Fivizzano, along with the Italian President Sergio Mattarella. It was a landmark visit by a German head of state, especially as he asked for forgiveness for the war crimes committed by his fellow countrymen in Italy. Steinmeier was a perspicacious and determined politician: he'd handled thorny issues, from relations with Iran and Russia to climate change, before. Now he was taking the bull by the horns again. He was in Fivizzano on the seventy-fifth anniversary of the beginning of the massacre carried out there and in Vinca by the 16th SS. Speaking in Italian, he addressed a large and surprisingly appreciative crowd – and then surprised them and everybody else in Germany and Italy who was listening. By 2019, as has been written in previous pages here, apologies and memorial celebrations in places such as Vinca, Fivizzano and Sant'Anna di Stazzema had followed a carefully established narrative: admission, acknowledgement, apology.

But Steinmeier went further. Much further. He stood and gave a speech in which, for the one of the first times since the Second World War, a German politician admirably admitted responsibility for not doing enough, faster, to deal with the country's legal duty to investigate and prosecute war crimes. What he was effectively saying was that everything done or said by the legal institutions in his country have been insufficient. He pulled the carpet out from under the feet of parts of his country's judicial and legal system in his following speech:

I stand before you here today as president of the Federal Republic
of Germany and can only bow my head in shame at how Germans
treated you.[6]

He added, 'With sorrow, I pay tribute to the victims of the massacres
in Fivizzano,' before acknowledging that Germany had taken too long
to thoroughly investigate the crimes committed by Germans in Italy
during the Second World War.[7] He did not qualify the word 'thoroughly', as finding out the details of the 2012 Stuttgart prosecutor's
office investigation has proved fruitless – to German prosecutors and
Italian prosecutors, too:

It is with a very heavy heart that I as a German and as President of
the Federal Republic of Germany have come to this place to speak
to you. But I am deeply grateful to have the chance to be here today.
I would like to thank you, the citizens of Fivizzano. And I would like
to thank you, President Sergio Mattarella, that we are able to follow
this path of remembrance and commemoration together in the interests of a better future.[8]

So far, Steinmeier had not deviated from the accepted path of apology,
admittance and asking for forgiveness. Then he did:

'*Non possiamo capirlo*'. Those were the words of the great Italian
author Primo Levi, writing about the hatred of the National
Socialists – that indescribable, unbridled hatred to which he himself
was subjected, and which he survived. No, we cannot understand the
hatred that consumed Germans here in Fivizzano seventy-five years
ago. Members of the 16th SS Panzergrenadier Division, under the
command of Walter Reder, pillaged, plundered and murdered their
way through the Apuan Alps.[9]

Steinmeier did not mention Max Simon, pardoned by the British.
Nor did he mention the fact that the one key war crimes trial at
which Primo Levi, the man he was quoting with such reverence, gave

testimony was that of Friedrich Bosshammer, the Gestapo chief from Verona who had overseen the deportation of some of the Italian Jews. Steinmeier did not mention that the failure by German prosecutors to find, try, convict and imprison Bosshammer after the war was just one of his country's many errors and failings as regards to its handling of the war crimes issue. Bosshammer, as we have seen, disappeared for twenty years, protected by former SS and Gestapo colleagues who worked in Germany. However, Steinmeier's overarching message was what most counted:

> Their [the 16th SS'] task was clear: to exact revenge on the partisans for their resistance, in this case on the so-called Gothic Line.
>
> It was a terrible, inhumane form of revenge, and defenceless women, children and old people bore the brunt of it. On their way to Vinca, the soldiers slaughtered practically everyone who crossed their path. They set houses on fire and destroyed churches. In Vinca they rampaged for four days, returning again and again, also killing those who had dared to emerge from their hiding places. Even pregnant women and small children were butchered, according to survivors' accounts.[10]

The German President was flanked by Italian carabinieri policemen in full dress uniform, cavalry helmets tumbling with horse-hair plumes, swords, smart tunics racked with rows of medals:

> More than 160 people fell victim to the fury of these units, which left smouldering piles of rubble and a dark red trail of blood in their wake. Mommio, Bardine San Terenzo, Valla, Vinca, the Nazi henchmen set upon many villages, brutally murdering more than 400 people. Yet the list of the sites of terror in Italy is much, much longer. Sant'Anna di Stazzema, Marzabotto, Civitella – I have visited several sites of National Socialist crimes, and each time I was deeply moved. Dear Sergio Mattarella, at the Fosse Ardeatine we grieved together. These places stand for many others which are lesser known, too little known.

We think we know what Germans did in these times. *And yet we are not sufficiently informed* [italics author's own]. That is why I believe it is so important to be here today in Fivizzano, a place which many Germans have never heard of. Few Germans are aware of the brutal atrocities committed here by Germans.[11]

One of the reasons why he was in Fivizzano was to try to discover and understand more about what happened there, so Germans could never say they didn't know what took place:

I stand before you here today as President of the Federal Republic of Germany and can only bow my head in shame at how Germans treated you. With sorrow I pay tribute to the victims of the massacres in Fivizzano. I ask for your forgiveness for the crimes perpetrated here by Germans. To all of you, the survivors, the victims and their descendants, I want to say this: we Germans *are aware of the responsibility that we bear for these crimes* [italics author's own]. It is a responsibility that we will never shake off.

You, the victims and their descendants, have a right to remembrance and commemoration. You have a right that people in Germany, too, learn about what you had to endure. All of you associate the events of that time with untold suffering and untold pain. That suffering, that pain lives on in your collective memory. Above all, it lives on in your families. We have just heard about that in conversations with some of you, and those conversations moved me deeply.

Some of you no doubt feel the pain even more acutely because most of the perpetrators were never called to account for their deeds. In Germany *it took far too long to remember the crimes against humanity committed by Germans in Italy. The judicial examination of these crimes in Germany was also far too late in commencing. Germany did not embrace its responsibility in this area* [italics author's own].[12]

In a very long speech, in stifling August heat, the President took a long time getting to what was this fundamentally vital, and new point. Looking at the three passages in italics above, they summarise an official admittance by the German state that, since 1945, and at least since the creation of the new Federal German Republic in 1949, the country has not done enough, soon enough, well enough, to remember, investigate and take responsibility for the war crimes of the Third Reich. Simply put, it hasn't done enough to investigate, try and convict a lot of people it should have, a long time ago. It was a blanket explanation, a blanket apology, and Steinmeier was saying it in summer 2019. This was despite the fact that every single German formally wanted for war crimes committed in Italy between 1943 and 1945 was now reportedly dead. Was this too little too late, or better late than never? Steinmeier spoke further, and seemed to prove and persuade that it was, indeed, the latter:

Yet, as improbable as it may seem – I also sense another emotion in this place: thankfulness.

For Fivizzano is now not only a place of remembrance, but also a place of reconciliation and interaction.

That gives me hope, it gives us as Germans hope – and I believe that it can give hope to everyone.

We owe this hope above all to you, the survivors and descendants, so many of whom were willing to reach out across the abyss created by our past.

… We Germans are deeply grateful for this willingness for reconciliation and we are grateful for the friendship between our two countries that has grown out of it.

'*Se comprendere è impossibile, conoscere è necessario.*' Primo Levi wrote that, too.

'*Even if it is impossible to understand, it is necessary to know.*' – '*Wenn es schon unmöglich ist zu verstehen, so ist doch das Wissen notwendig.*' – This one sentence of Primo Levi I am deliberately also stating in German. I am addressing it to my compatriots, particularly the younger generation. They need to know what happened.

The German–Italian Commission of Historians has laid the foundation for joint efforts to come to terms with our past – and therefore also for our common future as friends and partners. Many of its recommendations have already been implemented, but we can't afford to stop there.

It is our responsibility to create a joint culture of remembrance and to pass on our knowledge to coming generations, in the interests of a better future in a united Europe.

I am therefore delighted that next year German pupils will be visiting Fivizzano to learn through dialogue and interaction what happened during that chapter of history and how indeed it was possible.[13]

So, having told the audience in Fivizzano, and the assembled Italian, German and European media, that Germany had categorically failed in its obligations to deal with its legal duty to the past, he assured them that there would be unexpected benefits: German students could visit Tuscany to examine the scorching stain of history their country had left there, and other initiatives were in progress, too. One was the funding and development of *The Atlas of Nazi–Fascist War Crimes in Italy*, a joint endeavour between Rome and Berlin. The project listed online and in a printed book all of the sites of war crimes and killings of civilians carried out by the Germans and Italian Fascists, and the latest estimated death toll, of 22,000 people.[14] Steinmeier concluded:

Those who are acquainted with the past will be better equipped for a common European future. But those who forget are weaker and more susceptible to intolerance and violence.

Sergio Mattarella, you recently reminded us of this fact.

We must not forget. We must not forget, in order to ensure that our consciousness cannot again be deceived and clouded.

Our common Europe is based on a promise: never again unbridled nationalism, never again war on our continent, never again racism, hatemongering and violence! We need to remember that, particularly at a time when toxic nationalism is seeping back into Europe.

And we need to fight for freedom and democracy, for human rights and humanity, for our united Europe – now perhaps more than ever before. We owe that to the victims. And we owe that to you, the survivors and their descendants. Thank you very much.[15]

Again, better late than never. And a brave better-late-than-never.

19

TUSCANY TODAY

October 2019, Sant'Anna di Stazzema, Pietrasanta and Valdicastello

There were around 2,000 victims of the 16th SS' trail of massacres across Tuscany in summer 1944. At Sant'Anna, at least six of the children who survived the massacre are still alive today: two of them are Adele and Cesira, the sisters of Anna Pardini, the 3-week-old baby who was the youngest victim of the massacre. The other four are men, including Enrico Pieri and Enio Mancini. They're alive, in Tuscany, in Pietrasanta, and they visit the village of Sant'Anna di Stazzema constantly. They talk to the Italian and German prosecutors, lawyers, relatives, historians, old partisans and government ministers involved in the case. What happened that summer seventy-five years ago must not, they insist, ever be forgotten, simply because Germany would not extradite the guilty former SS men. To find them and talk to them, to hear their story? They'll tell you, because each person they tell may well be somebody who can learn from it, take their experiences and use them to shape a better future, to try and understand what happened, and why it must never be allowed to happen again.

The road to see them goes from Pietrasanta to Valdicastello, and it's warm in the October morning. The sun coming off the sea is still that of late summer, the sky a bright cerulean, a shining cobalt blue. From the old, cobbled Piazza del Duomo, where the Italian partisans raised their flag in August 1944, the streets lead out in all directions.

Head south towards the sea, and then turn, and the long road that leads up towards the Apuan Alps goes left. Past the cemetery, and out past vineyards filled with purple and white grapes, there's little traffic by the beginning of the morning.

A farmer putters by at the controls of his Vespa Ape, or 'Bee'. A modified design of the eternally popular scooter, the Ape is named because the sound of its engine is a familiar buzz heard all over Italy, like an omnipresent motorised bee. This version is a three-wheeler, with a small cab, and a cargo container set above its two rear wheels; the farmer has been to tend vines, for in the back are plastic baskets of early grapes, a rake and a fork. The whine of the engine hangs in the morning air, where the dew still sits on the blackberry brambles that line the road. Apricot and walnut trees stand guard. After a mile the road starts to climb gently, and curves to the left, bringing the foothills of the mountains into view. It was this road, which leads from Valdicastello to Pietrasanta, that was taken by the families fleeing Sant'Anna di Stazzema and the mountain villages in summer 1944. An hour's walk in the bright Tuscan morning leads to the houses and gardens that sit outside Valdicastello, and then, in front of a garden gate, and a three-storey house, waits Enio Mancini.

The first impression of a man who has lived the life he has is that he looks younger than his 83 years. He's calm and welcoming, but, despite the warmth of the morning, suggests we go and sit inside. At a long table in the sitting room, windows still shuttered, he sits down, a man who has a story to tell and who has told it many times before. He gestures around the room at some photographs of the old days in Valdicastello, some framed certificates, books of photographs. Yet what draws the eye the most is a life-size cardboard cut-out of a small boy, the image enlarged from a photograph and attached to its background. It's Enio as a child, taken in the 1940s, before, he says, the days at Sant'Anna di Stazzema changed forever. It sits by the fireplace now, and has clearly stood there for years. It seems to watch over us as we sit, and as he begins to talk.

He has his own narrative, and his own way of telling his story, as though he is putting together in his mind a verbal jigsaw puzzle, where only he knows how all of the pieces fit together. He leans on the long oak table, his hands raised, as he starts. The explanation comes out in blocks of speech, and to interrupt him, and request clarification, it's almost nec-essary to raise your hand. Born in 1938, he had lived all of his childhood in Sant'Anna, the 'village away from the world', as he describes it. He only went to the sea at Pietrasanta for the first time when he was 10, he says, after the war. 'We put on our shoes only to go down the mountain. From Sant'Anna you can see the Mediterranean,' he says, 'and by mid-summer 1944, when there were an estimated 2,500 people in the small scattered village, it was always there, over the trees.'

With the family members in his house, and the additional displaced people, there were sixteen in all. He pauses, stares down at his hands, thinks of the next episode in the familiar, painful, story that he is telling, the one that has been the narrative of his entire life, that like an eternally repeated soundtrack he has to play again, and again, and again. There was no running water, or electricity, and he and his mother helped to take care of their cow. At night, the partisans and the adult males hid in the village. The Germans took some of the men off to build fortifications on the Gothic Line. His father somehow escaped being press-ganged, and so along with the women of the village – who toiled like men – they grew maize, they harvested chestnuts, they bartered milk from their beloved cow. Some of the men produced charcoal in the woods, and ground the soft, yellow chestnuts down into flour. Life seemed peaceful.

'Yes,' he says, 'of course everybody knew the war was just beyond our doorstep; in January and February 1944 we had our first news of the partisans, and on 17 April there was a battle on the neighbouring mountain. The Germans searched our village. At night we boys opened our windows to hear the noise of the battle.' But he says, again, they were cut off from the world, except for the thousand extra displaced people who had poured into the village by April. 'They came,' he says, looking up from the table, 'from everywhere. Genoa, Naples, La Spezia.'

For them Sant'Anna was a foreign land, and still. And still. Another pause, as he turns his head to the left and looks out of the open front door into the sunlit garden, where pink bougainvillea hangs entwined on the balcony. And still the war seemed to be noise from far away. 'For us,' he says, looking at his hands, about to begin another episode of the story, where you feel the tempo will change. 'For us, it was just a game.'

And then, he says softly, 'It wasn't a joke. On 30 July the Germans arrived at Sant'Anna, and by 8 August posters were put up telling us that anybody who harboured partisans would have their house burned down. I remember,' he says, 'that photograph of all of the children dancing in a circle, it was taken in 1943.' He pauses, widens his eyes, and continues.

At 6.30 in the morning on 12 August, his father rushed into the room where he was sleeping with other children, rushing him awake, telling him not to be frightened, to take some clothes. His father then fled. At 6.45 the SS arrived. The children were turfed out of bed, no shoes, some with no clothes, they lined them up, and screamed, '*Raus, schnell, raus, schnell, Valdicastello.*' And then with flame-throwers they began to burn the houses.

'They killed our cow – it suffocated from the smoke – and I wanted to save the house and save the cow.' But along with a group of children they were taken outside by the young teenage soldier, the one who seemed almost an adolescent, the one whose nephew would eventually come to the village to try and make peace, to find some reconciliation. The one who fired the burst of shots into the air, telling the children to run away, to get lost, to hide, to escape. So he went home, the house was burning and the cow was dead. And then he went down to a position where he could see through the trees, and see the bodies, the carbonised, almost skeletonised children. His father found almost all of his family alive – he was almost the only one who did, says Enio – 'and that night we slept out under the stars, under the chestnut trees, before we prepared a mass grave'.

Forty days in the caves above and around Sant'Anna followed, eating at night, beans and potatoes. And then eventually, he heard the group of four or five soldiers approaching, speaking a language he didn't know. It was the American war crimes investigators. And afterwards? Afterwards? His story leaps forward, nearing another episode, about how in 2008 and 2009, at the invitation of the Hamburg prosecutor, he went to try and see Gerhard Sommer in his nursing home, but the German staff wouldn't let him in. Sant'Anna for him remains a 'why?' A lifetime of trying to explain it to other people, and to himself. 'It was not a reprisal,' he says quietly, 'it was done for hatred. And what gets us all is the absence of justice.'

Enio Mancini has been telling the story of the massacre his whole life: it has, indeed, *been* his whole life. From German and Italian politicians to parties of school children, aid workers, humanitarians, soldiers, journalists, policemen and women, priests, parties of pilgrims, nuns, film crews, and those thousands of people who come every day, every week and month of the year to see and to mourn, and to wonder too why it happened. The monumental nature of the killings seem to be able to dwarf whatever agenda or feeling or opinion people bring to the village: it silences, because when there isn't justice, and there is nothing more to be done, and every avenue and every option has been tried, then silence is sometimes the only answer.

The road from Pietrasanta to the village of Sant'Anna di Stazzema climbs and winds through olive groves, stands of chestnut trees with burnished green leaves, already dropping their spiky fruit on to the carpet of fallen leaves below them. The sea and Pietrasanta lie far below, spread out on a flat coastal plain. The serpentine route curves and rises, and cannot seem to get steeper, until the car arrives on a flat open area where buses are parked. They cannot make it any further up the narrow route to the village. Then there's a stretch of green space, a small church behind a statue, a wall separating the church garden from a gorge behind it, and a little piazza.

A café has set its chairs and tables outside. Knots of young Italian teen-agers mill around, school backpacks, jeans, Converse All-Stars, mobile phones. They're more subdued than normal, though: they know why they are here, and they know what happened. Looking at the scene in front of the church, you realise it all looks very familiar, and then recall that it's been pictured in countless photographs. It's the open space of green grass, where in 1943, in a sepia photograph, a group of young boys and girls danced round in a circle, hand in hand. All gone, bar one. Behind the parking spaces, there's a bigger building that houses the Museum of Sant'Anna di Stazzema, and the offices of the National Park of Peace. There are a lot of people around in front of the church, but somehow the place feels empty, as though it forever belongs without humans, left by itself to mourn and endlessly to try and understand.

That afternoon, Enrico Pieri is doing what he does sometimes two or three times per week: addressing a large group of children who have come on a school trip to visit Sant'Anna di Stazzema. They wait until he's ready, and then file into the church, and sit in the pews, on the floor, leaning against the font. They're silent as he begins his story. Like Enio Mancini, you get the feeling of a crusader with a story that he must tell, and never stop telling, who has been given a task by the gods that he will carry with him all his life, to try and explain to people, while inside he still tries to understand himself. The church has a memorial stone to Anna Pardini, the 3-week-old baby who was shot by the masked Italian outside the house that stands close by. Large pieces of figurative commemorative sculpture stand in the garden. Inside the church, with light blazing in through the door, Enrico tells his story. Hiding under the stairs, running for shelter in the runner beans, as groups of Waffen-SS men prowled through and around the village shooting everybody.

The schoolchildren wait until he's finished, and clap loudly and appreciatively before beginning with a small blizzard of questions. 'Which of the perpetrators are still alive?' asks one girl. 'Where? When was the last time somebody from Sant'Anna had direct contact with anybody from the Italian or German government who could tell them whether any of these perpetrators are alive or dead?' Afterwards, a short drive up a winding road leads to the monument set on top of the hill of Sant'Anna, where there is memorial stone listing the names of everybody who died here.

Across the wooded valley is the village of Farnocchia, where part of the German attack began the night before 12 August 1944. On the memorial stone there are lists of identical surnames that continue all the way down the vast piece of granite. It's so large, and so heavy, that when it was time to put it in position in the memorial garden, a Chinook helicopter from the Italian military was brought in to swing the stone down into place, the heavy, underslung load swaying in the mountain wind. The monumental stone that had been there before it had fallen over and cracked on one night of a tempestuous storm that blew up from the sea below.

Enrico always thought that Sant'Anna would never and could never happen again, but then, he says, you look at Yugoslavia. He remembers what it was like just after the war, *povero e rosso*, he says, poor and socialist. He's a consummate man of the people, and unlike Enio, he doesn't appear to have packaged his story, his feelings, to have ordered them or balanced them. He's still furious, inside, and he admits that the years after the war, as a child, were desperately difficult. He emigrated and spent twenty-two years in Switzerland, where in the 1960s and '70s Italians were like the Moroccans or Albanians of today, the perpetual immigrants always in need of something.

He wanted Sant'Anna to be rebuilt because after the war it was deserted and destroyed. It is almost how he feels about the curse that life has given him, the Ancient Mariner of Tuscany, forever narrating, forever telling his story, because if he doesn't, then there's a danger that the world could forget, and when it forgets then it means it doesn't care. But Enio found, if not peace, satisfaction and contentment in a marriage that has lasted fifty years, since he and his wife were married in 1969. He laughs as he thinks about it, winding his sleek Volkswagen Polo back down the hill, through the olive groves, the sea sparkling below us. 'We never run out of things to talk about,' he says, 'even if it's just about what to have for lunch.'

In the Piazza Duomo in Pietrasanta afterwards, he sits outside at a café, drinking an Aperol Spritz, the Campari-style aperitif that is somewhere between vermillion and scarlet in colour. You can feel the levers in his brain cranking to settle, to find balance, to lay things in place, but watching his face and listening to him talk, it's clear that they never will. Pietrasanta is a stylish seaside haven of modern art galleries and chic clothes shops. Some late American tourists, bundled together with the bustle and clamour and amiable getting along of a Tuscan population who live by the sea, live off the seaside, and shrug their shoulders gently at the vicissitudes of life. Everybody knows of Sant'Anna, and everybody knows of all of the people and all of the characters in the story. It seems to sit far away from the warm, sleek pace of life in Pietrasanta, hiding out on its mountain promontory, never going away, never at peace, never the recipient of justice.

Just on the northern edge of Pietrasanta sits the little town of Seravezza, where Adele Pardini lives. One of nine children, of whom seven were girls, she had lived in Sant'Anna di Stazzema for two or three generations. Nowadays, she lives in a small, comfortable two-storey house in the town, where the streets are interspersed with small allotments and fields of olive trees. She smiles and stretches as we arrive, her back is hurting, she says, from picking olives all day in the 32° heat. The bright sun is still beaming down, even in the late afternoon. Adele tells her story too, although in a different way from those of Enio and Enrico. She tells it because she wants to, but will not waste her breath and her words if she thinks that those in front of her are not listening. The inside of her house is filled with maps, photographs, certificates, municipal decorations.

She narrates what happened to her, and her family, watching her mother and her baby sister killed in front of her. And she too tries to make sense of what happened, and why it happened. The old men who did it were all dead or dying in Germany, and here she was, picking olives in the sunlight. Who was the winner, the victor, if there had to be one? With Adele, however, there is not the feeling that she has been burdened through life by the weight of her experience: she has dealt with it, as she has got older. She has lived and survived. There isn't any triumph, there isn't any happy ending with the story of Sant'Anna di Stazzema, but there is a resolute affirmation of the continuing strength of the human spirit.

In Wollin, outside Potsdam, the television footage of ex-SS man Karl Gropler showed a scurrying, almost rat-like figure, desperate to escape the cameras, shoulders bowed by age, and a life spent working in the fields. He was alive, but he looked dead. The same was true of Gerhard Sommer and Alfred Concina, angry, unintelligent, ill-looking men; a very long way indeed from the photos of their youth with the skull and crossbones on their collars and caps, men who had spent their younger years being exploited and killing, in the name of extreme nationalism, and then the rest of their lives hating everybody and everything because of it. It's a story in which, predominantly, Italy and the Italians have behaved with humanity, toughness, maturity, patience and a ton of forbearance in the face of appalling obstacles and events. And Germany? The country that waxes long, loud and lyrical about learning from history, and making sure that 'Never Again' really means something? It comes across, wrongly and sadly, as duplicitous, and chronically insecure of itself and its past, as represented by the men of the 16th SS. This is everything it works so hard not to be, and fundamentally is not.

After nearly three hours of sadness, wisdom and no small amount of laughter with Adele, it's time to return to the centre of Pietrasanta. The sun is coming low, the warmth of the day creeping out to sea. As it does so, one last question seems to hang over the town, the mountains, the question that one of the schoolchildren asked up in Sant'Anna the day before. Which perpetrators are still alive, or not? All are reputedly dead, says the affable and efficient director of the Sant'Anna museum, sitting over an elegant Tuscan breakfast the following morning. And Gerhard Sommer? So a message is sent on WhatsApp to Gabriele Heinecke in Hamburg. A minute later the museum director's phone whoop-whoops with an incoming message:

Gerhard Sommer died in March 2019.

20

Epilogue

What Became of the Characters in this Book?

Enio Mancini
He still lives in Valdicastello, outside Pietrasanta, is President of the Museum of Sant'Anna di Stazzema, and continues to keep the flame of memory burning as bright as he can.

Adele Pardini
She lives with her son in Seravezza, and at the time of writing was 81, and still growing and harvesting olives with great humour and determination.

Enrico Pieri
With his wife of fifty years, sprightly, wry and eternally questioning, he still lives in Pietrasanta.

Marco De Paolis
He has now been promoted the chief military prosecutor of all of Italy, based in Rome. One of his latest investigations involved Italian victims of the massacre at Oradour-sur-Glane in France in 1944.

Gabriele Heinecke
She practises law and human rights law in Hamburg.

Gerhard Sommer

He died in March 2019 at the retirement home in Volksdorf, and his daughters buried him in the same graveyard as his wife. He was unrepentant to the end.

Ludwig Goring

He died in 2006, reportedly haunted by nightmares and post-traumatic stress disorder.

Karl Gropler

He died in 2013 in Wollin, outside Potsdam, aged 90. Again, he was unrepentant.

Werner Bruss

If Werner Bruss is alive, then he was 100 in May 2020. No date of death is possible to find, and the telephone at his home in Reinbeck still rings.

Alfred Concina

He died in 2012, near Chemnitz.

Karl Gesele

He died in 1968 at Friedrichshafen on Lake Konstanz.

Anton Galler

He fled to Denia on the east coast of Spain, where he died in 1995 and is buried in the local cemetery.

Max Simon

He died in 1961. HIAG, the SS comrades association, attempted to place an obituary of him in the *Frankfurter Allgemeine*. The newspaper declined.

Karl Wolff

Wolff gave evidence at Nuremberg, then spent time in a British prison, was released in 1947, but then re-arrested by the Germans, serving a short sentence under house arrest. Subsequently he got another four years for his membership of the SS. He worked in PR, before new evidence at the Eichmann trial in Jerusalem tied him to his complicity in the Holocaust. He was arrested in Germany – again – and in 1964 given fifteen years on charges related to the deportation of Italian Jews to Auschwitz, the killings of Italian partisans, and the deportation of 300,000 Jews to Treblinka. He served only five years. He died in 1984 in Rosenheim, in Bavaria.

Milton Wexler

The US investigator retired from the military, and returned to being a physicist. On his return to the United States after the war, he met Albert Einstein to tell him about the fate of his cousin and his family in Tuscany.

Walter Reder

He was released from prison in Italy in 1985, after expressing repentance to the citizens of Marzabotto in a letter. He returned to Austria, where, on arrival, he then declared himself unrepentant for his crimes. He died in 1991.

Bibliography

Among the many works of historical non-fiction written about Italy in the Second World War and its aftermath, the following stand out as exceptional examples of good writing, excellent research, engaging storytelling and analytical interpretation of history.

In English

The Day of Battle: The War in Sicily and Italy, 1943-1944, by Rick Atkinson (Henry Holt U.S., 2008). The second volume in Atkinson's Liberation trilogy, this book begins with the American and British armies as they depart from North Africa to invade Sicily and then the Italian mainland. It progresses northwards from Salerno and Monte Cassino to the liberation of Rome.

Italy's Sorrow: A Year of War 1944-1945, by James Holland (Harper Collins, 2009). The first-hand accounts of Italy's civilian population caught up in the fighting in Italy make a powerful counterpoint to Atkinson's military perspective: together these books explain most clearly the Allied strategic and tactical decision to invade Italy, the complete uncertainty of the campaign's outcome, and what it was actually like for the soldiers and civilians of all sides who fought and lived there.

A House in the Mountains: The Women who Liberated Italy from Fascism, by Caroline Moorehead (Chatto & Windus, 2019). Probably the best book in the English language about the Italian girls and women who fought and operated with and for partisan groups. In Moorehead's account, the

lives of four women in wartime revolve around their role as couriers with
resistance groups in and around Turin.

Fatal Decision: Anzio and the Battle for Rome, by Carlo D'Este (Harper Collins,
1991). The Allied amphibious landing at Anzio, their failure to push
towards Rome, and the subsequent five-month battle was one of the great
missed opportunities of the war. D'Este's exhaustively researched book tells
what happened and why.

Mission Accomplished: SOE and Italy 1943-1945, by David Stafford (Vintage,
2012). A fascinating and beautifully in-depth look at what the Special
Operations Executive actually did on its many missions inside Italy. It is
so good because Stafford has had complete access to SOE's records and
describes the idiosyncratic deployments of the even-more-idiosyncratic
agents and exactly what they did and didn't achieve.

*Hunting Evil: How the Nazi War Criminals Escaped and the Hunt to Bring them
to Justice,* by Guy Walters (Bantam Press, 2009). A comprehensive 700-page
account of the hunt for the major German war criminals after the war
and the efforts to track them down. It concentrates on the high-profile
individuals such as Eichmann and Josef Mengele, while also providing one
of the best accounts of the 'Rat-Line' escape routes that enabled wanted
criminals to escape to South America and Spain.

The SS: A New History, by Adrian Weale (Little, Brown, 2010). To understand
the military operations, policing and internal security duties of the SS, a thoroughly researched and clearly explained account of its history, background,
motivations and *raison d'etre* is needed. Adrian Weale provides just that.

Black Warriors: The Buffalo Soldiers of World War II, by Ivan J. Houston (iUniverse U.S., 2011). The fighting in Tuscany in summer and autumn 1944
described from the point of view of a junior NCO serving with the
African-American soldiers of the U.S 92nd Infantry Division. A unique
and rare look at the unit and what it was like to fight with them, as well
as what Tuscany was like in that year of war.

*Allen Dulles, the OSS, and Nazi War Criminals: the Dynamics of Selective
Prosecution,* by Kerstin von Lingen (Cambridge University Press, UK, 2013.)
The German author is a Professor of Contemporary History, living and
working in Germany and Austria, who studies, teaches and writes about
war crimes, genocide, and international justice, particularly with regard
to Nazi Germany, and Italy, in the Second World War. This book, which
covers the centre of the curious Venn Diagram occupied by American

intelligence, Karl Wolff, the SS, the war in Italy and the Nuremberg Trials, is as good as it gets on the subject: full of academic rigour while being colourful, detailed and well-written.

In Italian

Four people alone have done more and better than anybody else, often almost single-handedly, to investigate, research, document and narrate the events that took place at Sant'Anna di Stazzema in August 1944. Their work has defined the historical documentation of what happened and includes the operational and historical prelude to the operation; the German, Italian and Allied perspectives; the experience of the Italian victims and survivors; the participation of the SS and Italian Fascist soldiers; and the enormous legal, judicial and political process that followed from 1944 to the present day.

Sant'Anna di Stazzema: Storia di un Strage [*Sant'Anna di Stazzema: Story of a Massacre*], by Paolo Pezzino (Il Mulino, 2013), is one. The author is a historian who assisted as a consultant during some of the judicial proceedings.

Sant'Anna di Stazzema: Il Processo, la Storia, i Documenti [*Sant'Anna di Stazzema: The Trial, the History, the Documents*], by prosecutor Marco de Paolis and Paolo Pezzino (Viella, 2016) is probably the most definitive and authoritative work on the massacre written to date; the sub-title is exactly what the book provides.

I crimini di guerra tedeschi in Italia 1943–1945 [*German war crimes in Italy 1943–1945*], by Carlo Gentile (Einaudi, 2016) is another definitive account of German war crimes committed in Italy. The author is a professor at the University of Cologne, and the author of several books and academic papers that investigate and examine not just the massacres committed in Italy by the Germans, but the motivations and operational rationale of the soldiers who carried them out.

In German

Das Massaker von Sant'Anna di Stazzema [*The Massacre of Sant'Anna di Stazzema*] was compiled and researched and written by prosecutor Gabriele Heinecke, journalist Christiane Kohl, survivor Enio Mancini and by Maren Westermann. It was published in 2014 by Laika-Verlag.

ENDNOTES

Prologue

1 *La Repubblica* (Florence edition), 25 April 2020.

2 Agenzia Nazionale Stampa Associata (ANSA) is Italy's leading wire news service. This quote is from 25 April 2020, also carried by *La Repubblica* in Florence.

3 Quoted on the website www.comune.pistoia.it, 25 April 2020, also carried by *La Repubblica* in Florence.

4 *La Nazione*, 25 April 2020.

5 These figures are taken from *The Atlas of Nazi and Fascist Massacres* (*Atlante delle Stragi Naziste e Fasciste in Italia*). This encompasses the findings of a huge research project begun in 2012, funded by the German Ministry of Foreign Affairs, aimed at improving historical understanding between Italy and Germany. The atlas is in the form of a database that includes photographs, maps, documents and videos. The database documents the killings and massacres of Italian civilians and some resistance fighters by German and Italian Fascist troops from 8 September 1943 onwards. It can be found at www.straginazifasciste.it

6 *The Atlas of Nazi and Fascist Massacres* lists the names, sexes and ages of 391 people killed at Sant'Anna di Stazzema; the Historical Museum of the Resistance at Sant'Anna di Stazzema, and its website, www.santannadistazzema.org, holds what it terms an 'incomplete list' of 393 dead; prosecutors in Germany from 2002 onwards estimated that former SS men could be charged with 354 deaths; a figure of 560 people killed in and around Sant'Anna di Stazzema on 12 August 1944, including in neighbouring villages, is also used on the museum's website, and this figure has become commonly used as the accepted total of dead. This includes all of the casualties from Sant'Anna, and from SS killings in the area around it on the same day, carried out by the SS units en route to, or returning from, the village. Given that many of the bodies could not be identified at the time of the killings, the total of 560 includes those identified post-war using forensic analysis.

7 See Chapter 18, in which the German President's speech is excerpted in full.

Italy Surrenders

1   The information on Luftwaffe signals intercepts is taken from the US Target Intelligence Committee (TICOM) document number IF-179, Volume IV, Part I of the Seabourne Report on the Luftwaffe's Signals Intelligence Service.
2   This version of the communique is from ANPI, the Italian National Partisans' Association.
3   Copies of these orders from both Hitler and Field Marshal Kesselring are held in the Museo Storico della Liberazione di Roma in Via Tasso, Rome, housed in the former Gestapo headquarters in the city.
4   Details of the killings are in the archives of Il Memoriale Della Deportazione, in Borgo San Dalmazzo outside Cuneo.
5   Personnel files on Karl Gesele are held in the Bundesarchiv Military Archives in Freiburg and at the Deutsche Dienstelle in Berlin.

Reprisals

1   Documents detailing the attack on Via Rasella and the subsequent reprisals at the Ardeatine Caves are held at the Museo Storico della Liberazione di Roma in Rome.
2   Interviews carried out by the author at the Historical Museum to the Resistance at Via Tasso.
3   The drawings and messages are preserved there to this day, visible to see in the former cells.
4   Documents about the story of the priest are held in the museum of the neighbouring town of Bardonecchia.
5   A children's playground, sitting under the pine trees near the ski slopes in Bardonecchia, is named after him.
6   Copies of Kesselring's orders are held in museums and archives across Italy, including in the Museo Storico della Liberazione di Roma in Rome.

Partisans

1   SOE & OSS reports held, inter alia, in ANPI archives in Milan, Rimini, Turin and Bologna. Extensive details of the operating conditions for SOE and OSS officers with partisans can also be found in *Mission Accomplished: SOE and Italy 1943–1945*, David Stafford, Vintage, London, 2012.
2   Extract from the War Diary of the 1st Derbyshire Yeomanry, 6th Armoured Division dated 16 July 1944; also from Leslie Newman, 20 September 2005, BBC People's War.

The SS Division

1   In research for his book *At War on the Gothic Line: Fighting in Italy 1944-1945*, Osprey, Oxford, 2016, the author interviewed, among others, a surviving veteran of the 92nd Division, Ivan Houston, who recounted lengthy descriptions of the fighting in Tuscany in 1944. Houston's own account of the campaign can be found in his autobiography, *Black Warriors: the Buffalo Soldiers of World War II*, iUniverse Publishers, Bloomington, Illinois. 2009.

2 Theodor Eicke's quote about weakness in SS men appears in *Leaders and Personalities of the Third Reich Vol. 1*, Charles Hamilton, R. James Bender Publishing, San Jose, US, 1984, p.263.

3 Details of Max Simon's SS career are in the Bundesarchiv, but also in the documents and notes from his post-war trial in Padua in 1947. During his time in prison in 1949 Simon wrote a battle memoir of his time in Russia, France and Italy.

4 This estimate about local auxiliaries at Stalingrad comes from *Eastern Troops: Hitler's Russian & Cossack Allies 1941–1945*, Nigel Thomas, Bloomsbury Publishing UK, London, 2015, pp.13–15, 57.

5 The background information on Gerhard Sommer, inter alia, is from the Italian Ministry of Defence documentation of the defendants in the 2004–2005 trials in La Spezia, and from the Bundesarchiv. The Italian MoD reports are on the War Crimes & Justice section of their website, at www.difesa.it/Giustizia_Militare/Rassegna/Processi per *crimini di guerra*

6 Among other sources, the profiles of the SS NCOs and men come from the Italian Ministry of Defence documentation of the trials in La Spezia in 2004-2005 into killings in Tuscany, at www.difesa.it/Giustizia_Militare/rassegna/Processi/Sommer_Schoneberg_Bruss/Pagine/10Laposizionedegliimputati.aspx. There are, altogether, twenty different sections on this section of the website concerning the investigations, legal process, tribunals, sentencing and background of the case of the massacre at Sant'Anna di Stazzema.

7 *Ibid*. Bruss' description of his motivation, and the information about his fellow SS men, is from the same section of the Italian MoD website.

8 The British officer's description comes from the British War Crimes Group Report of 1945: A Report on German Reprisals for Partisan Activity in Italy, National Archives, WO 204/11465, p.9, with another copy in. NA, WO 32/12206, referring to a report dated 9 July 1945.

9 The description of the beginning of the operation at Sant'Anna di Stazzema comes from Sections 9 & 10 of the Military Justice section of the Italian Ministry of Defence website as quoted above, concerning the case of the massacre at Sant'Anna di Stazzema.

The Children of Sant'Anna di Stazzema

1 The author first visited Sant'Anna di Stazzema on 24 October 2019, when the season and weather were still that of late summer, and early Tuscan autumn.

2 Sheep, cattle and pigs were highly prized commodities in 1944 in wartime Italy – not just for their meat and milk, but for their value as bartering items.

3 The information in this chapter comes from personal interviews with three survivors of the massacre at Sant'Anna: Enio Mancini, Enrico Pieri and Adele Pardini. These were carried out by the author between 24 and 26 October 2019 in Sant'Anna di Stazzema, Valdicastello and Pietrasanta. They and fellow survivors of the massacre have been interviewed and given statements, testimonies and personal accounts from 1944 to the present day. What is extraordinary is the consistency of their accounts over the years. These have appeared in newspapers, on television, radio, latterly on websites, and in books, with many of these accounts from them – and other survivors – gathered in the archives of the Museum of Sant'Anna di Stazzema. They are also on the Military Justice and War Crimes Trials section of the Italian Ministry of Defence

archives, found on the website link above. Where survivors' testimony appeared in either an American, British or Italian military, police or intelligence investigative report this is either stated in the text, or endnoted below.

4 The author interviewed Enio Mancini at his home in Valdicastello on 25 October 2019, and Enrico Pieri in Sant'Anna di Stazzema and Pietrasanta on the same day.

5 The author interviewed Adele Pardini on 26 October 2019 in her home in the area where Pietrasanta becomes Forte dei Marmi.

A Trail of Massacres

1 ANPI archives in Carrara and *The Atlas of Nazi and Fascist War Crimes* – Episode of San Terenzo Monte Fivizzano 17–19.08.1944, pp.1–9.

2 The breakdown of the casualty figures from the operations at Vinca & Fivizzano can be found in *The Atlas of Nazi and Fascist Massacres*: www.straginazifasciste.it/?page_id=38&id_strage=4857&lang=en

3 One of many accounts of the SS raid on the monastery was published in 2005 in the Weekly English Language Edition of *L'Osservatore Romano,* the Rome newspaper traditionally close to Vatican sources. (pp.4–5, 2 February 2005, by Giuseppina Sciascia.) This was then reprinted by American Carthusians in 2006 as one in The Carthusian Booklets Series: http://transfiguration.chartreux.org/Publications/10-SilentSummer.pdf

   A full account has been written by Luigi Accattoli in his book, which in Italian is entitled *La strage di Farneta: Storia sconosciuta dei dodici Certosini fucilati dai tedeschi nel 1944*, Soveria Mannelli, Rubbettino Editore s.r.l., 2013 (The massacre of Farneta: Unknown stories of the twelve Carthusians executed by the Germans in 1944).

   In 2000, The Vatican wrote a request to the Carthusians at Farneta to finally write a detailed report of what had happened in 1944. Accattoli is a journalist specialising in Vatican affairs and he was the first person outside of the Vatican or Carthusian community to see the report, which he details in his book. He also interviewed two surviving witnesses to the executions of the monks.

4 The Historical Institute for the Resistance and the Contemporary Age in the Province of Lucca (ISREC) www.isreclucca.it/luogomemoria/i-martiri-di-farneta Among the documents in Lucca is an essay by Nicholas Lagana, published in the January–April 2009 edition of Quaderni di Farestoria, itself published by the ISRPt, or Historical Institute for the Resistance & the Contemporary Age, in the Province of Pistoia, 2009. The description of the SS operation against the monastery and the subsequent massacre is on pp.9–17.

   istitutostoricoresistenza.it/wp-content/uploads/2016/12/QF-2009-n.-1-Lucca.pdf Also: *The Atlas of Nazi and Fascist Massacres in Italy* – Certosa di Farneta 02–10/9/1944

5 Investigative reports from the British Intelligence Corps Field Security Sections, Sept–Nov 1944, synthesised in *A Report of British War Crimes Section of Allied Force Headquarters on German Reprisals for Partisan Activity in Italy,* National Archives, WO 204/11465, p.9, with another copy in. NA, WO 32/12206, referring to the report dated 9 July 1945.

6 A clear breakdown of the casualty figures, and the towns, cities and countries of origin of the dead, can be found in *The Atlas of Nazi and Fascist Massacres*: www.straginazifasciste.it/wp-content/uploads/schede/SAN%20LEONARDO%20AL%20FRIGIDO%20MASSA%2016.09.1944.pdf

7 *Ibid.* www.straginazifasciste.it/?page_id=38&id_strage=4623&lang=en

The Americans Investigate

1 The story of SS deserter Willi Haase's interrogation by the US Army – itself drawn from the original US Army War Crimes Commission investigative report of 1944, compiled by Majors Milton Wexler et al – is on the Italian Ministry of Defence website, in the Military Justice section detailing the case of Sant'Anna di Stazzema, and trial proceedings at La Spezia in 2004–2005. Haase's mention comes in Section 9 of the Sant'Anna case, entitled 'The Individualisation of those responsible for the killings at Sant'Anna', in sub-section 9/2: The 2nd Panzergrenadier Battalion and its Companies. www.difesa.it/Giustizia_Militare/rassegna/Processi/Sommer_Schoneberg_Bruss/Pagine/9individuazionedeiresponsabili.aspx

2 The details of the US and British investigations are partially published on the War Crimes and Justice Section of the Italian Ministry of Defence website, which details the respective investigations carried out into the massacres at Marzabotto, Sant'Anna di Stazzema and Fivizzano.

3 Letter to Professor Albert Einstein from Major Milton R. Wexler IGD, US Army letter no.55/048, dated 17th September 1944, original held in the archive of the Jewish National University Library in Jerusalem.

4 Italian MoD website – War Crimes and Justice Section., dealing with the case of Sant'Anna di Stazzema. Section 7/5 'Previous investigations into the facts' details in Italian the American investigation – the interviews with Alfredo and Marino Curzi are from this section: www.difesa.it/Giustizia_Militare/rassegna/Processi/Sommer_Schoneberg_Bruss/Pagine/7Laricostruzionedeifatti.aspx

The official resting place of the US Army report from summer and autumn of 1944 is in two locations in the US National Archives and Records Administration: Record Group 153, Judge Advocate General's Dept. War Crimes Branch, Cases filed 1944–1949, Location: 270/1/25/3-4, Entry 143, Box 527, Case 16–62 (Santa Anna). It's also recorded as being in Records Group 238, Office of the Chief of Counsel for War Crimes, Location: 190/10/34/25, Entry 2, Box 10, Case 16–62 (Santa Anna).

5 The description of his actions are in the Archives of the Italian National Partisan Association, ANPI (Associazione Nazionale di Partigiani) in Pietrasanta – their war diaries of the liberation of Pietrasanta is online at: old.anpiginolombardiversilia.it/documenti/La%20Liberazione%20della%20Versilia.pdf

Salvatori's version of events appears on p.34.

6 *Ibid.* His diary is also online at the same site, and his story of the liberation of Pietrasanta is on pp.36–37.

7 This testimony of Milena Bernabo and Mauro Pieri, as provided to the British and thence American and Italian investigators, can be found in Italian on the Italian MoD website, in the War Crimes and Justice section detailing the case of Sant'Anna di Stazzema. It opens Section 8: The facts resulting from briefings during the (court) hearings. www.difesa.it/Giustizia_Militare/rassegna/Processi/Sommer_Schoneberg_Bruss/Pagine/8Ifatticomerisultantiistruzione.aspx

8 Letter from Major John B. Bergin, 2nd Armoured Group, to HQ 2nd Armoured Group & HQ Task Force 45, and to the Commanding General and Assistant Chief of Staff, IV Corps, letter referenced JBB/jef. A copy of the original can be seen at: www.wanderingitaly.com/blog/article/722/sant-anna-di-stazzema

9 Interview with Enio Mancini by the author, Valdicastello, Tuscany, 25 October 2019.

10 The testimony from Giuseppe Vangelisti, Ettore Salvatori and Garibaldi Aleramo are included on Section 7/5 'Previous investigations into the facts', of the Italian MoD website's Military Justice Section, in the documentation detailing the court proceedings in the case of Sant'Anna di Stazzema. This lays out details of the American investigation in 1944 and 1945. www.difesa.it/Giustizia_Militare/rassegna/Processi/Sommer_Schoneberg_Bruss/Pagine/7Laricostruzionedeifatti.aspx

On the Plateau at Monte Sole

1 This extract from an account by Willfried Segebrecht was also included in a collection of personal descriptions of service in the 16th SS Division compiled after the war in Bavaria, and then published. It was entitled *In Step Together, United, or TruppenkameradenSchaft, Im gleichen Schritt und Tritt. Dokumentation der 16.SS Panzergrenadier Division 'Reichsfuehrer SS'*, Munich, Schild, 1998.

2 Testimony of Adriano Lipparini collected by Luciano Bergonzini in Luciano Bergonzini, *La Resistenza a Bologna*, 5 volumes, Volume 2, Bologna, Istituto per la Storia di Bologna.

3 *Ibid.*/Lipparini. His testimony is also quoted on the historiana.eu case study.

4 National Archives Washington, Massacre of Monte Sole, HQ US 5th Army, G-2 Section, Interrogation Centre, 1 November 1944, Prisoner of War Reports.

5 The National Archives, Kew, London, War Office Documents 235/538, Trial Documents for Max Simon, Statement of Pte. Legoli Julien, Infantry Gun Platoon, 5th Coy/16 Recc Regt/16th SS, 1 October 1944.

6 The German actions against civilians as they advanced into and through each location is documented on the database of *The Atlas of Nazi and Fascist Massacres*, with an entire section of eighteen locations listed under the Monte Sole operation: www.straginazifasciste.it/?page_id=338&grande_strage=1&lang=en
The database, website, photographs and video of the project entitled Storia e Memoria di Bologna (History & Memory of Bologna) contains a timeline of the operations on and around Monte Sole, from which parts of the description in this chapter is taken: www.storiaememoriadibologna.it/cronaca-della-strage-di-monte-sole-287-evento

7 Personal testimony of Cornelia Paselli, interviewed in 1945 and held in the Fondazione di Scuola di Pace di Monte Sole, Bologna, also quoted in Jack Olsen, *Silence on Monte Sole,* Putnam, New York, 1968, pp.192–3.

8 German after-action report on Monte Sole.

9 *The Atlas of Nazi and Fascist Massacres* lists each individual death in each of these eighteen locations: www.straginazifasciste.it/?page_id=338&grande_strage=1&lang=en

10 His testimony is in the archives of ANPI in Bologna, and in the Fondazione di Scuola di Pace di Monte Sole.

11 Von Halem's first cousin was, however, opposed to Mussolini and Hitler; he was executed for his part in the July 1944 attempt on Hitler's life.

12 Il Resto di Carlino, Giorgio Pini, 1 October 1944. The text appears in Italian on Storia e Memoria di Bologna: www.storiaememoriadibologna.it/da-il-resto-del-carlino-11-ottobre-1944-270-testimonianza

13 Dino Fantozzi wrote the confidential letter to Benito Mussolini on 10 October 1944, and sent it to him in the Headquarters of the Salo Republic; it was evacuated with other documents by the Allies and now is in the Archivio Centrale dello Stato, at the Ministry of Culture building at Piazzale degli Archivi in Rome. The contents of the note is also quoted in *The Hidden Wars*, Mimmo Franzinelli, Mondadori, Milan, 2002.

14 The testimony of different survivors and witnesses is split between this and three other chapters, those that detail the trials of Walter Reder and Max Simon, and the 2007 La Spezia court hearings into the Marzabotto massacre.

15 Tullio Bruno Bertini, *Trapped in Tuscany, Liberated by the Buffalo Soldiers*, Dante University Press, Boston, 1998, p.215.

16 Victoria Belco, *War, Massacre & Recovery in Central Italy 1943–1948*, University of Toronto Press, 2010, p.135.

17 *Ibid.*, pp.139–142.

18 Tullio Bruno Bertini, *Trapped in Tuscany, Liberated by the Buffalo Soldiers*, Dante University Press, Boston, 1998, p.229–230.

19 The account of the Bertuzzi family returning home is contained in the archives of ANPI in Bologna, at Storia e Memoria di Bologna, and is quoted at length in Jack Olsen's book, *Silence on Monte Sole: The First Complete Account of the Massacre at Monte Sole*, Putnam, New York, 1968, published in Italian in 1970 as *Silenzio su Monte Sole*, Garzanti, Milan.

20 *Ibid.*

Getting Away with Murder

1 The Museum at Brettheim has devoted a website to archival material, books and a film project about 'The Men of Brettheim', available in German at brettheimmuseum.hohenlohe.net

2 Under the authority of the Allied Control Commission in Caserta, the Field Sections of the British Intelligence Corps had, in October 1944, issued arrest warrants for Max Simon that held authority in any area occupied by the Western Allies.

3 The National Archives: War Crimes Trials, the Trial of Max Simon, Padua 1947 Documents 235/538. The details of Simon's capture and imprisonment are included in the proceedings of his trial in Padua in 1947.

4 Details of the inmates and conditions and history of Special PoW Camp XI can be found at www.hut9.org.uk and www.islandfarm.wales

5 *Allen Dulles, the OSS, and Nazi War Criminals: the Dynamics of Selective Prosecution*, Kerstin von Lingen, Cambridge University Press, Cambridge, UK, 2013, p.116, footnotes 140 & 141. These in turn quote, respectively, documents from The National Archive/Public Records Office, WO 310/127, a Judge Advocate General's memo from 13 January 1946, and 310/123, a statement given by SS-Obersturmführer Hans Joachim Richnow on 17 July 1946.

6 *The SS: A New History*, Adrian Weale, Abacus, London, UK, 2010, p.322.

7 Letter from Wolff to Albert Ganzenmuller, quoted in *Allen Dulles, the OSS, and Nazi War Criminals: the Dynamics of Selective Prosecution,* Kerstin von Lingen, Cambridge University Press, UK, 2013, p.216.

8 *Allen Dulles, the OSS, and Nazi War Criminals: the Dynamics of Selective Prosecution,* Kerstin von Lingen, Cambridge University Press, UK, 2013, p.117, & footnote 45.

9 Kerstin von Lingen, *Conspiracy of Silence: How the Old Boys of American Intelligence Shielded SS General Karl Wolff from Prosecution,* included in Holocaust and Genocide Studies 22, No.1, Spring 2008, p.84. This in turn quotes an OSS report: OSS R&A Report No. 3133.7, 'Principal Nazi Organisations Involved in the Commission of War Crimes: Part Four: The Nazi Party,' 10 Sept. 1945 (draft for internal use), 87: 107, Donovan Archive at Cornell Law School, Ithaca, New York.

10 Kerstin von Lingen's accounts stand among the most authoritative on Operation Sunrise – Livermore's assessment here was included in an OSS report, itself quoted on p.85 of *Conspiracy of Silence.*

11 The CIA's account of the story of Roderick Hall can be found as one of their Featured Stories of 2010: the information here is drawn from this account. www.cia.gov/news-information/featured-story-archive/2010-featured-story-archive/oss-heroes-stephen-hall.html

12 The story might have been exaggerated or embellished, yet the *Herald Tribune* chose to repeat it in a longer investigative article, published on 23 January 1962, written by Gaston Cobentz and Seymour Friedin, entitled 'The Strange Story of an SS General'.

13 Kerstin von Lingen, *Conspiracy of Silence,* pp.79–80, in turn quoting a statement given by Heinrich Andergassen: National Archives, War Office documents 310/123, PW Interrogation/SS-Andergassen, February 1946.

14 The CIA Interagency Working Group File on SS-Lieutenant Guido Zimmer, US National Archives and Records Administration, IWG Record Group 263: Records of the Central Intelligence Agency, Records of the Directorate of Operations – Analysis of the name file of Guido Zimmer, provides an excellent insight into the machinations behind Operation Sunrise.
Zimmer's correspondence, in the form of memos and diaries kept between May 1944 and March 1945, covering the period of Operation Sunrise, illustrate his dealings with the Allies, his German colleagues and Italians: www.cia.gov/library/readingroom/docs/ZIMMER%2C%20GUIDO_0059.pdf

Victors' Justice

1 Investigative reports from the British Intelligence Corps Field Security Sections, Sept–Nov 1944, synthesised in *A Report of British War Crimes Section of Allied Force Headquarters on German Reprisals for Partisan Activity in Italy,* National Archives, WO 204/11465, p.9, with another copy in. NA, WO 32/12206, referring to the report dated 9 July 1945.

2 In December 1946 the US files on the massacre were closed because the case had been handed over to the Italian authorities.

3 Edmonson dated his report 12 June 1945, and says at the beginning that he started enquiries on 5 February 1945. The report from him is referenced SIB/HQ/X/44/44.

The First War Crimes Trials

1   The National Archive – Foreign Office document No. 371/57557, letter from
    Colonel Richard Halse, Army Legal Corps, to the Judge Advocate General's
    Department, 30 October 1946.
2   The Trial of Albert Kesselring: British Military Tribunal in Venice, Italy,
    17 February–6 May 1947, website of the Italian Ministry of Defence, Military
    Justice & War Crimes Trials Section (text in Italian, drawn from Documents of the
    UN War Crimes Commission 1949); Section A – Description of the Proceedings.
    www.difesa.it/Giustizia_Militare/rassegna/Processi/Kesserling/Pagine/default.aspx
3   *Ibid.*, Section A.
4   *Ibid.*, Section A.
5   Outline of the Proceedings, British Military Court at Venice, Italy,
    17 February–6 May 1947, Case No. 44, The Trial of Albert Kesselring.
6   Oliver Leese's quote appears in *Kesselring's Last Battle: War Crimes Trials and Cold
    War Politics, 1945–1960*, Kerstin von Lingen, University Press of Kansas, Lawrence,
    Kansas, 2009, p.130.
7   The National Archives, War Office 220/11 'Military Courts: Atrocity and
    War Crimes Trials, Volumes 1 and 2, 1943 Dec–1945 March', Voluntary
    Statement by PW LD 1687 Max Simon, 'Report regarding the battles of
    16 Panzergrenadier-Div 'Reichsfürhrer SS' against the Italian partisans during the
    period 28 May–31 October 1944', p.10.
8   PRO/NA/JAG Office War Crimes Case Files 235/584-588.
9   Pen-in-Hand Publishers, London, January 1950.
10 Norbert Frei, *Adenauer's Germany and the Nazi Past: the Politics of Amnesty and
    Integration*, Columbia University Press, New York, 2002, p.3.
11 Operation Unthinkable: Russia: Threat to Western Civilisation. British War
    Cabinet, Joint Planning Staff (Draft & Final Reports: 22 May, 8 June and
    11 July 1945) Public Record Office CAB120/691/109040/002.
    The thirty-eight pages of the report can be downloaded individually from this
    link below; copy also in the author's possession.
    web.archive.org/web/20101116155514/ www.history.neu.edu/PRO2/
    pages/002.htm

Amnesty in the New Italy

1   The Italian Ministry of Defence website, War Crimes Section, pertaining to the
    German defendants in the La Spezia trials in 2004–2005.
2   Office of the Historian, Foreign Relations of the United States 1946, the British
    Commonwealth, Western and Central Europe, Volume V, Telegram 865.00/7-1946
    US Embassy in Rome, accessed online here: history.state.gov/historicaldocuments/
    frus1946v05/d628
3   *Ibid.*

The Trial of Walter Reder

1 See the Supplement to the *London Gazette* dated 4 June 1950, No. 38937.

2 Testimony collected by Captain Archer of the British Military Police SIB, War Crimes Commission/Judge Advocate General's Dept, U.K War Crimes Unit Caserta, Walter Reder Trial IV, 63, Bologna.

3 It was also included in a collection of personal accounts of service in the 16th SS Division compiled after the war in Bavaria, and then published. It was entitled *In Step Together, United, or TruppenkameradenSchaft, Im gleichen Schritt und Tritt. Dokumentation der 16. SS Panzergrenadier Division 'Reichsfuehrer SS'*, Munich, Schild, 1998.

4 Calisto Migliori describing the massacre at Marzabotto, quoted in Marzabotto Parla, (Marzabotto Speaks), by Renato Giorgi, originally published in 1955 in Bologna; the latest edition came out in 2019 from Franco Cosimo Panini Publishers. The interview is also in ANPI archives in Bologna

5 historiana.eu/case-study/rights-civilians-and-responsibilities-armies-during-war-wwii-and-onwards/attitudes-italian-partisans-amongst-german-officers

6 *The Atlas of Nazi and Fascist Massacres* – in the large section of the database dealing with Monte Sole, there are eighteen sub-sections, one of them for San Giovanni di Sotto e Casoncello: www.straginazifasciste.it/?page_id=38&id_strage=5285

7 Quoted in Luca Baldissara & Paolo Pezzino, *Il Massacro – Guerra ai civili a Monte Sole, Il Mulino* (The Massacre – War Against Civilians on Monte Sole), Biblioteca Storica, Bologna, 2009, pp.141–142 and also at: historiana.eu/case-study/rights-civilians-and-responsibilities-armies-during-war-wwii-and-onwards/29-september-1944-through-multiple-perspectives-2

8 Quoted in and translated from, one of the editions of *Marzabotto parla*, (Marzabotto Speaks) by Renato Giorni, Marsilio, Venice, 1985, p.129.

9 F.J.P. Veale, *Advance to Barbarism: The Development of Total Warfare from Sarajevo to Hiroshima*, Mitre Press, London, 1968.

SS Men in the New Germany

1 Norbert Frei, *Adenauer's Germany and the Nazi Past: the Politics of Amnesty and Integration*, Columbia University Press, New York, 2002, p.3.

2 Divided Memory: The Nazi Past in the Two Germanys, Herf, Jeffrey, Harvard University Press, Cambridge, Mass., 1997, pp.289–90.

3 *Ibid.*, Herf, & Frei.

4 See Herf, pp.289–90.

5 The exchange of letters between the German foreign ministry in Bonn and their Rome embassy are in the archives of the German Ministry of Foreign Affairs in Bonn. They can also be found on the 2003 Italian government report into the concealment of war crimes documentation in the 1950s–1960s in the so-called 'Cupboard of Shame': www.straginazifasciste.it/wp-ontent/uploads/2015/02/relazionediminoranza.pdf

6 The details of the meeting between Tringali and Klaiber emerged in 2015 after German historian Felix Bohr wrote the story for *Der Spiegel*, which was run across the Italian media, including in *La Repubblica* and *La Nuova Sardegna*: www.repubblica.it/esteri/2012/01/15/news/germania_spiegel_accusa_italia_su_ardeatine-28158045

www.lanuovasardegna.it/regione/2012/01/16/news/ardeatine-inchiesta-insabbiata-per-scelta-del-governo-italiano-1.3639462

7 The 2003 Italian government report, linked above at note 5, provides context and further clarification of this meeting.

8 The article linked here – in Italian – contains a rare copy of a Deutsche Bank report from 1957 that confirms on p.4 Winden's status within the company:
anpi.it/media/uploads/patria/2012/50-53_CASSARA.pdf

9 The government report, in Italian, can be found at:
www.straginazifasciste.it/wp-ontent/uploads/2015/02/relazionediminoranza.pdf
Subsequent references to it include a chapter and/or page number.

The Cupboard of Shame

1 Parliamentary Commission of Inquiry on the Causes of Concealment of the Files Relating to Nazi & Fascist Crimes, 430pp, 2003. Chamber of Deputies and Senate of the Italian Republic.
www.straginazifasciste.it/wp-content/uploads/2015/02/relazionediminoranza.pdf

2 *Ibid.*, p.67.

3 *Ibid.*, p.68.

4 *Ibid.*, p.138.

5 *Ibid.*, p.224.

6 Marco De Paolis, *Sant'Anna di Stazzema: the Investigation, the History, the Documents,* Paolo Pezzino, Viella, Italy, 1996.

7 *Corriere della Sera*, Milan, 14 April 2001.

8 Chemnitz Homicide Department investigation no.220/AR 3581/03, 15 December 2003, questioning of suspect Matthias Alfred Concina by the military prosecutor of the Italian Republic working with the La Spezia Military Tribunal, hearing process number 315/0s ma3/RNR447.

The Trials

1 The entire summary of the court proceedings, the investigations that preceded it, the documentation, and the crucial interviews with the former SS men have been gathered on the website of the Italian Ministry of Defence, in the section dedicated to Military Justice and War Crimes trials. The section about the ten defendants at the La Spezia trial, and the trial itself, is divided into some twenty sections:
The opening is from Section 2, 'The Opening of Proceedings':
www.difesa.it/Giustizia_Militare/rassegna/Processi/Sommer_Schoneberg_Bruss/Pagine/2iniziodeldibattimento.aspx

2 This is from Section 7, 'The Reconstruction of the Facts', and Section 9, 'The Individualisation of Responsibility'.
www.difesa.it/Giustizia_Militare/rassegna/Processi/Sommer_Schoneberg_Bruss/Pagine/7Laricostruzionedeifatti.aspx
www.difesa.it/Giustizia_Militare/rassegna/Processi/Sommer_Schoneberg_Bruss/Pagine/9individuazionedeiresponsabili.aspx

3 *Ibid.* The testimonies that follow are also from these sections.

4 Also included in Sections 7 & 9.

5 The information from them is included across Sections 7, 8, 9 & 10.

6 Quoted in *The Guardian*, Rome, by Barbara McMahon, 23 June 2005: www.theguardian.com/world/2005/jun/23/secondworldwar.italy

7 The court sentence is from Section 18 of the trial proceedings: www.difesa.it/Giustizia_Militare/rassegna/Processi/Sommer_Schoneberg_Bruss/Pagine/default.aspx

8 Testimony of Antonio Politi, La Spezia Military Tribunal, September 2006.

9 *Im gleichen Schritt und Tritt. Dokumentation der 16.SS Panzergrenadier Division 'Reichsführer -SS'*, Munich, Schild, 1998.

Voices of the SS

1 *Das Massaker von Sant'Anna di Stazzema,* by Gabriele Heinecke, edited by Christiane Kohl, Laika Verlag, Hamburg, 2014.

2 Quoted in *The Guardian,* Rome, by Tom Kington, 2 October 2012.

3 Statement from the Stuttgart Regional Prosecutor's Office, quoted *inter alia* in the Italian newspaper *Il Giornale,* 1 October 2012.

4 Quoted on the English language website of *Deutsche Welle,* 7 August 2014.

5 Gabriele Heinecke, quoted in *La Gazzetta di Viareggio,* 19 March 2016, on the occasion of her receiving the honorary citizenship of Sant'Anna di Stazzema.

6 *Ibid.*

7 These include *I crimini di guerra tedeschi in Italia 1943–1945, Einaudi, Turin 2015. (Trans: German war crimes in Italy 1943–1945).*

8 The Rosenburg Project – Information on the work done by the Independent Academic Commission at the Federal Ministry of Justice and Consumer Protection regarding the critical study of the National Socialist past; Forward, page 1. www.bmjv.de/SharedDocs/Publikationen/DE/Rosenburg_Broschuere_englisch.pdf?__blob=publicationFile&v=5

9 Interview with the author, 25 October 2019.

10 www.straginazifasciste.it/?page_id=9&lang=en

11 ARD Contrasts, 11 April 2004.

12 taz.de/Ein-Fall-von-Ruhestoerung/!293897/, published in Taz-Nord on 14 April 2007, by Friederike Graff, Culture Editor. The headline reads as 'A case of a disturbance'.

13 Author's note: the translation is exact as possible, with any words inserted marked in brackets.

14 Interview on Deutsche Welle radio with Gabriele Heinecke, June 2013, Hamburg.

15 *Ibid.*

16 Heinecke further elaborated her arguments in June 2014 in an article in *Betrifft Justiz,* on pp.57–61. betrifftjustiz.de/wp-content/uploads/texte/Ganze_Hefte/BJ%20118_web.pdf

17 Deutsche Welle English Service website, 29 May 2015/Agence France Presse, 28 May 2015

18 Deutsche Presse Agentur (dpa), 28 May 2015, as quoted and run by *The Local,* one of Germany's leading English language newspapers.

19 Interviews with Gabriele Heinecke on Deutsche Welle, 28 May 2015.

20 Interviews carried out by ARD Contrasts, 15 July 2014.

21 Quoted in *La Gazzetta di Viareggio,* 19 March 2016.

German Apologies and Reconciliation

1 *Corriere della Sera*, 19 December 2012, quoted on the website of the German Federal Foreign Office: www.auswaertiges-amt.de/en/newsroom/news/121219-corriere/252934

2 *Il Crimini di Guerra Tedeschi in Italia 1943–1945 (*German War Crimes in Italy 1943–1945), by Carlo Gentile, Einaudi, Turin 2015.

3 Mancini's, Pardini's and Berlusconi's quotes, though originating in *Corriere della Sera*, *Il Fatto* and *Il Giornale*, were all carried simultaneously by one newspaper: www.iol.co.za/news/world/outrage-after-germany-shuts-file-on-nazi-massacre-1394793

4 Interview with the author, Valdicastello, Tuscany, 25 October 2019.

5 www.bbc.com/news/world-europe-33143473

6 The speech appeared on many outlets, including the German Presidential website; www.bundespraesident.de/SharedDocs/Reden/EN/Frank-Walter-steinmeier/Reden/2019/08/190825-Fivizzano.html,
Deutsche Welle; www.dw.com/en/italy-german-president-marks-75th-anniversary-of-ss-massacre/a-50159581. And the Italian government's site: www.quirinale.it/elementi/35355

7 *Ibid.*

8 *Ibid.*

9 *Ibid.*

10 *Ibid.*

11 *Ibid.*

12 *Ibid.*

13 *Ibid.*

14 www.straginazifasciste.it

15 Quoted on the English language website of *Deutsche Welle,* 7 August 2014.

INDEX